CHAIWAT SATHA-ANAND

THE LIFE OF THIS WORLD

Negotiated Muslim Lives in Thai Society

ISLAM IN ASIA SERIES

mc **Marshall Cavendish**
Academic

© 2005 Marshall Cavendish International
(Singapore) Private Limited

Published 2005 by Marshall Cavendish Academic
An imprint of Marshall Cavendish International
(Singapore) Private Limited
A member of Times Publishing Limited

Times Centre, 1 New Industrial Road,
Singapore 536196
Tel:(65) 6213 9288
Fax: (65) 6284 9772
E-mail: mca@sg.marshallcavendish.com
Website:
http://www.marshallcavendish.com/academic

ISBN: 981-210-355-4

A CIP catalogue record for this book is available from
the National Library Board (Singapore).

Printed by Times Graphics Pte Ltd, Singapore
on non-acidic paper

**London • New York • Beijing • Shanghai
• Bangkok • Kuala Lumpur • Singapore**

Marshall Cavendish Academic

ISLAM IN ASIA SERIES
Series Editor: Omar Farouk Bajunid

The *Islam in Asia* series features quality original works on Islam and Muslims in Asia by regional scholars and other specialists. Focusing on empirical studies and addressing the whole range of contemporary issues affecting Muslim communities within and across national frontiers in the region, the areas of discussion include discourses on Islam and political violence, Muslim diversity, international Islamic networks, the role of Muslim minorities, the role of Islam in pluralistic societies and Islam and inter-religion dialogues.

OMAR FAROUK BAJUNID is Professor of Comparative Politics at the Faculty of International Studies, Hiroshima City University.

Contents

Acknowledgements

How do you express gratitude to those who have been kind to you in various ways in the past ten years? Their names could be listed, institutions credited, and thanks offered; but surely this would not be sufficient nor complete. Still, apart from doing the normal thing, I really don't know how. If the academic life is seen as an ongoing journey, responding to challenges, addressing the problems of the day we deem as significant with theoretical insights, research findings, and values held, then I have had many helpful companions on this journey.

While pursuing my graduate study at the University of Hawaii, several teachers helped form my views about both the social sciences and life in general. Profs. Glenn D. Paige and Michael J. Shapiro showed me how to be both a good social scientist and a political theorist. Prof. Manfred Henninsen and his wife Kareda, through their thoughts and lives together, helped me to understand the relationship between my complex identity and the search for philosophical meaning.

Among those who have contributed much to my journey on the subject of Muslims in Southeast Asia—as organizers of international conferences, editors of journals or books published where earlier versions of these essays appeared—I am most grateful to Prof. Charles F. Keyes, Prof. Hans Dieters Evers, Dr. Sharon Siddique, Prof. Mohamed Ariff, Prof. Mitsuo Nakamura and Dr. Imtiyaz Yusuf. In getting this book published I owe my gratitude to Prof. Craig Reynolds of the Australian National University for taking the time to advise me on both the process of publishing academic works and contents of the introduction; Prof. Omar Farouk, the series editor for believing in me all these years, as well as his determination which, in some ways, make it possible for this book to come out in the present form; and Prof. Thongchai Winichakul for his support and guidance. I am also grateful for the comments and suggestions made by the two anonymous reviewers of the manuscript.

I wish also to thank the Institute of Southeast Asian Studies (Singapore), the University of Hawaii Press, Sasakawa Peace Foundation, the International Movement for a Just World, and the College of Islamic Studies, Prince of Songkhla University Pattani campus for permission to reprint the essays that appear in their publications in earlier versions.

There are those without whose assistance and support I would not have been able to undertake my work. They are my friends in Bangkok and Southern Thailand; my mother, who might not fully understand what I have been doing but loves me unconditionally; and my wife, Suwanna, who has seen me through the agony and ecstasy of my life and my work as a Muslim and a social scientist.

Chaiwat Satha-Anand

Origins

Chapter 1 was first published in Isma-ae Ali et al., (eds.) *Islamic Studies in ASEAN: Presentations of an International Seminar* (Pattani: College of Islamic Studies, Prince of Songkhla University, 2000), pp. 89–98.

Chapter 2 was originally published as "Pattani in the 1980s: Academic Literature as Political Stories," *SOJOURN: Journal of Social Issues in Southeast Asia*, vol. 7, no. 1 (1992): 1–38. Reproduced here with the kind permission of the Institute of Southeast Asian Studies, Singapore.

Chapter 3 was first published in *SOJOURN: Journal of Social Issues in Southeast Asia*, vol. 8, no. 1 (1993): 195–218. Reproduced here with the kind permission of the Institute of Southeast Asian Studies, Singapore.

Chapter 4 was originally published as "Hijab and Moments of Legitimation: Islamic Resurgence in Thai Society," in Charles F. Keyes, Laurel Kendall, and Helen Hardacre (eds.) *Asian Visions of Authority: Religion and the Modern States of East and Southeast Asia* (Honolulu: University of Hawaii Press, 1994), pp. 279–300.

Chapter 5 was originally published as "Bangkok Muslims and the Tourist Trade" in Mohamed Ariff (ed.) *The Muslim Private Sector in Southeast Asia* (Singapore: Institute of Southeast Asian Studies, 1991), pp. 89-121.

Chapter 6 was originally published as "Spiritualizing Real Estate, Commoditizing Pilgrimage: Globalisation and Islamic Responses in Asia-Pacific?" in Joseph A. Camilleri and Chandra Muzaffer (eds.), *Globalisation: The Perspectives and Experiences of the Religious Traditions of Asia Pacific* (Petaling Jaya: International Movement for a Just World, 1998) , pp. 135–146.

Chapter 7 was originally published as "Defending Community, Strengthening Civil Society: A Muslim Minority's Contribution to Thai Civil Society," in Nakamura Mitsuo, Sharon Siddique and Omar Farouk Bajunid (eds.), *Islam and Civil Society in Southeast Asia* (Singapore: Institute of Southeast Asian Studies, 2001), pp. 91–103.

List of Tables

Foreword

It is ironic that although the Muslims are a significant minority in Thailand—historically, politically, culturally and numerically—there seems to be a dearth of good academic literature, especially in English, on their contemporary role in the kingdom. It is not surprising therefore that they continue to be either poorly or not at all understood, or, even worse, totally misunderstood, not just by outsiders but also by their fellow citizens in Thailand. It is doubly tragic that it often takes negative events, such as the recent escalation of political violence in the Muslim-dominated provinces of the deep south, to remind the Thai nation and the world not only of their existence in Thailand but also what appears to be an unresolved crisis of their political integration into contemporary Thai polity.

Even in terms of basic data on Thai Muslims, there still seems to be a lot of confusion, if not controversy, in the air. Official Thai government statistics invariably place the number of Muslims in Thailand at no more than 3.8 per cent of the total population, whereas Muslim sources insist that they actually constitute well over 10 per cent of the nation's population, arguing that they have been deliberately under-represented to trivialize their role and significance. Even on the basis of the government's conservative version, the Muslims would still number some 2,464,889 people (the Thai population stood at 64,865,523 in July 2004), which, by any criterion, is not an insignificant figure. Covering the trouble in the Muslim south, foreign as well as local media kept suggesting, albeit erroneously, that there are 6 million Muslims in the south. There may well be more than 6 million Muslims in Thailand, but they are definitely not confined to the southern provinces only. The error is not so much in the numbers but in the geography. It has also been invariably claimed that the Muslims in the south speak "Yawi," a dialect of Malay, in apparent ignorance of the fact that Yawi, which is the Thai rendering of the Malay term "Jawi," is essentially a script and not a language or even a dialect. The principal medium of communication among the Muslims of the south, with the exception of Satun, is Pattani Malay, which is akin to Kelantan Malay. The general misperception that the Muslims are essentially a homogeneous community also continues to prevail. It is easy to sense that there seems to be considerable ambivalence—if not ignorance—on the part of the Thai public of the place of Islam in Thailand and its role in the lives of the ordinary Thai Muslims. The image of Islam in popular Thai imagination seems to be mostly negative. It is probably due to their lack of knowledge of who the Muslims really are and what their religion represents that the majority of Thai-Buddhists tend to view them as the problematic "other."

Thailand's Muslim-dominated provinces of Yala, Pattani, Narathiwat, and parts of Songkhla, have had a history of chronic unrest brought about by a complex interplay of various factors. There was always a mix of separatist insurgency, local banditry, crime, and political violence in the deep south, a situation that has been compounded by endemic corruption, ethnic prejudices, bureaucratic tyranny, and bad governance. Partly on account of this, there has long been a high level of suspicion and distrust of the government, especially the local officialdom, among the Muslims in the south. However, the political liberalization and consolidation of democracy in Thailand in the post-1992 decade, which created the necessary political institutions, mechanisms and climate to facilitate the participation of the Muslims in Thai national politics, appeared, at least initially, to have significantly contributed toward the de-radicalization of Muslim political behavior and the emasculation of the separatist cause, that then began to be increasingly viewed as no longer viable. Yet, the recent outbreak of a series of unexpected events in the south threatens to undermine all this. The most serious incident occurred on 4 January 2004 when an organized group of more than 50 men, according to some sources, raided an army depot in Narathiwat, killing four soldiers and stealing some 100 rifles and a large quantity of ammunition. 18 schools were also simultaneously burned down in what appeared to be well-coordinated attacks. Although it was not immediately clear who was responsible for these daring attacks, the accusing finger was already pointed at the Muslim insurgents with nuanced allegations that international terrorist groups, including Al-Qaeda and Jemaah Islamiyah (JI), might have been behind this incident. As sporadic incidents of violence continued unabated, the kidnap and presumed execution of a prominent Muslim lawyer, Somchai Neelaphaijit, allegedly by the police—at the time of his disappearance, Somchai Neelaphaijit was responsible for the defense of five suspected JI terrorists under detention—and the allegation that a few Muslim Members of Parliament were behind the unrest further exacerbated tensions in the Muslim south. The situation took a turn for the worse with the outbreak of another major incident on April 28, when Thai security forces killed 107 suspected militants, some of whom were members of a local soccer team, who were accused of planning acts of terrorism. 32 were gunned down inside the historic Kru-ze mosque in Pattani. A new wave of violence including arson, bombing, killing of government officials and security forces, and beheading and murder of innocent civilians erupted following the above incident.

The latest episode in this vicious cycle of violence occurred on 25 October, 2004 in Tak Bai, Narathiwat when the Thai security forces resorted to excessive violence to break up a demonstration at the Tak Bai Police Station staged by about 1500 protesters who were demanding the release of six men accused of giving weapons to Islamic militants. Six protesters were shot and over 1300 were detained under trying conditions, packed like cattle into a number of military trucks, and transported to a military camp. The journey, which should have taken just two hours, took five hours, causing severe stress and pain to the detainees. As a result of this, almost 80 people died of suffocation amidst claims that many more had disappeared. When news of the incident broke out, the government came under relentless criticism from the media, civil society, and the international community, although there was a good deal of support from the Thai public. Muslim governments from Iran to Indonesia protested what they considered as unacceptable treatment. The government was caught openly on the wrong foot and had to be on the defensive. To be fair, the government had earlier tried to introduce various policies and measures to resolve the crisis in the south but to no avail; the situation continued to deteriorate. Following the Tak Bai incident, there was an even more severe wave of violence with rampant revenge killings of the innocent. In all, from January to the middle of November 2004, about 500 people have been killed, and a general climate of fear and insecurity has emerged in the south. The credibility of the government has been badly undermined and ominously, ethnic tensions between the Muslims and the Buddhists in the south have reached unprecedented heights. The high degree of religious tolerance that used to characterize Buddhist-Muslim relations in Thailand has suddenly become very fragile. The government seems to be running out of options. The king, a highly-revered figure in Thailand who normally stays out of politics, has come forward to appeal for calm and to help restore normalcy in the south. All the indications are that the situation in the south is still unpredictable and explosive. Something seems to have gone badly wrong somewhere in the Muslim south. What actually contributed to this imbroglio is still anyone's guess. There are indeed many ways of trying to make sense of what has happened and is continuing to unfold in Thailand's Muslim-dominated provinces. It is, however, obvious that it would be impossible to understand the recent events without understanding the historical and political backdrop that shaped them. This is where Dr. Chaiwat Satha-Anand's book, *The Life of This World*: *Negotiated Muslim Lives in Thai Society*, becomes indispensable.

In terms of its currency, content, approach, and relevance, the publication of this book could not be more timely. By any consideration, this is indeed a unique volume. First, although it is basically a compilation of earlier published papers, it is by no means an 'instant' volume hastily prepared to respond to the immediate market demand due to the present situation in Thailand's Muslim region. This is a work which contains thoroughly-researched and well-documented papers, on a range of critical issues that affect the Muslims in Thailand, that were undertaken over a period of almost two decades. Although every paper seeks to address different concerns, it is not difficult to see the thematic connection between all the papers and the balanced blend between the empirical and the conceptual. What is strikingly remarkable about the book is that apart from examining real issues on the ground, it also provides insights into the mind of a Western-trained Muslim scholar trying to understand his own society and striving to help others understand it too. Although it may not mean much to others, this book demonstrates that Western-trained Muslim scholars often have to grapple with the question of having to know and perhaps even to accept the limits of their expertise, particularly as defined by boundaries between Islamic Studies and Muslim Studies. Most attempts to examine the sociological or political state of Muslims empirically tend to operate within the parameters of Muslim Studies. Although it may be tempting to try to also use the lens of Islamic Studies to analyze Muslim communities, hitherto this has rarely been attempted. Content-wise, the review article on Pattani in Chapter 2 represents an excellent introduction to the state of existing works on Thailand's Muslim south. Although Chapters 3 and 4 appear to examine different issues, their common focus is on the fundamental question of Muslim identity. Concerns addressed elsewhere in other chapters shift the traditional focus of discussion from the south to the national scene.

Another distinctive feature of the book is that although it is about the Muslims in Thailand, its conceptual framework is such that it allows people who may not be familiar with Islam—or Thailand, for that matter—to understand the problems facing the Muslims in a broader perspective. It is specific in examining certain local issues, like the problem of the Kru-ze mosque, in Chapter 3, but the analysis is presented in such a way to show that the main issue was not really the mosque but the attempt to renegotiate Muslim identity using the mosque as the theatre to achieve that. This unique analytical approach that Dr. Chaiwat has adopted should make it easier for people who are not too familiar with the specifics of the situation to comprehend its actual underpinnings and universal relevance. It should also be noted that Dr. Chaiwat's 'theatre' became a "battlefield" on April 28, 2004. Likewise, in Chapter 7 when Dr. Chaiwat examines the problem of the Ban Krua Muslims resisting what they perceived as a mega-development project which would destroy their residences and livelihood in Bangkok, he presents their case as a civil society phenomenon rather than a Muslim problem, thus making it easier for a wider audience to understand the real dynamics and dimensions of the problem rather than constrict it to the religious sphere. Dr. Chaiwat's informed understanding of the relevant theoretical literature and conceptual tools of analysis coupled with his ability to use the universal language and idiom to highlight what are essentially local problems have contributed to enhancing the quality of this book.

Finally, Dr. Chaiwat Satha-Anand's unique personal traits, exposure, and solid academic credentials enables him to demonstrate a sophisticated level of scholarship that is rare in this part of the world as reflected in this volume. Although he comes from a devout Muslim family and is a practising Muslim, he grew up in a Buddhist social environment and went to a leading Catholic school in Bangkok for his early education. He graduated with a First Class Honours degree from Thammasat University before proceeding to do his doctorate in Political Science at the University of Hawaii in the United States. Unlike the majority of his co-religionists in Thailand who are of Malay ethnic origins, he is a Bangkokian of non-Malay origin. He is a leading authority on Nonviolence in Thailand and is a strong advocate of its philosophy. He currently teaches at the Faculty of Political Science, Thammasat University. Although Dr. Chaiwat Satha-Anand tries to understand the problems facing the Muslims in Thailand as a Muslim, he essentially does so as a Western-trained political scientist and as a peace scholar but without being unmindful of his Islamic background. It is this unique combination of the scholar and his scholarship and the conscious relationship between the observed and the observer that has helped make this volume rich in terms of content, creativity, analysis, approach, and perhaps most important of all, its universal appeal and relevance, especially in an era characterized by increasing conflict and violence. This book is compulsory reading for anyone interested in Thai and Southeast Asian Studies, Islam, and the Muslim world as well as current issues of peace and conflict.

Omar Farouk Bajunid
Hiroshima City University

PART I

Thesis, Methodology, and Perspective

Introduction: "The Life of This World …"

On February 8, 2002 while travelling as a participant of an international conference on "A Gandhian Alternative to Terrorism and War", in a bus from Gandhi Bhavan in Thiruvananthapuram to Rangaprabhat in Kerala, South India, I was having a long conversation with a senior Gandhian who, among other things, spoke about Muslim children wearing *hijab* (Muslim women's head covers) to schools in that state. He surprised me with his remark that these Muslim children should follow school uniform and India should not allow religious identity to manifest itself over and above national identity. I was surprised for two reasons. First, to subsume religious identity under a dominant national identity would reflect more a nationalist than a Gandhian attitude which has always been sensitive to religious beliefs. Second, it seems that the issue of wearing *hijab* continues to be contested as it once was in Thailand more than a decade ago. The question is why wearing the *hijab* continues to be an issue,¹ not only in India, but also in France, Singapore, and many other places. *The Life of this World*, in a way, speaks to this question, by focusing on the ways in which Muslims in a minority negotiate their lives in a non-Muslim society, using different sites where their identities as Muslims are contested while facing various challenges that call into questions their connectedness with the local, the national and the global contexts.

If "negotiated life" means steering a difficult path between a dominant universal idiom and an ethnocentric particular resistance, then it cannot but engage in continuing conversations with others. In these conversations, voices are heard, not dominated nor drowned by power. The British political philosopher, Michael Oakeshott, in a gem of an essay written in 1959 titled "The Voice of Poetry in the Conversation of Mankind", has argued that the excellence of conversations, "springs from a tension between seriousness and playfulness. Each voice represents a serious engagement (…); and without this seriousness the conversation would lack impetus. But in its participation in the conversation, each voice learns to be playful, learns to understand itself conversationally and to recognize itself as a voice among voices."²

The tension between seriousness and playfulness which emerges in the negotiated life of this world as conversations is curious because it seems to echo a striking Qur'anic injunction. In *Al-Qur'an*, there is an *Ayah* (verse) in *Surah* (chapter) "*Al-An'am*"(Cattle), a late Meccan chapter said to be an admonition to the Muslims to expound the Unity of God doctrine to pagan Arabs,[3] which says:

> What is the life of this world
> But play and amusement?
> But best is the Home
> In the Hereafter, for those
> Who are righteous.
> Will ye not then understand? (VI: 32)[4]

A commentator points out that this verse does not mean that earthly life has nothing serious about it. But compared with the true Life in the Hereafter, it is but "a sport or a transient pastime" with which to amuse oneself before turning to serious business. Muslims therefore should not be misled by it.[5] Another comments that since the Eternal Home where everyone is going is much more important than the seductive ephemeral pleasures of this world, "play and amusement", though not serious in themselves, are for the purpose of preparing the human minds for the serious things of life.[6] In addition, since the Ultimate Reality is hidden from humans, there are people with misconceptions who would indulge in a variety of actions which are so blatantly senseless, their lives would then seem to consist of but sports and pastime. For these people, one who assumes the position of a king in this world should understand that he is no different from the person playing the part of a king on the stage of a theatre.[7]

In addition to heeding the religious teaching that the life in this world is but a temporary phase, a preparation, I would also underscore the problematic notion of "play and amusement". The life of this world, as play and sport or amusement, is at once serious and playful. As rule-governing activities, play, sport and amusement could be serious. In sports, if rules are not taken seriously, players will be thrown out of the field, and therefore lose. In plays, if a thespian does not act the part by following the script, he/she will have to be replaced and therefore no longer "play". As a matter of fact, even if the position of a king in life is to be conceived as a theatre, it still has to be taken seriously because an ordinary person wrongly engaging with a king could result in punishments as evident in some societies.

The tension which characterizes treating the life of this world as play or sport is also governed by two kinds of attitude: playfulness and seriousness. The former is crucial if gains and losses are to be confronted knowing that all things must pass and changes seem to be the only invariant in human affairs. The latter is important if one wants to continue to meaningfully engage with others in this life. A life which exists, or rather lives this tension, beautifully captured by the Qur'anic injunction which serves as the title of this volume, needs to be a negotiated life not unlike the lives of Muslims in Thai society examined here.

Then and Now

Some of the materials included in this volume were written approximately ten years ago. A question could be raised as to their relevance, given changes that have taken place both in Thailand and the world during this period of time. When I wrote Chapter 5, the number of tourists coming to Thailand in 1988 was 4.3 million bringing in 65,000 million baht in revenue.[8] But in 2002, there were 10.8 million international tourists bringing in approximately 323,484 million baht with the set target of 383,900 million baht from 12 million visitors in 2004.[9] When I first wrote Chapter 3, the per capita income of the four Southern provinces was 12,839 baht compared with the national figure of 40,125 baht.[10] Half a decade later in 1996, per capita income of these four provinces was 43,947 baht,[11] and in 1998 number of Malaysian tourists dropped by 4.41per cent with a 31.91 per cent increase in Singaporean tourists.[12] Moreover, there is precious little about violence in the South in this book, while there has been a rising tide of violence in the South to the extent that almost never a day goes by in early 2004 without headline news about killings in the area. In fact , violence in the South has assumed a new level of danger since January 4, 2004, the day when there was an elaborately planned, well-organized attack on a military camp in Narathiwat, taking away more than 300 firearms, killing 4 soldiers, while 20 schools across 11 districts of that province were simultaneously torched.[13] From January 4 to March 6, 2004, a Thai newspaper reports 32 violent incidents with 50 people killed.[14] An official source, on the other hand, reports that from January 4 to March 1, 2004, there have been 154 violent incidents in the same three Southernmost provinces, killing 48 people with 30 more injured. [15] Even at the time of this writing on March 19, 2004, there were 39 minor arson attacks, thirty in Pattani, eight in Songkhla, and one in Yala.[16]

There have been several past attempts to explain the recurring violence in Southern Thailand. The 1999 Senate Special Commission, for example, concluded its study of the Five Southern Provinces by saying that, although the issue of "social psychology" remains the "core", both chronic poverty and lack of education are conducive to the problems of the area.[17] In a recent research on problems in the South from the villagers' own perspectives, involving 589 villagers from 9 districts in Pattani, Yala, and Narathiwat discussing their views in 13 different public forums, the researchers conclude that most pressing problems are poverty-related. More than 40 per cent of the people there have to work outside their villages while some 70 per cent of the youths were unemployed.[18] Poverty indeed continues to plague this area. From 1994 to 2001, there have consistently been more poor people in the three Southernmost provinces than the average national figure. In 2001, for example, the number of people under poverty line were 21.35 per cent in Yala , 30.47 per cent in Pattani and 53.19 per cent in Narathiwat compared with the average 13.48 per cent in the country.[19] Other problems, in the villagers' perceptions include irrelevant secular education and lack of support for religious education; corrupted government officials; lawlessness resulted from availability of war weapons, organized crimes involving drugs, the abuse of power and money; and inappropriate government policies.[20] The continuing violence and the recognition of existing economic problems, among others, lead the government to both continue with implementing martial law in the area and to come up with the approval of 28 billion baht development projects to be implemented in these provinces over the next three years.[21]

A social scientist at the Prince of Songkhla University, Pattani campus, commented that the state of knowledge concerning societies in Southern Thailand has been pitiful. The issue of political conflicts in these Southern provinces as well as the official security framework normally used , tend to dominate the academic landscape such that local cultures and the lives of ordinary people have been overlooked.[22] Discussing some notable contributions to Muslim studies in Thailand written in English such as Surin Pitsuwan's *Islam and Malay Nationalism* (1985) and W.K. Che Man's *Muslim Separatism* (1990), among others, an anthropologist echoes a similar opinion that political conflicts between

Thais and Malays have been the main focus of these works. In addition, he criticizes them for paying inadequate attention to heterogeneity among ordinary Thais and Malays other than the officials and the elites.[23] Reviewing studies on the Malay-Muslim provinces in Southern Thailand, edited volumes on Muslims in Thai society, as well as comparative studies of Muslim separatism in Southern Thailand and Southern Philippines, a respected Malaysian scholar with a longstanding interest on Thai society concluded that, the role of Malay-Muslims in the Southern provinces has been overemphasized, while the "complete picture of the role of the Muslims in Thailand is still far from clear."[24]

I would argue, however, that it is indeed the specter of extreme violence which prompts a rethinking of the relationship between violence and local culture/ordinary lives. Violence in Southern Thailand has mainly been a series of vertical conflict between state authorities and the local people, both Muslims and non-Muslims. This is perhaps one of the reasons why the Thai cabinet had recently approved a distribution of 20-page booklets on codes of conduct and prohibitions of government officials in their dealing with Muslims to help bridge cultural gaps and strengthen relations between them and the Muslims. These booklets, however, will be modeled on 1923 guidebooks which were distributed to public servants in the reign of King Rama VI.[25] It is important to note that in the communities, workplaces, markets and other public space, though prejudices among peoples of differences naturally exist, violent conflicts have been rare. This is due to the fact that non-Muslims and Muslims alike in the area possess a sufficiently high degree of cultural sensitivity necessary for living together in just such a context.[26] It is "necessary" because living together in a multicultural context means, as Horstmann's study shows, living in the communal cultural space that is shaped by identity politics where lives of ordinary people are presented and negotiated.[27]

It is now more important than ever to underscore such negotiation processes between Muslims and others because apart from the daily killings of officials and civilians as well as the disappearances of some 40 to 50 Muslims since martial law was enforced in January 2004 as estimated by a senator from Pattani,[28] the unprecedented killings of two Buddhist monks and a novice in Narathiwat and Yala cut deep into the cultural ties that bind communities of differences together.[29] Among many conversations I recently had with local people of different classes and religious persuasions, it is fear that has become the dominant

7

temperament in the area and could produce adverse effects not only on Muslims' negotiated lives, but also on relationship among peoples of differences in Thai society as a whole.

Although this work is by no means an attempt to portray "the complete picture" of Muslims in Thailand, it could be seen as an analytical description of the ways in which Muslims both in the Southern provinces and Bangkok engage in challenges coming from sources such as globalized forces or bureaucratic regulations. Descriptions of these engagements between Muslims and the others, or Muslims' negotiated lives, could elucidate the tensions both between Muslim minorities and their societies, as well as the challenges Muslims face as members of their given society. Muslims' negotiated lives are not confined to the South, however. Focusing on Cham Muslims and their struggle in Bangkok, Scupin points out that with an expanding corporate capitalism, aspirations for democracy stimulated by modernist trends and the influence of Islamic resurgence, their religious and ethnic identity have been reaffirmed with the rise of new ethnoreligious sentiments.[30] Both the reaffirmation and the new sentiments would contribute to the ways in which they live their lives in relation to others in the urban center of the country.

Moreover, negotiated lives in the sense of wearing *hijab* to schools, contested claims about ancient mosques/temples, or changing Arabic names into something else, are presently taking place in different contexts around the world. In Singapore, two very young schoolgirls who were wearing *tudong* (white long-sleeved shirt and ankle-length blue pinafore with head covers) to classes were suspended from school because "they continued to flout the school rules and turned up wearing the Islamic head-scarf." The third girl, Khairah Faroukh aged six, was given a week to conform to the school's common uniform rule.[31] The way Singaporeans handled this incident, among other things, led the Deputy Prime Minister Tony Tan to say that racial harmony and social cohesion in Singapore were being seriously challenged.[32] On February 8, 2002, some seventy Malaysian students gathered outside the Singapore High Commission in Kuala Lumpur to protest against Singapore's ban on schoolgirls' wearing *tudong*.[33]

On March 13, 2002, *The Economist* reported from Ayodhya, India, that Hindu "extremists" planned to perform a religious ceremony at the site of the old Babri mosque, demolished by a mob of Hindu activist in December 1992 which led to more than 2,000 people killed.[34] The

8

proposal of the Ramjanmabhoomi (Rama's birthplace) movement to construct the temple where the mosque once stood, has brought back the violence which began with the burning to death of fifty-eight Hindu pilgrims on the train from Ayodhya in late February, 2002 to the revenge killings in Gujarat which has resulted in more than 600 deaths. Equally important as the violence, is the question: Do India's Muslim minority of 120 million belong in a land of 820 million Hindus?[35] In London, the British Home Secretary, David Blunkett, urged South Asian families, a large number of whom are Muslims, who have been involved in arranged marriages to find partners in Britain and not in Asia. The new immigration proposals would also require would-be immigrants to pass English tests, take citizenship classes and make loyalty pledges. Muslim opinion leaders in Britain responded angrily saying that "we know what is best for our children" and the Home Secretary should not lecture "Asian families on how to carry out Asian traditions."[36] In the US, more than 5,000 Middle Eastern men were "interviewed" in the expectation of terrorist investigation after the September 11 attacks in New York and Washington D.C. An addition of more than 3,000 Middle Eastern men visiting the US after the terror attack have been targeted for these "interviews". The impact of such a policy and heightened sensitivity towards Muslim minority resulted in a growing number of people across the US changing their names to become less Arabic. A former "Bedir", now called "Mark", said: "I do not want an Arabic-sounding name anymore." A "Mohammed Khalil" could not get a job in Southern California until he changed his name to "Michael.".[37] It could be argued that, despite the obvious differences, these incidents do have something in common with those discussed in this book especially in the realities of negotiated lives.

As indicated earlier, most of the studies included here were written at the invitation of different regional and international organizations for a diversity of themes. These organizations considered it important to examine the ways in which communities of faith react to challenges coming from the forces of globalization, modernity, nation-state's grounds for legitimation, economic development, emerging places for civil society or some combinations of these, among others. Given recent incidents around the world, it seems that the issue of negotiated lives in different contexts has become increasingly relevant. Perhaps, it is relevant because negotiated lives have, by necessity, for many a people, become their realities. As a result, understanding negotiated lives of a faith-based minority in the contexts of both the rural South and cosmopolitan Bangkok could perhaps elucidate how Muslims live in Thai society and hint at how they do elsewhere in the world.

The Critique that Affirms

One of the advantages of a volume of collected essays is the fact that some of these writings have been alluded to in academic journals.[38] But these favorable academic responses, though important, are less interesting than the criticisms in Thai and Muslim popular magazines some of my writings have provoked. They are interesting because these criticisms are by themselves reflective of the theme of this volume.

After Chapter 3 was published in the academic journal *Sojourn* in 1993, it was translated into Thai under my authorization and published in a widely read and respected monthly feature magazine.[39] One of this magazine 's readers who claimed to have come from Pattani and to be a devout believer in the Chinese goddess, wrote a letter criticizing the piece on both factual and interpretive grounds. Most important, perhaps, he wrote: "Several things in Dr. Chaiwat's writing were not in accordance with what I know … because his writing was in favor of the Muslim side (because he is a Muslim)."[40]

Chapter 6 was first published in Malaysia in 1998. In May 1999, there was a round table discussion on "Religious Dimension and Economic Problems" in Bangkok. This article was circulated, and later it was partially reproduced in a newspaper column titled: "When Capitalism Fights Religions".[41] A Muslim writer wrote a letter which was later published in *Islamic Guidance Post*, a Muslim newsmagazine, criticizing "Chaiwat's logic" which led to the conclusion of the newspaper article on the antagonism between Islam and capitalism. The letter writer criticized "Chaiwat's logic" on the ground that to combine *Hajj* with real estate advertisement is acceptable because Islam as a belief system is not against trade. To provide opportunity for those who buy houses to go to *Hajj* should not be considered advertisement but religious support, and that it is un-Islamic to judge people's actions on the basis of their motivations, considered God's sole domain, and not on their apparent behavior.[42]

Putting the two criticisms together would suggest that my works were criticized by a non-Muslim as a result of my bias for the Muslims because I am a Muslim, and by a Muslim because "my logic" led to criticism of Muslim business that tries to do good things and perhaps, I have not been Muslim enough. It appears that for some, a Muslim writer will always write as a Muslim first. But for some Muslims, there exists a discrepancy between the religiocultural symbol adhered to by the *ummah* (Muslim community) and reality, which creates problems and sometimes perceived as chaos since religious symbols are perceived as symbolic system aimed at clothing reality with "an aura of factuality". Yet, the moods and motivations produced by religious symbols could also be seen to correspond to existing reality "by being adapted to it".[43] In other words, the "paradox of identities" could be maintained through living a negotiated life. In this sense, these criticisms are instructive as they highlight the reality of negotiated life of Muslims in a particular context, including mine.

Two decades ago a highly respected scholar on Islam in Southeast Asia maintained that the issue of identity—what is a Muslim?—is the kind of question common in the nineteenth century and in the early part of the twentieth because of the then existing administrative categories of colonial administration. But "they never made sense so far as identity was concerned".[44] This is perhaps a result of the fact that through the years Islam has become a "means of identity" characterized by both unification among Muslims and separation them from "the others" in order to either strengthen or oppose political structures depending on specific contexts.[45]

One of the basic paradoxes that shapes one's own identity is that while each component of a composite identity, and there are many components, helps connect the person to a larger collective, when these components are reconfigured together, the identity of that person becomes his/her own specificity. For example, by being a Muslim, I am connected to more than one billion people. As a Thai citizen, I am one of some 62 million people. As a professional social scientist, I am a member of hundreds of thousands of people globally, and perhaps several thousands in the Thai context. But by combining all these identities together—and there are many others—into that of a Muslim social scientist in Thailand, the emerging identity turns out to be much more specific.[46] This specific identity as a compact category is by and large a result of the ways in which each constitutive component faces and influences one another in different contexts. For example, when I offer my prayers or go to *Hajj*, it should be obvious that being Muslim is the most important component that dominates my identity at that particular time. But when I do research, it is possible that being a social scientist could be more important because academic research is governed by the rules, regulations, and language of academia. But since it is futile to compartmentalize each component of identity, negotiations take place within a person all the time. As a result, the shapes, forms and colors of identities, Muslim or otherwise, change in different contexts. The criticisms by a non-Muslim and a Muslim mentioned above, therefore, reaffirm the continuing negotiated life of a person who, in this case, is a Muslim in the context of the Thai public sphere.

The book *Negotiations* by the philosopher Deleuze is a series of texts of nearly twenty years of conversations. He believes that philosophy cannot battle nor converse with powers because it "has nothing to tell them, nothing to communicate, and can only negotiate."[47] For the purpose of my analysis, if Deleuze is correct, then negotiation takes place when conversation is not possible, but it need not be the case, however. It depends, to some extent, on what is meant by conversation. Oakeshott claims that conversation is humankind's "greatest accomplishment".[48] For him, conversation does not mean engaging in debate or inquiry. There is no "truth" to be discovered, proposition proved, no conclusion sought. It does not seek to inform, persuade, or refute others, and is therefore not a battle. Facts appear to be resolved into possibilities and "certainties" kindled by the presence of ideas of another order. Conversation for humankind is "the meeting-place of various modes of imaginings", the latter term understood as "self making" and recognizing the "not-self", or the other. Each has a voice and there is no voice without an idiom of its own. To understand the idiom of one is "to discern how it is distinguished from, and how it is related to the others."[49] Oakeshott's notion of conversation of humankind could perhaps be best understood as an attempt to "steer a difficult path between a hegemonically imposed universalism, governed by one idiom or voice, and an array of self-enclosed, ethnocentric particularisms where no voice would be willing or able to listen to others."[50]

The notion of "negotiated life" used here is a kind of conversation, especially in the sense of a steering of the path between a hegemonic idiom that oftentimes dominates and an ethnocentric voice that sometimes refuses to listen to the voices of others. I would say that it is theoretically next to impossible, on the one hand, to conceptualize a hegemonic idiom so complete nor, on the other, an ethnocentric voice so deaf that it drowns out all other idioms of resistance and voices of other peoples. Empirically, especially in this case, Islam understood as a universal faith practiced by the Muslim minority could not be seen as hegemonic because there will be forces at work in Thai society to counterbalance this possibility. In addition, their particular voices could hardly become enclosed in an ethnocentric manner, due to the realities of their continuing participation in political activities or business transactions. The life of this world, I would argue, is necessarily negotiated, especially in the case of Muslims living as a minority engaging in different conversations, facing various challenges.

The Thread that Binds

I write all but one of the essays that form this volume at the invitation of different organizations, both academic and otherwise, responding to issues considered challenges to communities of people connected by faith, though not shared by most of the Thai people. This volume could be seen as consisting of three parts. Part One attempts to set the tone of the studies which follow and the paradox involves in studying them. In this sense, Chapter 1 could be read as an entry into and a reflection on the Muslim studies project. Part Two, with its three chapters, deals with Muslim people's lives as the biggest minority in Thai society and a numerical majority in Pattani, both as a cultural geography and an administered space in the periphery. Part Three, also consisting of three chapters, focuses on Muslim lives as a minority in the center that is the urban national capital.

Chapter 1 was originally a keynote address at the seminar on "Viewing the Muslim World", part of a project to establish the Kalyani-wattana Institute of Language and Cultural Study together with the College of Islamic Studies, Prince of Songkhla University, Pattani Campus. In order to clearly carve out areas of study and research that would be possible without stringent religious constraints, it seeks to separate Islamic studies from Muslim studies. In fact, the studies that follow in this volume are situated along the line of Muslim studies project rather than Islamic studies. While studying the latter must posit sacredness of the texts, both *Al-Qur'an* and the Prophetic traditions among other things, as limits of scholarship, the former chooses to draw on such sacredness for its inspiration and thus sensitize the researcher to the beliefs and practices of Muslims in various contexts. As a Muslim studies' project with Muslim lives in their different manifestations and hybridities at the centers of studies/research, interdisciplinary methodology is used to view the phenomena, then expressed in the language of social science that is at once critical and sensitive to the place of faith in the lives of believers.

I wrote Chapter 2 when I was a researcher at the Institute of Southeast Asian Studies (Singapore) (ISEAS) in the early 1990s. What might set it apart from other literature surveys is that I chose academic literature review as a way to both tell the story of Pattani based on a decade of existing research and to elucidate the kinds of subtle imaginative acts involved that one usually employs in representing Muslim lives in Southern Thailand to the academic world. The story of Pattani thus told is not unlike other stories, for it has plots complete with heroes and villains contesting along the corridor of history for their pride of places in the politics of public perceptions.

Chapter 3 was written at the invitation of ISEAS to examine the ways in which religion has become more important in the last decade of the last century despite some academic beliefs that it would fall victim to either the processes of rationalization and modernization or the decline of meta-stories and the dissolution of normative connections.[51] I address the issue of religious revivalism in Southeast Asia by focusing on the case of "Kru-ze", the ancient unfinished mosque in Pattani said to be cursed by a Chinese goddess, which has been turned into a historical site mainly for the benefit of the tourism industry, with a large number of Chinese tourists coming in from nearby Malaysia and elsewhere. The protest at the mosque reflects an attempt to renegotiate Muslim identity amidst the changing local myths about the mosque resulting, in turn, from the rise in tourism industry and its official designation as a historical site at a time when global religious resurgence was on the rise.

Chapter 4, written at the invitation of the Social Science Research Council and American Council of Learned Societies Committee on Southeast Asia to explore the phenomenon of religious resurgence in East and Southeast Asia, further elaborates on the negotiating process discussed in the previous chapter. Raising the question why Muslim girl students chose to wear their *hijab* in defiance against official dress code in a Yala school and the ensuring protest which took place at that particular moment in time, this chapter connects " 'a crisis of authority' that has emerged as a consequence of the modernization and nation-building projects"[52] with a new moment in the process of legitimation. This new moment of legitimation appears at a time when being a religious "other" and a minority has been reaffirmed by a transnational religious force in a context where nationality and ethnicity is religiously defined by the majority. In this case, Islam serves as a ground to contest official ideology for a minority at a time when the notion of who they are, were reaffirmed by religious practices.

Chapter 5 is a study of Bangkok Muslims and the tourist trade. Written as a research essay within the "Islam and Economic Development in Southeast Asia Project, Phase III: On Islam and the Role of the Private Sector in Economic Development" organized by the Institute of Southeast Asian Studies in Singapore, this chapter seeks to explore how a minority in the urban context lead their lives as Muslims in tourist-related businesses where most facets of life, including hospitality, can be commercialized. Using data collected from field research in Bangkok covering tourist-related businesses involving Muslims, I analyze narratives of the ways in which their lives as Muslims are "compromised" in the restaurant, travel, souvenir, and entertainment businesses. It could be argued that in this case, the negotiated lives of Muslims in Bangkok are presented from an ethical perspective which highlights the "extent [to which] the Muslims of today are willing or prepared to compromise their faith".[53]

Chapter 6, written at the invitation of the International Movement for a Just World (Malaysia) and the International Christian Peace Movement (*Pax Christi*) (Australia) to explore the impact of globalization on religions and cultures in Asia and Pacific, is an attempt to elucidate possible contradictions when the modern economy is spiritualized using religious idioms while religion is being commodified as an appendix to business transaction. Through the marriage between advertising machines and spirituality in this case, negotiated Muslim lives in Thai society assume unusual forms when the formation of their identity is shaped and reshaped, among other things, by both the global rules of business transactions on the one hand; and local beliefs/values energized by global resurgence of Islam, on the other.

Chapter 7 was written for the Sasakawa Peace Foundation (Japan) to examine the role of Muslim civil society in enhancing the relationship between Islam and democracy. Against Ernest Gellner's thesis that Islam is somewhat incompatible with civil society, by analyzing a case of the Ban Krua Muslim community in downtown Bangkok, I argue that by the urban Muslims' participation in a public conflict to defend their own community against the onslaught of an expressway mega-project by relying on their particular history and Islamic inspirations, the Ban Krua Muslims could help bring about a stronger Thai civil society.

I write this book as a Muslim social scientist working in Thai society. On the one hand, I have to cope with people in academia who are on the verge of ignorance about Islam, in the face of rules enunciated in a society with little understanding of its minorities. There were some who had brushed aside a campaign for peace in the South on the ground that there was no use to talk about peace to the Muslims "because Islam teaches them to kill the non-believers so that they would go to paradise." On the other, I encountered a Muslim who condemned me as a non-Muslim merely because I was drinking coffee while standing.[54] But since the configuration of a person's set of identities cannot be compartmentalized, and different rules governing different identities do exist, living this "paradox" becomes perhaps a possible reality. Consequently, the methodological orientation, the language used in this volume and my belief in the limits of human knowledge resulting from the inherent paradox of the author writing as both a social scientist and a Muslim run through the volume. In addition, dwelling in-between these components of identity, among others, in itself could be seen as an act of negotiated life discussed here. It is safe to assume that my negotiated life does influence the ways in which negotiated lives of Muslims in Thai society in this volume are examined and represented.

1

Muslim Studies, Radical Social Science, and "Alterity"*

As the world has entered the so-called age of "clash of civilizations" between "the West" and "the rest" said by some to be spearheaded by an alliance between two ancient civilizations; Chinese and Islamic, to view the Muslim world through the eyes of critical knowledge rather than passion is essential for both academic excellence and proper policy by all concerned parties. Despite numerous shortcomings, Huntington's "clash of civilizations" thesis is academically useful because he argues that at the dawn of the new century, while the economy and ideology are declining as arbiters of human destiny, cultural or civilizational identity seems to gain unprecedented power in shaping the conflicts, cooperations or even demises of political entities that presently exist after the Cold War.[1] Although the Huntington thesis has been roundly criticized,[2] the fact that culture has been gaining significance as a unit of analysis in social science and influencing policies is increasingly becoming evident if viewed from the perspective of international scholarship.[3]

This paper maintains that Muslim studies should be thought of as a separate academic space where theoretical and highly critical analysis are accepted as a norm. I will begin by discussing the distinction between Islamic and Muslim studies from a social science and theological perspectives. Then the idea of a radical social science as an appropriate methodology for Muslim studies will be advanced. Finally, a crucial

---

* Originally written in Thai as a keynote address for the seminar on "Viewing the Muslim World: On the Road of the Body of Knowledge," organized by the Project to establish the Kalyani-wattana Institute of Language and Cultural Study with the College of Islamic Studies, Prince of Songkha Nakarin, Pattani Campus, June 26–27, 1997, this article is translated into English with some revisions by the author. The Thai original was published in *Songkhlanakarin Journal of Social Science and Humanities*, vol. 4, no. 1, (January–April 1998), pp. 1–10.

problem that lurks in the studies of Muslims and their societies, the "problematique" of "alterity" or otherness, will be examined.

TOWARDS MUSLIM STUDIES

Two very important books could well serve as points of entry in discussing the differences between Islamic and Muslim studies. The first is *Islam and Modernity*[4] by late Prof. Fazlur Rahman of the University of Chicago. The second is *Islams and Modernities*[5] written by Aziz Al-Azmeh, Institue of Advanced Study, Berlin. These two volumes were written by two noted scholars on Islam, based in world-class academic institutions and published almost 15 years apart. Superficially these two books are similar, especially their titles.

But under careful inspection, these two titles are quite different, most notably the singular and plural forms used. That modernity could take various shapes should come as no surprise to most social scientists, Muslim and non-Muslim alike. But that "Islams" in the title of Al-Azmeh's book is plural could engender strange reactions. Seeing "Islam" with an "s", non-Muslim social scientists could be reminded of the multicultural reality of Islamic civilizations. But for most Muslims whose conception of Islam is shaped by the longing for lost unity and the oneness of faith, Al-Azmeh's title could pose a serious problem.

I would argue that both authors did choose their titles correctly. Fazlur Rahman's work is a part of a large research project on Islam and social change at the University of Chicago. Rahman suggests in this work that it is the growth and uniqueness of Islamic thought that would determine the success or failure of Islamic education. He believes that this would be possible through well thought out methodology necessary for a correct exegesis of the *Qur'an*. His work begins with the basic belief, shared by every common Muslim,[6] that *Qur'an* is a sacred text because it is in fact the "Word of God" that was revealed by the "Pen of God" through the unlettered, and therefore pure heart of Prophet Muhammad, His last messenger.[7] *Qur'an* is the center of all guidances for human beings. It affirms what has come before and completes all other revelations.[8] Al-Azmeh, on the other hand, begins with an assertion that his work is based on a basic belief that there are as many Islams as the various contexts that constitute them.[9] He tries to underscore the Islamic cultural heterogeneity that exists even among British Muslims which resulted from multiple realities at the structural, institutional, and organization levels. He, in turn, claims to view these realities from the "Pakistani-British Muslim" perspective.[10]

I would say that Fazlur Rahman's starting point is in accordance with Islamic studies type research because of its theological implications. The object of study is Islam, a living faith of at least a billion believers worldwide. Under the framework of Islamic belief (*Iman*), there are several non-negotiable articles of faith: the belief in Allah as the Absolute Being beyond human comprehension; the Day of Judgement; the belief that all goods and ills are results of Divine Will; or that *Qur'an* is God's Words, final and cannot be altered in any way. For Islamic studies, these features are at once objects of study and faith. Any study that seeks to question these beliefs would result in all kinds of problems. Some might even be seen as shrouded in ignorance or lack of religious understanding. Others might even be perceived as conspiracies aiming to undermine Islam and the Muslim communities.[11] These may be consequences of the fact that Islamic studies begins with religious Truth which is thought by Muslims as those revealed by God through Prophet Muhammad. Islamic studies then focuses on attempts to construe God's commandments as they appear in the sacred text, explanations and elaborations of these commandments based on evidences scrutinized from the *Hadith* (Traditions of the Prophet), or sages' commentaries from times past. Conflicts which arise in Islamic studies are oftentimes consequences of different interpretations of the texts or rationales behind them.

Al-Azmeh's starting point is to study Islam in different social and multicultural contexts. For example, to conduct research on British Muslims involves a study of their linkages characterized by such questions as: where are they from? Are they Muslims from South Asia? or Africa? From Pakistan influenced by Pathan culture or Bengali's? From Khartoum or Alexandria? In the eyes of a social scientist, these backgrounds matter. Because social science in general assumes, on the one hand, that a human being is primarily a seeker of meaning and his/her future destiny , carrying burdens of the past from inherited histories which include language, cultures, or ethnohistories. On the other, he/she lives and struggles in the present social conditions. As a result, for Al-Azmeh, "Islam" for a Pakistani British Muslim would be different from "Islam" of a Sudanese British Muslim or "Islam" of an Albanian influenced by decades of Maoisam. Al-Azmeh's object of study is not "Islam" in the religious sense which emphasizes non-negotiable "religious Truth" as in the case of Fazlur Rahman's. It is the multiple social realities which are constantly changing that is his academic concern. This type of research belongs more clearly in the realm of Muslim studies than in Islamic studies.

While Islam does not change nor decline because God's Words and Truth remain unaltered through the ages, Muslims in different societies all over the globe could perform their religious duties or lead their lives somewhat differently. For example, the standing postures during prayers of Muslims from different places are not the same due to schools of thought which they adhere to. Muslim food in China are different from those among Malay or Indian Muslims. Most important, is the fact that Muslim societies such as the Mogul empire in South Asia or the Ottoman empire rise and fall just like other human societies have experienced in world history. Research and studies of things that are unchangeable or indestructible and those which change in accordance with histories and social conditions have to be dissimilar.

From the social science perspective, I would argue that Islamic studies is the study of Islam which takes into account at least 3 types of sacredness; *Qur'an* as Islam's sacred text; the holy city of Mecca (*haram*) where non-Muslims are not allowed to enter, the Prophet's city of Madina, or Jerusalem with Islam's third holiest shrine, *Bait al-Maqdis*, as sacred topography;[12] and sacred duties of Muslims which include sacrificing everything for the sake of Allah, Almighty. Violations of these sacredness would engender conflicts with the Muslims as reflected in the international controversy surrounding *The Satanic Verses* by Salman Rushdie more than a decade ago,[13] the status of Jerusalem in the eyes of the Muslims and the Jews,[14] or conflicts over the wearing of hijab among Muslim girl students in Yala in 1988.[15]

Muslim studies do not focus on the scholastic study of *Qur'an*, the *Hadith*, nor Islamic Law (*Fiqh*) all of which require profound religious knowledge as well as a high level understanding of the Arabic language, not to mention the fact that these are the domains of authority of religious scholars. Muslim studies seek to examine the lives of Muslims and their living societies. If that society has a Muslim majority such as those in the Middle East or Indonesia, then it is Muslim studies that conduct research and studies on Muslim societies. But if the Muslims constitute a minority in that particular society, such as in Thailand, the Philippines or Cambodia, then it is the study of Muslims in a Buddhist or Christian context. These studies could be research on people's belief. It would not be considered Islamic studies since it is not a study of Islam as a religion endowed with Divine Truth, but a study of the different Muslims' beliefs in Islam in various contexts. For example, belief in Islam among the Acehnese in Sumatra would be different from that among the Javanese Muslims in Jakarta. Understanding these differences could result from an analysis of numerous variables including the coming of Islam in Southeast Asia. Acehnese history, Sumatran geography, or unique Javanese cultures, among other things.

Another distinctive feature of Muslim studies is to focus on Muslims as ordinary people suffering from good and evil just like others in the world. This type of inquiry could be considered deeply Islamic. I would argue that being a Muslim does not mean that he/she is an unblemished believer and would not be punished in the Hereafter. As a matter of fact, in Islam there is a distinction between a "Muslim" and a "*Mumin*." In Islam's early history, Muslim societies had to face the issue of people who claimed to be Muslims and yet were corrupted and had committed evil deeds. The *Kharijites* believed that these people were not Muslims while the *Murjites* maintained that such verdict could not be made until God has revealed the whole truth for all to see. In the absence of Divine Truth, it had to accept that everyone who declared him/herself as a Muslim should be considered as such.[16] When these people committed sin, they will then be punished accordingly.

While Muslims could be those who declare themselves accepting Islam with a *Shahadah* (religious vow), they could do something unwarranted by the religion and would therefore be punishable. "*Mumin*," on the other hand, according to the *Qur'an*, are people who "humble themselves in their prayers," "avoid vain talk," "active in deeds of charity," "abstain from sex except with those joined to them in the marriage bond, or (the captives) whom their right hands possess,… "[17]

It could therefore be said that Muslim studies are attempts to study Muslims in social contexts which may be Muslim or non-Muslim, underscoring the people's behavioral patterns, beliefs, religious and social practices, among other things. It is ordinary people and societies which are being studied. They could be good or bad, saintly or evil, proper or decline because they are not sacred. Finding within the realm of Muslims studies are subjected to challenges because they are not "Truth" in the final sense. Quite contrary, these findings could be reviewed, criticized, or even negated. Muslim studies as an academic endeavor studying people and societies are, in some ways, as good as the methodology chosen. The question next is what kind of methodology would be most appropriate to Muslim studies?

TOWARDS RADICAL SOCIAL SCIENCE

More than a decade ago, I reviewed the discipline of political science, criticizing its dominant trend in terms of its sociology of knowledge and positivistic epistemology for relegating human beings, which constitute the subject of study, to marginal importance. I then advanced the idea of an alternative called "radical political science" re-positioning human beings in their contexts as the focus of study and research. The return to the most fundamental of units and issues of study, which is human beings in all their complexities, is "radical" in the original sense of returning to the "roots" of things, and the "root" of politics is none other than human beings themselves.[18]

My proposal in the field of political science is, in fact, not dissimilar to my suggestion to create a space for Muslim studies here. The Muslim studies I propose is based on a radical social science study of Muslim societies, focusing on Muslims as ordinary people in their contexts as the main subjects, taking into account at least three levels of variables necessary for any analysis of humans and their societies.

Level 1

The Muslims as human actors, underscoring their patterns of behavior as well as action,[19] should be studied. Psychological factors, needed to explain that specific behavior or biographical factors inevitable for a more comprehensive understanding of particular human lives, could be emphasized. For example, to understand the political role of a Muslim individual such as the Pattani senator-elect Mr. Den Tohmeena or the Thai Foreign Minister, Dr. Abdul Halim Surin Pitsuwan, would require a careful attention to each psychohistory, far beyond textbooks psychological modeling. Biographical details together with the subject's individual experiences could offer insights into the possibility to adequately construe a Muslim's leadership behavior.[20]

Level 2

Each individual certainly exists in a specific social context. Factors necessary for understanding an individual's or a group's action could lie at a level deeper than any personal preferences or psychohistory. These economic, sociological, and political factors, which form such a context, are related and structural. For example, a Muslim group's action engaging in conflicts over their rights to natural resources in the ocean might depend on the degree to which they are economically secured. If the structure of income distribution is unjust while political space for their rightful participation is limited, it is highly likely that their actions would turn out to be more aggressive. On the contrary, if the political space is expanded and channels do exist within the normal political system so that Muslim voices could be sufficiently heard and power fairly negotiated, the use of strong actions, or in some cases—political violence, as well as the reasons for using them in advancing their rights would decline in significance.

Level 3

While the socio-economic-political sphere constitutes a basic structure which serves as the context of an individual or a Muslim community as well as their behavioral pattern, there remains a "deeper" level of variables important for a profound social science reading. This is the cultural layer which serves as legitimization of other levels of variable, behavioral, and structural. As a set of variables, it operates at a "deeper level" because although it could change through times, the pace of change is much slower than variables at other levels. Since the focuses of study here are the Muslims and their societies, the process of legitimizing or de-legitimizing their behavior and structural context necessarily relates to Muslim cultures, characterized by the central role of Islam. But to deal with Islam here as a culture is not a search, criticisms, nor defense of Islam's "religious Truth." Rather, it is an attempt to comprehend the ways in which the Muslims lead their lives, legitimizing certain actions/behaviors, institutions and structures while consider some other unacceptable. For example, there are a number of Muslim restaurants in crowded areas in downtown Bangkok which only serve lunch and choose to close in the evening despite heavy demands for dinner. To construe such a phenomenon requires something beyond common economic reasoning informed by material profit motives. From a cultural perspective, it could be said that these Muslim restaurants do not merely operate for worldly gain but to serve the dietary need of Muslim minority during lunch time for those who work outside. Evening then is the time to be spent at home with families where eating and other religious duties, such as prayers and the preceding ablutions, could be carried out, preferably together and in convenience.

The idea of Muslim studies advanced here could depend on a methodology characterized by multiplicity and complexities, partly because Muslim societies, not unlike any other human society, are complex. Muslim studies that seek to analyze Muslim-related phenomena using these three levels of variables primarily attempt to find an ordered process to explain or understand Muslims' behavior or action and their structural contexts.[21] This very methodology is informed by various disciplines in social science and humanities such as, psychology, history, biography, sociology, economics, political science, cultural studies, and definitely some knowledge about Islam. These disciplines then form themselves into a web of social and human sciences that would provide meaning, supply relevant understanding, and generate rational explanations for the very problems under study.

This methodology proposal for Muslim studies could be seen as an ideal due to the fact that there may not be any researcher with sufficient expertise in all these fields of knowledge. Some might suggest a joint study with researchers drawn from diverse disciplines while others in some societies could sense that this "teamwork" itself is another impossibility. I would argue that perhaps the most important feature of radical social science is the researcher's awareness of his/her own discipline's limitation in understanding such a complex human phenomenon. In addition, the disciplinary territory in the interrelated world of social science and humanities itself is mainly illusory and should not be regarded as sacred. To understand social realities means, among other things, that these lines dividing the disciplines should not be petrified, and in fact, could be crossed. While a separation of Muslim studies from Islamic studies is important in terms of clarity of focus, attachment to these illusions that constitute the disciplines is not necessarily a virtue in Muslim studies. An awareness of the nature of methodology used, its weaknesses and limitations, is important if the academic quality of research and studies are to be maintained and indeed ad hoc. Awaiting further research, using novel theoretical perspectives or innovative methodology, all findings based on radical social science with the Muslims as the human center could be reviewed, criticized, and enriched. This methodology, in turn, would strengthen and broaden Muslim studies.

"ALTERITY"

One of the reasons for proposing the idea of Muslim studies is that within the framework of Islamic studies, a basic problem arises from the identity of the scholars who conduct the studies themselves. If the person is a Muslim, certain levels of Islamic knowledge and Arabic are fundamental for Islamic studies. A non-Muslim researcher, on the other hand, even with profound Islamic knowledge and Arabic capability, could be criticized from his/her perspective used. Perhaps, this is because in Islam, the constitution of the Muslim self is well defined. As a result, the line between a Muslim and "the other" as non-Muslim or non-believer (*kafir*) is sharply drawn. Anyone without faith in Allah Almighty, the Prophethood of Muhammad, the authenticity of *Qur'an* as Divine Message, among others, could be seen as "the other." They are "outsiders" with their own paths, different from the Muslims, and at times could even be considered "enemies."[22] Withinsuch a framework clearly demarcating "the other" from "the self," studies related to sacred texts, topography and duties conducted by "the other" could easily be suspected and contribute to future problems.

But will this very problem disappear within the framework of Muslim studies?

It is my contention that such a problem will continue to exist, though transformed. For example, two researchers, a Buddhist and a Muslim, studying the topic such as "Muslims as consumers" would encounter the alterity problem differently.[23] The first would have to face the alterity problem directly as a non-Muslim researcher studying patterns of Muslim consumers' behavior. He/she would have to try his/her best to understand their behavioral patterns. In the eyes of the Muslims who were being studied, the researcher would be the "other" while the Muslims would constitute his/her "others" at the same time. The researcher would have to deal with alterity which sometimes appears as something at once exotic, servile, or a mere object of study.[24] This alterity could at times be mysteriously beautiful or unrealistically frightening. This researcher then needs to reduce the gap between his/her own "alterity" and the Muslim community which he/she studies. An obstacle to be faced would be the strong cultural line dividing the Muslims from the others.

But if he/she is a Muslim, some forms of alterity would still exist. It could hide behind the existential otherness between the researcher and the people whom he/she studies. While the cultural line dividing the believers from the non-believers may not exist, the discursive line in most research works still does. The Muslim researcher will also have to guard against the study of the others as the study of one's own self when the line dividing the two completely vanishes. In studying the self, the researcher confronts another type of realities distorted in some other ways. It is important to note that in confirming the exotopy of alterity is to invite the others' subjective experiences upon the self of the researcher.[25] To engage in Muslim studies is then to situate the researcher at a "comfortable distance" so that social realities could be properly reflected while retaining the ability to relate to the people under study not as object but as human beings. Researcher the concrete social contexts is a distinctive type of cultural activity. The problem of studying other people or their communities, according to a noted anthropologist, is an attempt at "comprehension of the self by the detour of the comprehension of the other."[26] This approach, I would argue, is in line with radical social science methodology proposed for Muslim studies which do not ignore the humanity of the people to be studied and their powerful living faith and culture that is Islam.

CONCLUSION: VIEWING MUSLIM STUDIES

For the sake of clarity, let me state categorically that my theoretical proposal for the possibility of Muslim studies does not in any way mean that Islamic studies is no longer important or that its significance has declined. I propose Muslim studies as a separate field because there are two distinctive academic activities with different objectives. To sustain and strengthen faith in Islam with findings and answers relating to religious injunctions are the main objectives and worthwhile mission of Islamic studies since they are crucial for the spiritual lives of all Muslims adhering to Islam as their guiding light. But to study and do research on the Muslims and their societies under the influences of the socio-cultural-historical-economic-political context is indeed a social science mission in need of the guidance of studies is human beings, who are Muslims in this case. In the process, the "alterity problematique" may arise. But to work creatively with alterity means, among other things, to give significance to the others' human experiences which, in turn, means to genuinely respect the Muslims' living faith in Islam.

PART **II**

Negotiating Muslim Lives in Pattani: Cultural Center, National Margin

2

Pattani in the 1980s: Academic Literature as Political Stories*

INTRODUCTION

Pattani[1] has for centuries been regarded as one of the cradles of Islam in Southeast Asia. A Malay scholar, currently working in Brunei, suggests in his published Ph.D. thesis that "The Kingdom of Patani, it is believed, was officially declared an Islamic state in 1457."[2] What is interesting is not the specific date given, but the source the author uses. Using the same source to discuss the historical development of Pattani, another scholar states categorically in a note: "On the history of Patani, see Teeuw and Wyatt's *Hikayat Patani*... "[3] Teeuw and Wyatt, however, concluded the classic text they translated, which was referred to by these two scholars, with the following insightful words:

> It is a story in which the author worked very selectively and with a clear aim in mind. We have reason to believe that, moreover, he did not limit himself to historical facts, and that in his story fact and fiction occur side by side, although this distinction may have been irrelevant to the author himself.[4]

Most good academic works are sharply focused. Consequently, these works are normally selective in the subjects chosen and theoretical perspectives used.

---

* The research on which this paper is based was conducted while I was a Research Fellow in the Social Issues in Southeast Asia (SISEA) program at the Institute of Southeast Asian Studies (ISEAS), Singapore, from March to April 1990, supported by the Konrad Adenauer Foundation. I wish to thank ISEAS and the Konrad Adenauer Foundation for their kind support.

It is often said that the ordeal of Malay Muslims in southern Thailand is among "the most protracted and best documented."[5] If such is truly the case, it is important to pause and assess the body of knowledge accumulated on the issue. A review of the literature over a period of time (that is, 1980–89), though not the sole purpose of this study, is crucial in revealing the extent to which academic works are also "stories" with some normative functions.

THE PROBLEM AND SCOPE DEFINED

Teeuw and Wyatt argue that the primary aim of the author or authors of *Hikayat Patani* was "clearly" not to give a factual account of historical events, but to provide readers with "a political pattern as seen from the viewpoint of Patani."[6] Most academic works claim to do just the opposite. With few exceptions, they often present themselves in an "objective" fashion. To highlight the nature of academic works as stories, it is imperative to examine how the issue of Muslims in southern Thailand is raised. Taken as discursive practices, this paper argues that these academic works also provide readers with "political patterns" as seen from various viewpoints. In other words, in the process of reviewing the literature on Pattani, an attempt is made here to draw out the kinds of subtle imaginative acts which are involved in re-presenting Muslims in southern Thailand to the academic world.

The period of time covered in this study is approximately 1980–89.[7] The decade is important for two basic reasons, among others. First, except for a couple of abortive coup attempts, for much of the decade internal political conditions in Thailand were marked by relatively uninterrupted parliamentary democracy and a constitutional government, although under a non-elected prime minister. Second, following the success of the Iranian revolution in 1979, the tide of Islamic resurgence began sweeping throughout the world in the 1980s.[8] The impact of this resurgence was experienced by the Malay Muslims in southern Thailand, as in neighboring Malaysia.[9]

This study is concerned with the ways in which the issue of Muslims in southern Thailand is re-presented to the international academic community. The literature under review is, accordingly, all in English. There are three reasons for this. First, the Pattani issue is more than a Thai problem from a historical perspective. The British, and later Malaysian involvement, as well as the Meccan connection, are conspicuous. Second, an issue involving the Malay Muslims is necessarily related to the much larger Malay cultural world of Southeast Asia. Third, this issue is directly the story of the Muslims in the area and the ways in which their religion forms a significant part of their lives. It goes without saying that Islam is transnational in character. It is, however, important to note that the portrait of Malay Muslims in southern Thailand is necessarily incomplete because the literature on the subject in both Thai and Malay lie outside the scope of this study for reasons of space.

The main academic story of Pattani will be reconstructed from three major sources. Doctoral dissertations on the subject will first be discussed. Then monographs on the issue will also be taken into account. Finally, reviews and articles which appear in 13 international academic journals dealing with Asia in general and Southeast Asia in particular will be covered. In addition, attention will also be paid to an international journal specializing on the issue of Muslim minorities. These journals are published in North America, England, Australia, Southeast Asia, and the Middle East. Papers and chapters in edited volumes are beyond the scope of this study. Nonetheless, it is evident that the literature which has been drawn upon here tells the international academic community (and perhaps others) a story of Pattani which reveals the academic landscape of the past decade, and through this story the future course of academic endeavor on the subject may be meaningfully charted.

THE ACADEMIC LANDSCAPE

Theses

In the 1970s, there appeared to be only three major works popularly cited on the subject of the Malay Muslims in Pattani: Teeuw and Wyatt's *Hikayat Patani* (1970),[10] Arong Suthasasna's *Problems of Conflict in the Four Southern Provinces* (1976),[11] and Nantawan Haemindra's two-part essay entitled "The Problem of the Thai Muslims in the Four Southern Provinces of Thailand" (1976/77).[12] In contrast to this, however, the past decade saw the appearance of several theses on Muslims in southern Thailand. Perhaps the most notable of all these Ph.D. theses is Surin Pitsuwan's *Islam and Malay Nationalism: A Case Study of the Malay Muslims of Southern Thailand.* This 1982 Harvard Ph.D. thesis has received considerable attention for three reasons, apart from its scholarly quality. First, it is one of the most comprehensive treatments on the subject and the first to be published by Thai Khadi Research Institute, second, it has been translated into Indonesian, naturally broadening the number of its readers in the Malay-speaking world. Third, its author is a well-trained political scientist and a successful Muslim politician from southern Thailand.

While Surin's thesis was written in 1982, the most recently completed thesis in the 1980s was Che Man's Ph.D. thesis which was submitted to the Australian National University in 1988 and which was recently published (1990). Che Man compares the Moro of the southern Philippines with the Malays of southern Thailand.

Surin's thesis captures the essence of the Muslims' ordeal in southern Thailand by linking the two main factors which have helped sustain the people's distinctive character, namely, their ethnicity and religion with developments in various periods of Thailand's political history. He argues that political events which took place from 1902 (when the Malay Muslims were incorporated into the Thai state) up to 1982 decisively transformed the socio-economic structure of Thailand. Through a series of historical "accidents," the Malay Muslims of southern Thailand "have been living under the jurisdiction of a government that can hardly claim their loyalty."[13] As socio-economic conditions change, the Malay Muslims are forced to "adapt their tactics and orientation in pursuit of their goal of autonomy."[14] In the process of their struggle, Islam and Malay ethnicity constitute the "primordial ties" or "unreflective sense of collective selfhood" for them. However, he concludes that the strongest bond (in the sense of Abner Cohen's "articulating principle") that binds the Malay Muslims together has been Islam. In fact, this dissertation can be seen as an attempt to describe the role of Islam in the long process of independent struggle of the Malay Muslims within the "changing economic, political, and other social circumstances" of Thai political history.[15] While Surin emphasizes the recontextualization of the Malay Muslims' struggle, Chavivun Prachuabmoh claims that the existence and perpetuation of their identity cannot be sufficiently explained by history and cultural symbols because other media are needed to transmit and organize them. She indicates that the "southern Thai Muslims" maintain their distinctive ethnicity through various social organizations such as family, kinship, community, friendship networks, and religious education. This dissertation is also unique in its attempt to underscore the role of Muslim women. Based on women's commitment to maintain ethnic symbols such as clothing and language as well as the way they minimize interaction with outsiders and their strong opposition to intermarriage, they are regarded as crucial in maintaining ethnicity. In fact, she suggests that as a consequence of the socialization process, women are more inclined to maintain their cultural symbols better than men. They may also have greater influence on children because the teaching and learning of ethnicity through women is a more intimate and emotional process while make ethnicity is more heavily oriented towards formal organizations.

But beyond this, Chavivun's dissertation is most impressive as a remarkable story of prejudice. Using the concept of "ethnic boundary," she provides a fascinating account of mutual estrangement between Buddhists and Muslims. She narrates, for example, how a Buddhist hairdresser living in the Thai quarter in Pattani for more than twenty years could not manage to have any contact with her Muslim neighbors. Another Thai trader living in a "Thai" village surrounded by Muslim villages "hates Muslims without specific reason except for such differences."[16]

Such attitudes are amply illustrated in the attributes accorded to *khaek* in Thai perception. In discussing ethnic conflict, Horowitz points out that *khaek* is pejorative,

> not because it connotes utter inferiority—though it also means "dark" (cf. "khaki") and thus refers to skin color but because to call the Malays visitors is to undercut their legitimate place in the country.[17]

Chavivun shows that in the eyes of the Thai, *khaek* are ethnocentric, lusty (male), lazy, dirty, selfish, untrustworthy, poor, narrow-minded, cruel, uncooperative, stupid, unfriendly, and very religious. In addition, they do not eat pork, cannot touch dogs, close their house doors, do not speak Thai, are good at magic and disloyal to Thailand.[18] This list of attributes, in many respects, explains much better the "pejorative" connotations of *khaek* in everyday life than Horowitz's analysis which ultimately rests on a notion of the legitimacy or illegitimacy of Malay Muslim presence.

On the other hand, the Muslims also view the Thai unfavorably. Such an attitude is nurtured by common stories narrated and communicated among themselves. These stories include, for example, the past invasion of Pattani by the Thai when many Muslims were killed and taken captive, the erosion of Islamic education with the introduction of compulsory Thai secular education, the enforcement of Rathaniyom by Field Marshal Phibun Songkhram, and the murder of Haji Sulong. Chavivun concludes that hostility among groups do exist and therefore avoidance is "their strategy for coping with potential conflict."[19]

She then returns to the characteristics of Islam and asserts that compared with Buddhism, it does become the source of ethnic identity and boundary maintenance, while providing mechanisms for organizing an ethnic group. Indeed, when Islam is part of a complex pattern of relations in which cultural differences are significant, "the ethnic boundary is greatly sharpened regardless of political sensitivity."[20]

In discussing the nature of Malay ethnicity, language is perhaps the mode in which all other interactions such as rituals or familial socialization are carried out. Seni Mudmarn chooses to investigate the loyalty of the Muslim Malay people of southern Thailand towards the Malay language. He does so by assessing the degree of Malay language loyalty in terms of a causal relationship between socio-demographic variables and the language behavior of his respondents. Then he compares the degree of loyalty between the population of the two geographically and historically different speech communities, namely, "Patani" and Satun.[21]

Seni maintains, theoretically, that language loyalty is a phenomenon in which a group of people persistently resist change to their language in either function or form. Language loyalty is awakened either when the mother tongue is considered superior to the dominant language or when it is threatened by a rival language. Using both quantitative and qualitative methods of investigation, he found and extremely favorable attitude towards the Malay language. He also found that rural residence, language use in childhood, parents' language(s), and the level of Islamic/religious education are the major factors which determine the degree of language loyalty.

Perhaps the most important implication of his study is the way the "Muslim Malays" view their language. For them, the Malay language is strongly associated with the notion of Malay ethnicity and the religion of Islam:

> The Malay language functions as a boundary marker between those who are Malay and those who are not. It links their present existence with their glorious past, reminding them of their history as a separate sovereign polity. Furthermore, Malay is considered a source of cultural heritage, of positive values and of pride for the Muslim Malays.[22]

The close association of the Malay language with Islam is also emphasized. After the Islamization of the Malay peninsula, Arabic script was adopted for the Malay writing system. Then the Malay language written in the Jawi script became a language associated "not only with the communicative and symbolic aspects of the Malay culture but also with Islamic learning, propagation, and rituals."[23] Now that the ethnic boundary has taken upon a religious dimension and the fusion between the two (religion and ethnicity) has strengthened the identity of the Malay Muslims, the story of the Thai Government's policies and practices in dealing with them remains to be told.

Among persistent and long-term government policies are family planning and education. While Thailand is considered successful in both policies, demographic trends in southern Thailand leave much to be desired in the eyes of Thai policy-makers. According to Krich Suebsonthi's thesis, the "Thai Muslims" tend to unite and keep on protecting their own tradition because of their rigid belief in Islam. Those who call themselves "Thai Malays, " face more restrictions concerning their tradition and customs. As a result, the level of secular education is rather low among them. He concludes that it narrows their view in accepting and adopting any kind of innovation such as family planning.[24]

Focusing on education as a means of national integration, Kanniga Sachakul attempts to compare the use of education to assimilate the Chinese and the Muslims in Thailand. Among other things, she tries to study the central government's efforts to "solve" ethnic problems and examine educational programs designed by the central government for ethnic minorities. She finds that the "Malays" have striven to maintain their religion, language, and cultural identity and have resisted policies and administrative practices intended to foster assimilation into the larger Thai society. This leads her to conclude that educational policies, like most government policies, have been greatly affected by political influences which are intricately linked to the issue of national security. The Thai Government, which requires the minorities to be able to speak Thai and has pressured them to be loyal to Thailand, is then recommended to be "flexible and compromising" and to work "toward integration rather than total assimilation." And, without a trace of irony, it should also provide the southern people with ample opportunities to be educated at all levels.[25]

Panomporn Anurugsa's case-study of the "Malay Muslims" is an attempt to examine the integrative strategies and methods pursued by the Thai Government and the consequences of such strategies and methods as well as assessing various social programs in relation to creating loyalty or disloyalty among the Malay Muslims. This dissertation views political integration as a process emphasizing various aspects of the government's efforts to create loyalty among the minorities. She asserts that in southern Thailand,

> the success of political integration generally is to erase the Malay ethnicity of the Malay Muslims according to which political integration will be successful at the point when most Malay Muslims identify themselves as Thais (who profess Islam) or Thai Muslims, not as Malay Muslims.[26]

She points out that many government policy-makers are attached to the ideal outcome of assimilation in the tradition of nation-building suggested by Leonard Binder and Rupert Emerson because "there is no doubt that, if successful, assimilation would be the best way to guarantee nation-building of the country."[27] However, she thinks that the costs would outweigh the benefits. On the other hand, an autonomy model which ultimately requires an alteration in the very form of the state is too ambitious because "for a unitary state such as Thailand, autonomy is considered a breaking down of a united territory and of the boundaries of the country."[28]

She then suggests that an accommodation model is most appropriate because in a heterogeneous state it proposes to build a nation out of diversity while each group can still enjoy control over its distinctive institutions. In communal conflict, then, the state will assume a conciliatory role. The government will become a broker in the articulation of the interests of various ethnic and cultural groups. The model also implies reciprocal benefits for ethnic groups in creating loyalty and support to the system through political participation, among other things.

Panomporn then goes on to analyze "four sequential stages of integrative efforts" from the late nineteenth century to 1982. The analysis includes a consideration of government policies on *pondok* education, youth programs, the creation of a new administrative organization at the beginning of the decade, economic policy aiming at dependency of the Malay Muslims on the Thai economic system, as well as development projects under the patronage of the king and the "serene south policy" under General Harn Leenanond. It is interesting to note that her analysis is uncommonly straightforward regarding the royal project in the Malay Muslim provinces.[29]

She points out that the sole purpose of the rice-growing project in the Malay Muslim provinces (the royal project) was to create economic self-sufficiency in rice production for the Thai Buddhists in the land settlement area. This was because the government believed that the security in the Malay Muslim provinces could not be established unless the Thai Buddhists resided along the boundaries of the land settlements in the area. In her view, with this established, "the Thai Buddhists in the area will thus become a natural ward of the government."[30]

This dissertation maintains that although the present government does not directly pursue a solely assimilationist policy, most of its policies effectively undermine accommodative premises. Policies are utilized to transform parochial loyalties among the Malay Muslims into national loyalty. The most important approach of the government in nation-building is

> ensconcing Thai Muslims in those who are willing to accept Thai legitimacy. Every policy (in education, economics, administrative reform, and security) works toward this goal

and those who do not comply with this, such as "the orthodox Muslims, the theological graduates from abroad, the separatists," are politically suppressed.[31] Unless important corrective measures are taken, ethnic conflict is likely to persist in southern Thailand.

Government policies analyzed by Panomporn are but parts of the trajectory that Thai society has taken during the past three decades. That trajectory can be characterized as a process of modernization. Conventional theories maintain a negative relationship between the persistence of ethnic loyalties and modernization. But Uthai Dulyakasem believes that certain aspects of modernization processes produce conditions under which ethnicity can become most effectively utilized by the group as the basis for political mobilization. In his dissertation, he examines the relationship between the expansion of modern education, economic modernization, and political modernization on the one hand, and the degree of involvement in separatist activity on the other.[32]

What is unique about this work is its methodological contribution. Uthai utilizes historical, quantitative methods (panel analysis, cross sectional analysis, and pooled time series data using regression analysis as a major tool), and qualitative methods (case-studies through field observations and interviews) as part of a framework informed by an "ecological-competitive model." This model posits that

> economic and political modernization create the conditions under which ethnicity is seen as the most viable and effective political instrument for the periphery to oppose the penetration from the center.[33]

His study reveals that the degree of ethnic nationalism is not only related to aspects of modernization processes, but also to the development of the particular history of the communities and their linguistic identification. Nevertheless, one of his most intriguing findings is that ethnic political conflict has led to and expansion of modern education because the government believes, along the lines of some theses mentioned above, that education would help integrate or assimilate the "Muslim Malays" into "Siam" proper. However, the expansion of education into Malay Muslim areas has not only failed to bring about peaceful assimilation, "but it also intensified, if not created, ethnic conflict between the Muslim Malays and the central government."[34]

Most of the theses discussed above analyze different conditions or sets of conditions which give rise to ethno-religious conflict in southern Thailand. Some writers, such as Surin and Uthai, discuss the separatist movements in the south. However, the separatist movements themselves have not been their main object of study. There seems to be a missing episode in the story.

Che Man's Master's thesis in 1983 focuses on the specific historical and political roots which gave rise to the secessionist conflict in the south. He maintains that the secessionist movement in Pattani "has its roots from the incorporation of the Patani state into the expanding Thai kingdom."[35] Colonization of the "Malay Muslims" and their incorporation into the "Thai Buddhist state" took place without their values being made a part of the civil society of modern Thailand. Following Thailand's forced integration of the south, resistance movements flourished. The thesis emphasizes one movement in particular, the Barisan Nasional Pembebasan Patani (BNPP), which Che Man considers as the potentially strongest and most influential. He argues that the base of the movement which was originally restricted to Malay aristocrats had been transformed so that it now includes popular support. Religious élites assumed leadership positions in the movement consequent on the increasing importance of Islam as its ideological basis. Finally, he argues that Muslim religious élites constitute the core of contemporary liberation politics in the south.

In his published Ph.D. thesis, which compares the Moros of the southern Philippines and the Malays of southern Thailand, Che Man sees these movements basically as a type of ethnic minority community which results from the incorporation of autonomous peoples or tribes inhabiting a hitherto alien territory by a state. For these people then, separatism becomes a political possibility because of

> a socio-historical logic, the coincidence of geography and cultural plurality, distance from the center of authority, and the support of an external community.[36]

In essence, Che Man maintains his original position regarding the emergence, transformation, organization, and promise offered by the Malay Muslim separatist fronts, placing more emphasis, however, on the significance of the BNPP, perhaps because his field study in 1985–86 was confined mainly to them.[37] One of the most impressive features of this work is the information concerning the front, its orientation, leadership, and organization. For the first time, the academic world is able to "read" the internal structure of the movement itself which is a major "actor" in the story of modern Pattani. He informs his readers that the BNPP is a loosely knit front which is unable to control the behavior of the various factions or to have a well-defined chain of command. The front's policy-makers, who are largely religious leaders, "satisfy themselves with furnishing broad policy outlines, giving the local leaders the power to make their own decisions."[38]

Similar to Uthai's theoretical outlook,[39] Che Man points out that "modernization, in the form of increases in social mobilization, intensifies ethnic tension and fosters ethnic competition which can be conducive to separatist demands."[40] Moreover, Islamic resurgence and external assistance from Muslim countries contribute much to the movements. He regards economic exploitation and a response to cultural degradation as of marginal importance in giving rise to the separatist movements. The main "cause" is "a conflict of cultures which is seen as the continuation of centuries of confrontation between Muslims and foreign intrusion."[41] In this struggle, the movements have integrated Islamic concepts and symbols into nationalist dogma. Despite factionalism, which has become "one of the dominant features of ethnic-minority separatist struggles,"[42] Islam and nationalism reinforce each other in their fight against "foreign rulers," while at the same time linking them with the wider Islamic *ummah*.

At this point, the story of Pattani which may be discerned from these theses comes full circle.[43] While some stories tell of the inability of the Malay Muslims to "adapt" themselves to changing times and the government's family planning and education policies have therefore not been successful, others see the policies themselves as being inappropriate and poorly administered or that the country's trajectory towards modernization itself may not yield the expected results. Instead, ethnic conflict will continue. Given Islam and Malay nationalism, which have always been unified and nurtured by the Malay language and transmitted through the family as well as other media, distance between the Malay Muslims and the Thai will continue to exist. When such social distance is situated in a turbulent political history of involuntary incorporation into a modern nation-state, which is considered foreign to the Malay Muslims, and when democratic space for the minority to operate is sometimes a function of brute force and political ambition, then ethnic conflict results and eventually violence erupts. Under such circumstances, people who learn from their tragic history that requests for autonomy are futile then choose separatism as their most logical option. Separatist movements thus claim to operate under the guidance of Islam and Malay nationalism, which then serve as a platform to mobilize both popular as well as external support. Additional aspects of the academic story of Pattani emerge in the research monographs published in the last decade.

Research Monographs

During the last decade there have been only four research monographs on the subject. These publications were not earlier academic works submitted for the fulfillment of higher degrees. One of these was published in Thailand, two in the United States, and the fourth in Malaysia.

A monograph on traditions influencing social integration between the Thai Buddhists and the "Thai Muslims" maintains that reciprocal relationships can emerge from participation in religious activities different from that which marks each group's religious affiliation. These researchers from Prince of Songkhla University attempt to find forms of traditions that can constitute a common practice leading to peaceful relations between the two ethnic communities. They believe that such relationships will "help to set aside" social conflict between the two groups.[44]

After describing numerous traditions in Pattani, Yala, and Narathiwat, the researchers classify them into those which will "facilitate the highest, moderate and lowest degrees of social integration."[45] One of their findings is that "the more social activities involved in a custom, the better the custom will facilitate social integration."[46] Obviously this monograph, published in Thai in 1981, aims at practical results in lessening ethnic conflict between the two groups. It is not certain how the authors would come to terms with Chavivun Prachuabmoh's findings on prejudices as well as the fact that there are times when communication may negatively affect social integration. Or, how could these traditions be measured against past stories of forced incorporation of the Malay Muslim area in the eyes of the people as evident from Ibrahim's account of Pattani history?

Ibrahim's *Sejarah Kerajaan Melayu Patani* or *History of the Malay Kingdom of Patani*, written in 1949, was banned both in Thailand and Malaysia.[47] According to Wyatt, this book

> gives the voice to the pained historical consciousness of Patani in the late 1940s and early 1950s, when the full force of Thailand's policies of national integration began to bear upon the Malays of the peninsula.[48]

This "pained" historical consciousness" is reflected throughout the book especially when the author traces the period of "decline" to that of the "re-awakening" of Pattani.

The last chapter discusses the little-known history of Pattani in the early twentieth century and the Malays' resentment of the Thai Government. Ibrahim writes:

> The officials of Siam-Thai never tried to understand the Malay people and the Islamic religion, because in the period of autocratic rule there was no such concern.[49]

Regarding the well-known *Dusun Nyior* uprising in April 1948, Ibrahim maintains that

> close to 400 Malays, including old people, women, and children, were killed in the battle, and more than 30 Siamese police were killed

for which he blames "the Siamese government" because it "tried to keep secret the events which led up to the battle and lied to the world by saying that it was simply a battle between a group of bandits and the guardians of peace."[50] His final position on the situation in Pattani is well described at the very end of the book. He writes:

> If studied in depth, since the fall of Patani in the eighteenth century until this day, it is clear that the government of Siam has misgoverned during this whole period of time. No progress has been made in Patani to provide well-being for the Malays. In matters of health, education, association, and economy, Patani has lagged far behind the progress of its neighbors in Malaya. The actions of the Siamese government, which allow the Malays to live in backwardness, definitely gives a large profit to them, but this has grieved the hearts of the Malays.[51]

Ibrahim doubts whether the Pattani Malays will be forever satisfied "to live imprisoned under the conservative democracy of Siam." He closes his book with a call for the people of Pattani to place their fate in their own hands.[52] The story given by Ibrahim and the direction he pointed at four decades ago are significant if Chavivun Prachuabmoh's stories of prejudices, Surin's account of Malay nationalism, and Che Man's logic of Muslim separatism are to be comprehended. Ibrahim's historical anger in his story is no doubt illuminating as a story of Pattani told by an educated and politically conscious Pattani Muslim. This historical anger, together with other factors, can crystallize the phenomenon of Malay nationalism which gives rise to violence in the region but it does not explain the place of Islam in the process of the justification for violence.

Strictly speaking, *Islam and Violence*,[53] also published in Thai in 1984, is not a study of the Malay Muslims in southern Thailand. Rather, it is an attempt to understand the relationship between Islam and violence *using* events which took place in the Four Southern provinces of Thailand from 1976 to 1981 as a case-study. The theoretical position is that conflict and violence are two different concepts. Conflict is sociologically natural while violence is not. As a result, a complex set of factors can cause conflict but not violence. The problems of poverty, lack of education, and social injustice in the Malay Muslim area are basically no different from those existing in other parts of rural

Thailand. But this conflict assumes a different manifestation when factors such as Islam, the Malay language, and the people's subjective appreciation of "their" history are taken into consideration. Nevertheless, for conflict to be translated into violence, justifications are needed. Based on clandestine pamphlets issued by the separatists, "a logical process of using Islam to justify their violent actions" is reconstructed. These step-by-step justifications then

> serve as a structure of meaning through which Malay Muslims give shape to their experiences and history. Such structure publicly unfolds in the arena of politics where Malay Muslims sympathize (or even join forces) with the actors of violence. Like other religions or ideologies, Islam does not cause violence. Instead, it has been used to justify violence.[54]

In short, the work tells a story of how the Malay Muslims who use violence as a means of struggle utilize Islam to justify their actions. However, the possibility of non-violent actions does exist in its tradition and therefore a creative interpretation of Islam is much needed.[55]

Violence leads to death, among other things. Wayne Bougas is not interested in ethnic conflict or death as such but he is interested in describing cemeteries found in Pattani. His focus is on structures and items such as pavilions or tombstones and seeks to explain how they evolved and came to be part of Islamic cemeteries. He found that almost everything in the graveyards in Pattani can be traced to some Islamic concepts.[56] However, indigenous and pre-Islamic elements did survive and influence the form cemeteries took. In fact, Islamic concepts were realized and expressed in indigenous forms, basically derived from Hinduism and Buddhism. For example, the pagoda roof was substituted for the dome and *bai sema* type structures were used as tombstones.[57]

Bougas' research is significant because it emphasizes the multi-civilizational origin of Pattani. It attests to Pattani's past greatness from a different angle than that of Ibrahim. In this sense, Ibrahim's position is confirmed by a somewhat "apolitical" treatment of an unusual research subject of Pattani's past. It also shows the importance of Islam, which many writers of theses discuss. Islam governs both life and death of the people in Pattani. Existing layers of culture have been incorporated into the Islamic framework, which is a sign of the vitality of the people's faith. Such vitality, if properly harnessed, can become effective in the political arena.

A distinctive pattern seems to emerge. Writers of all the theses and research monographs discussed above are mostly Thai nationals, except for Wayne Bougas. A few of them are Muslims. But this pattern changes when journal articles are examined.

Journal Articles

In this study, 14 English language academic journals are covered. These journals deal primarily with social and political issues in Southeast Asia, Asia, and the Pacific. Six of these are North American journals. Five are from Southeast Asia, of which two are published by the Institute of Southeast Asian Studies (ISEAS) in Singapore and the other two by the National University of Singapore, while the fifth, the *Journal of Contemporary Asia*, lists the Philippines as one of its editorial bases. The rest are from the United Kingdom, Australia, and Saudi Arabia. The *Journal Institute of Muslim Minority Affairs* is included for the obvious reason that the issue under consideration here is the specific focus of interest of the journal. *Southeast Asian Studies* published by the Center for Southeast Asian Studies, Kyoto, is listed in Table 1 but cannot be discussed because it is written in Japanese. However, the fact that only one article on the subject appears in the journal during the period of nine years is itself worth noting. In fact, the presence and the absence of articles dealing with the Malay Muslims in southern Thailand are equally revealing. The table summarizes the general findings on academic treatments of the subject from these journals during the past decade.

From Table 1, it is clear that four international journals specializing on Asia or Southeast Asia, *Asian Affairs, Bulletin of Concerned Asian Scholars, Modern Asian Studies,* and the *Southeast Asian Journal of Social Science* carried no articles or reviews on the subject during the past decade. The prominent *Journal of Asian Studies* published only two reviews on the subject during that time.[58] Of all the 22 academic writings which appeared in these journals, nine were published in *Crossroads* and *Journal Institute of Muslim Minority Affairs*. Of all the 14 articles, only three directly addressed the Malay Muslim issue in southern Thailand. During the past decade, only nine reviews appeared in these journals. These were reviews of only three works: Surin's *Islam and Malay Nationalism* received four reviews, two of which were by Ray Scupin; Ibrahim's *History of the Malay Kingdom of Patani* received three reviews; and *Islam and Violence*, two. It

TABLE 2-1 Articles related to Muslims in southern Thailand in fifteen international academic journals on Southeast Asia, Asia, and minorities issues

Journal	Period Covered	Type (Article: A Review: R)	Author	Title	Year Published
Asian Affairs	1980–89	—	—	—	—
Asian Survey	1980–89	A	R. Scupin	The Politics of Islamic Reformism in Thailand	1980
		A	A. Forbes	Thailand's Muslim Minorities	1982
		A	H. Federspiel	Islam and Development in the Nations of ASEAN	1985
Bulletin of Concerned Asian Scholars	1980–89	—	—	—	—
Contemporary Southeast Asia	1980–89	A	M. Ladd Thomas	Cultural Factors Affecting the Rural Interface of Thai Bureaucrats and Thai Muslim Villagers	1985

TABLE 2-1 Articles related to Muslims in southern Thailand in fifteen international academic journals on Southeast Asia, Asia, and minorities issues (cont'd)

Journal	Period Covered	Type (Article: A Review: R)	Author	Title	Year Published
Crossroads	1983–89	A	M. Ladd Thomas	Political Violence in Thailand	1983
		A	R. Scupin	Thailand as a Plural Society	1986
		A	R. Scupin	Interpreting Islamic Movements in Thailand	1987
		R	G. Olson	Chaiwat's *Islam and Violence*	1989
Journal Institute of Muslim Minority Affairs	1980–89	A	Arong Suthasasna	Occupational Distribution of Muslims in Thailand	1985
		A	W. Kraus	Islam in Thailand	1984
		A	W. K. Che Man	The Malay Muslims of Southern Thailand	1985
		R	Imitiyaz	Surin's *Islam and Malay Nationalism*	1987
		R	R. Scupin	Surin's *Islam and Malay Nationalism*	1988
Journal of Asian Studies	1980–88	R	Shaharil Talib	Ibrahim's *History of the Malay Kingdom of Patani*	1986
		R	R. Scupin	Surin's *Islam and Malay Nationalism*	1988

TABLE 2-1 Articles related to Muslims in southern Thailand in fifteen international academic journals on Southeast Asia, Asia, and minorities issues (cont'd)

Journal	Period Covered	Type (Article: A Review: R)	Author	Title	Year Published
Journal of Contemporary Asia	1980–86	A	G. Gunn	Radical Islam in Southeast Asia	1986
Journal of Southeast Asian Studies	1980–89	R	D. Lewis	Ibrahim's *History of the Malay Kindom of Patani*	1987
		A	D. Welch and J. McNeil	Archaeological Investigations of Patani History	1989
Modern Asian Studies	1980–88	–	–	–	–
Pacific Affairs	1980–89	A	D. Brown	From Peripheral Communities to Ethnic Nations	1988
Review (ASAA)	1980–87	R	V. Matheson	Ibrahim's *History of the Malay Kingdom of Patani*	1986

TABLE 2-1 Articles related to Muslims in southern Thailand in fifteen international academic journals on Southeast Asia, Asia, and minorities issues (cont'd)

Journal	Period Covered	Type (Article: A Review: R)	Author	Title	Year Published
SOJOURN: Social Issues in Southeast Asia	1986–89	R R	A. Cornish A. Cornish	Chaiwat's *Islam and Violence* Surin's *Islam and Malay Nationalism*	1988 1988
Southeast Asian Journal of Social Science	1980–87	—	—	—	—
South-East *Asian Studies*	1980–88	A	T. Hashimoto	The Problems of the Southern Border Provinces of Thailand and the Integration Policy toward the Malay Muslims	1987

would appear that the number of reviews a book receives depends on the time it is published, among other things.

Surin's work is generally praised by all reviewers. But it is severely criticized for its lack of "Islamic analysis" and the partiality of his conclusion in disregarding the totality of the Muslim *ummah* in Thailand by Imitiyaz Yusuf.[59] Raymond Scupin praises him lavishly in two different journals and then remarks that the work could have more historical depth if the global process affecting Islamic regions throughout the world and aspects of Thai Malay relations before the nineteenth century were included.[60] However, a thorough analysis of Thai-Malay relations, where Pattani was discussed along with Kelantan in relation to the failure of tributary relations, was only written as a doctoral thesis at Universiti Sains Malaysia in 1986 and recently published.[61]

Andrew Cornish reviewed Surin's work together with *Islam and Violence*.[62] He comments that neither work brings out the heterogeneity of Thai society, and that the use of the phrase "Malay Cultural World" by both authors tends to ignore "the very real differences in local culture"[63] in which a consideration of villagers in local communities was neglected, while the case of Satun was not discussed.

Grant Olson, on the other hand, underscores my attempt to explain how Islam has been associated with violence and then to try and transcend this. He concludes,

> Chaiwat wants to suggest that Islam is a religion of action, but that this action need not lead to violence. Ultimately, this fascination, albeit brief, study is really about nonviolence.[64]

The *Sejarah Kerajaan Melayu Patani* by Ibrahim Syukri (or Shukri, according to one reviewer) was reviewed thrice. All reviews were full of praise for the book and its translators. It is considered most important as a Malay text which has much to teach about the Malay community in southern Thailand.[65] It is also seen as "a study in the articulation of ethnic consciousness" and

> a further example of the many "local" histories which were written, and are still being compiled, by "amateur" historians throughout the region, particularly since World War II.[66]

But Shaharil Talib argues that the book does not fall within the *hikayat* tradition as suggested by the translators. Rather, it is "the *People's Tribune* version of history" because it was "written by a person who had an active relationship with the past."[67]

Contrary to Ibrahim, most of the writers in academic journals have no "active relationship" with the past. Journal articles are written in an academic fashion by interested scholars. But they too constitute the "story" of Pattani. There are 14 articles on the subject during the past decade covering the issues of Thai society in relation to the Muslims, the Islamic movement in Thailand and Southeast Asia, as well as theoretical aspects of the study of separatism.

Thai society is seen as heterogeneous and the ethnic Thai as being demographically and politically dominant. Since each ethnic group responds differently to Thai hegemony, Scupin argues that educational policies which have facilitated acculturation and assimilation in the northeast have failed miserably among the "Malay Muslims" in the south. In fact these policies "have influenced the development of ethnic resurgence and secessionist sentiments."[68]

Ladd Thomas, however, views secular education in the four southern provinces as a preventive measure, among others, against the growth of the separatists. Yet he cautions that dissatisfied, educated "Thai Muslim" élites will be susceptible to separatist blandishments.[69] Elsewhere, he maintains that cultural factors among the Muslims hinder the Thai Government's socio-economic development attempts. The problem of language remains an obstacle to communication while the religious factor seems to be weakening due to governmental efforts to provide "Thai Muslims" with a secular education.

However, Muslims in Thai society are not solidary homogeneous, or uniform, according to several socio-economic indicators. In an attempt to paint a broad picture of Muslim occupational patterns in Thailand, a Muslim sociologist points out that they face serious problems in the job market. They occupy low-level positions whether in the bureaucracy, industry, or agriculture compared with others with equal qualifications because of language problems, lack of funds, poor attitudes towards certain jobs, and the fact that they suffer from negative stereotyping on the part of non-Muslims.[70]

Furthermore, the separatists are not a solidary group either. By tracing the historical background of Pattani, Che Man shows that the separatists do not have a single origin and that differences exist among them. Under Thailand's domination, policies of cultural assimilation are persistently pursued while Islamic institutions under government

50

patronage are regarded with increasing cynicism. He is certain that the Muslim separatists' struggle will persist "as long as Bangkok continues to treat Pattani as its internal colony both in cultural and socio-economic terms."[71] In fact, with their emphasis on Islam, resistance movements in the south are gaining broad-based, popular support.

It should be noted that the story of Pattani is more complex than just about separatist politics. Recent archaeological investigations focusing on ancient Pattani suggest that the Yarang complex

> may have been established as a religious center as early as the sixth century and later developed into a center of Mahayana Buddhism similar to Buddhist sites in central Java and Srivijayan Sumatra.[72]

During the sixteenth and seventeenth centuries, the Pattani area produced gold while serving as one of the best harbors on the east coast of the Malay peninsula.

With the Islamization of Pattani, a new sense of ethnic identity that distinguished the Muslims of Pattani from Thai Buddhists emerged.[73] But the development of Islam in "Pattani" can be subdivided into three periods: the "magical period" from the late thirteenth century to the late eighteenth century; the theological period from the late eighteenth century to the late eighteenth century to the 1920s, the highlight of which was the life and times of Sheikh Daud ibn Abdullah Patani, "the crown of Patani scholarship;" and the modern period from the 1920s onwards, a period marked by the presence of Ahmad Wahab, an expatriate from Sumatra who came to Pattani in 1908.[74] This third phase marks the beginning of the *khana mai* ("new group") discussed by Scupin.[75] Characterized by its urban base, educational levels, and politically "left of center" orientation, the *khana mai* differs markedly from the "old group" which tried to maintain links with traditional authority structures in order to legitimize symbolically the social position of Muslims in Thailand. While Scupin is not certain whether the reformism of the *khana mai* will have an impact on the various Muslim separatists in the south, Kraus argues that due to rapid modernization they will have to confront urban culture and modern values. Perhaps alienation will be their common problem. Emerging new resurgent groups may be able to integrate better the Muslims from both urban and rural areas.[76]

Scupin, however, believes the rise of Islamic resurgence is a Muslim reaction to Westernization. Contemporary Islamic movements express themselves in a newly found pride in Islamic symbols and identity. This may lead to critical attitudes towards "Westernized" Muslims as evident in their virulent criticisms aimed at the West as well as Buddhist and Muslim élites in Thailand.[77] Islam serves as both a powerful vehicle of criticism as well as a link to a larger Muslim world, thereby lending the grievances of Pattani their regional and transnational character.[78]

In the eyes of the ASEAN governments, Islam as a carrier of values is significant

> as an institution of society that needs to be modernized to conform with other elements of society, and as an instrument of the modernizing process itself.[79]

In the Thai case, Islam constitutes a value system that is strikingly at odds with the dominant culture. Muslim élites may accept Thai political controls but not civic values. The government's call for the Muslims' transformation of values is hindered by the intense global revivification of Islam. Nevertheless, "radical Islam" in Pattani, as in Aceh and Mindanao, represents a case of Muslim people in the Malay world who are marginalized by the country's center which then results in the people's grievances antedating contemporary external factors.[80] Though exceedingly fractionalized along doctrinal, geographic, and sectarian lines, at present Muslim élites seem to be able to voice their concern on behalf of the Muslim community, among other things.[81]

Much of the literature discussed above is mainly concerned with the Malay Muslim case, government policies, or identifying patterns of Islamic resurgence in the region. They do not, however, attempt to advance comprehensive explanations for the separatist phenomenon.

Using the cases of the Karen, the Moros, and Pattani, Brown[82] provides a fine theoretical discussion of ethnic separatism in three stages. First, the mono- ethnic character of the state, deriving from the circumstances of its formation, ensures that state penetration of peripheral areas is disruptive of communal authority structures at the periphery. Second, élite groups in the peripheral community resolve crises of identity at the mass level and crisis of legitimacy at the élite level which result from the assimilationist expansion of the mono-ethnic state by articulating an ethnic nationalist ideology and mobilizing confrontation against the state. Third, factionalism among élite groups results from aspiring groups which seek to legitimate their élite status. Most importantly, Brown argues that the explanation for the separatism to be found in, for example, Pattani, is to be found in the character of the state.

Given then the "academic literature" of the past decade, the process of re-presenting the Malay Muslim issue of southern Thailand as "stories" may now be analyzed.

THE STORY OF PATTANI FROM ACADEMIC WORKS

Towards the end of *history of the Malay Kingdom of Patani*, Ibrahim quotes Barbara Wittingham-Jones, an English reporter for the *Straits Times*, on the situation of Pattani. He claims that the article was in the *Straits Times*. Bailey and Miksic, the book's translators, note:

> The Singapore *Straits Times* of 1 December 1948 does not contain an article of Barbara Wittingham-Jones. A search through microfilms of that paper several weeks in either direction failed to turn up this article. However, Wittingham-Jones did write an article in the April 1948 edition of *Eastern World* consistent with the statements the author ascribes to her.[83]

The translators attempted to confirm Ibrahim's source but failed. This failure needs to be explained. First, Ibrahim did not claim that the article was published in 1948. He merely stated that it was published in the *Straits Times* on 1 December. Bailey and Miksic failed to find the article because it was not published in 1948 but in 1947. In fact, Ibrahim's wording also suggests the correct year. Second, he in any case failed to give the correct date because Wittingham-Jones's article was published in the *Straits Times* on 30 October.[84] So there was such an article and the source can be traced. Ibrahim is therefore inaccurate in the reference he provided but perhaps time to verify the source was not a luxury he had at the time of writing. Or, accuracy was not a priority because he simply wanted to tell a story for political purposes.

The extent to which the book is a text on history by conventional standards is limited. The translators state clearly in their introduction that

> Syukri's presentation is at times unabashedly biased, but this is not
> exceptional within the Malay *hikayat* tradition. The SKMP places
> the conflict between Malay and Thai in an historical perspective
> and casts the Thais as villains of the plot.[85]

As a story, Ibrahim's work is splendid with a powerful plot and identifiable
villains. Using works in the field of history as an example, the question
raised here is not to assess the academic quality of works such as Ibrahim's
History of the Malay Kingdom of Pattani or Teeuw and Wyatt's *Hikayat
Patani*. Rather, the question is to what extent can academic works be
considered stories in the sense of containing loaded vocabularies,
questionable data, and narrative directions.

Take the number of Muslims in Thailand as an example, a Muslim
writer on the subject of Muslim minorities claims that there must have
been six million Muslims in 1982 in Thailand while the government
gives a figure of two million. He then reasons that "this is part of the
Thai establishment's effort to reduce the importance of its Muslim
population."[86] Another Muslim author estimated the number of Muslims
to be close to three million but added that according to the Muslims it is
an underestimation.[87] This is not the place to verify any of these figures.
Suffice it to say that apart from being a demographic category, the Malay
Muslims also constitute a political entity in the Thai state. As a result,
figures of Muslims in Thailand are not mere numbers. They are politically
significant. Consequently, it is highly likely that in a mono-ethnic state,
official figures of a minority group will be smaller than what members of
that group may maintain it to be.

It is suggested here that the extent to which these academic works can
be treated as stories can be determined by two basic "acts of imagination."
First, the ways in which the word "Pattani/Patani" are spelt will be discussed.
This reflects the politico-historical consciousness of the academic works.
Second, the ways in which the "object of study"—the Malay Muslims—are
termed will be examined. This reflects the ethno-religion consciousness of
the works. Using these two modest indicators, the plot of the story of Pattani
as seen by the academic writers can be identified.

When I was writing *Islam and Violence*, I was not aware of the
subtleties involved in the spelling of the word Pattani. Like many other
academicians such as Forbes or Thomas, whose works are discussed above,
I was using the "common spelling," namely, "Pattani," unaware of its
political significance.

Chavivun Prachuabmoh writes in her dissertation that "I have used the word 'Patani' to identify the old state and 'Pattani' to refer to the present province".[88] Che Man, a Muslim from the area, notes that "'Patani' is the Malay version; 'Pattani' is transliterated from the Thai spelling." He deliberately chooses "Patani" in his book.[89] Writers who care to explain their spellings are sensitive to their implications. Nevertheless, these explanations are merely indicative and do not reflect the extent of the political implications associated with how the term is spelt,

> Seni, a Muslim linguist, is able to convey the "deep implication" of the spelling of the word. "Patani" is used with historical connotations preserving the sense of a former Malay sultanate comprising the present-day provinces of Yala, Narathiwat, and Pattani. On the other hand, the word "Pattani" is a "Thai-ified" spelling. It merely signifies the name of a province in southern Thailand.[90]

In other words, "Pattani" refers only to an administrative entity and a sense of a struggle already ended. If one were to trace historically how this sense has come to be, then the route to take would have to be Thailand's history of administrative reform. "Patani," on the other hand, reflects the grandeur of this Malay kingdom in the past, refuses the present administrative arrangement which, in turn, means that to some extent the possibility of change can still be thought of. Following this subtlety, it may not be to difficult to find the story buried beneath the writers' academic works.

Although less subtle, the terms "Malay Muslims" or "Thai Muslims" are more complex. Che Man has a view of the differences. He writes,

> The term "Malays" applies to Patani Muslims of southern Thailand who are Malays, while the term "Thai Muslims" means non-Malay Muslims or Muslims who consider themselves Thais. The Muslims in Thailand are divided into two categories: the Malays and the non-Malays. The Malays from the majority, while the Thais, Pakistanis, Indians, Chinese, and other constitute roughly 40 per cent of the Muslim population.[91]

There are some, like Ladd Thomas, who are aware of the fact that the people under study are "ethnic Malays who follow Malay customs and mostly speak a local dialect of Malay as their first or only language" but continue to call them "Thai Muslims."[92] Perhaps this is a conscious act.

THE LIFE OF THIS WORLD

If such is the case, its political implication is quite clear. But then a more complicated case is to be seen in Chavivun Prachuabmoh's work. She is sensitive to the implications yet tries in a rather convoluted way to explain her adherence to the use of the term set by the Thai state. The subtitle of her dissertation reads: "A Case of Thai Muslims (The Malay-Speaking Group) in Southern Thailand."[93] As an anthropologist, she is well aware of the distinctive character of the people but she chooses to emphasize the notion which is officially accepted. This suggests a tendency to underestimate the role of language in determining identity on her part although for the Muslims in southern Thailand, the Malay language functions as a boundary marker between those who are Malay and those who are not.[94] In this sense, Chavivun's attempt to use two terms at the same time contains an inherent and inevitable contradiction. It is interesting to note that in trying to discuss ethnic boundaries, she attempt to de-emphasize a major component of ethnicity of her subject. But the most insensitive academic work discussed above maintains that Thai Muslims in the south call themselves "Thai Malays."[95] The contradiction inherent in the term is that they are an ethnic group with two competing ethnic labels.

More than four decades ago, Haji Sulong, one of the most important modern Pattani leaders, remarked:

> We Malays are conscious that we have been brought under Siamese rule by defeat. The term "Thai Islam" with which we are known by the Siamese government reminds [us] of this defeat and is therefore not appreciated by us. We therefore beg of the government to honor us with the title of Malay Muslims so that we may be recognized as distinct from the Thai by the outside world.[96]

As a matter of fact, apart from Uthai, who emphasizes ethnic nationalism and thus uses the term "Muslim Malays." the only other academic work which uses "Malay" as a noun and not as an adjective is Seni's. The Muslim linguist explains that the word "Malay" reflects the major ethnic traits and characteristics of the people as a distinctive ethnic group. But the adjective "Muslim" emphasizes the fact that their religion is inseparable from their ethnicity.

> Thus, one never hears the expression "Malay Buddhists" or "Malay Christians" used for they would be self-contradictory. The term Muslim and Malay always complement each other.[97]

Seni's position, however, creates some problems. First, where semantic fields are concerned, few would place race above religion. If the encompassing quality of a word is a measure of its significance, then Islam is undoubtedly more universal while "Malay" is less so. Second, by equating "Malay" with "Muslim", the usage itself is conceptually narrow because it also forecloses the possibility of conversion of the Malays to other religions. Ethnicity is, taxonomically, less accommodating than religion. At the same time Seni seems to elevate the notion of a particular race at the expense of the universal appeal of Islam.

Other academic works use the more familiar "Malay Muslims." Apart from taxonomical considerations, the notion Malay Muslims enables the analysis to be connected with both the theory of Islam and praxis among Muslims. In Surin's case, as well as Che Man's, this provides a channel for them to connect the grievances of Malay Muslims with the Muslim world. As a result, external support from other Muslim countries can be discussed.[98] Such an emphasis on Islam is crucial to Che Man's comparative study between the Moros and the Malay Muslims.[99] For Federspiel[100] and Gunn,[101] this allows them to link the particular case of Malay Muslims in Thailand to a much broader context in which Islam is pivotal. In Chaiwat,[102] the Malay Muslims' struggle is used as an empirical example to substantiate the argument concerning Islam, violence, and non-violence. Moreover, by underscoring the Islamic component of the issue, it allows a non-Malay Muslim such as myself to be able to empathize better with the problems under analysis. In the phenomenological method, an analyst's capability to empathize with the subject under study is essential.

The two indicators discussed above are but signposts to the story. There are many others, but these two are subtle and ubiquitous. Accordingly, they can be used effectively to decode the significant but less obvious features of the plot embedded in the academic story of Pattani.

CONCLUSION: THE STORY
OF PATTANI AS POLITICS

The Malay Muslims are profoundly different from the Thai Buddhist majority. Manifestations of such differences are evident in the symbolic sphere, among others. For example, a mosque built by the Thai state as a gesture to promote Islam can be perceived by the Muslims as an unwholesome place of worship due to the builder's "unclean" intentions. Such perceptions can be substantiated by authentic Islamic teaching. The dome of a mosque in Satun, designed by the Thai Government's architect in the shape of a lotus, can be considered a symbolic affront to the Islamic crescent.[103] Such a symbolic clash emerges out of a complex context full of economic, cultural, and historical differences. Given existing inequalities and social injustice, political solutions through normal channels, though possible, are more difficult for Malay Muslims than others and thus recourse is sought in separatism.

Analysts caught within these complex differences need to be cautious in their collection of data and in the theoretical frameworks they select. Uthai, who explicitly rejects the cultural pluralist or cultural diversity models, cautiously states at the beginning of his dissertation that despite his considerable efforts to analyze the data objectively, "it is undeniable that my basic value premises do affect the way I view and study ethnic nationalism in southern Siam."[104]

There are times when such explicit statements are absent, but the tone of the works can also reflect the ways in which the subject is addressed. Imitiyaz Yusuf's criticism[105] of Surin is based primarily on his understanding of Islamic values. On the other hand, the attempt by Chaveewan et al.[106] to find traditions conducive to social integration between the Buddhists and the Muslims clearly reflect an adherence to the Thai state and perhaps ignores the state's goal of substituting the "Thai Muslims" in place of the "Malay Muslims" as analyzed in Panomporn.[107]

In short, it is difficult for any academic work on the Malay Muslims in southern Thailand to present its analysis without becoming, at the same time, a story. Although comprehensive data collection, sophisticated theories, and multi-dimensional analyses, together with appropriate academic language can reduce the likelihood of such an outcome, the story-like quality of these academic works is none the less usually reflected in their more subtle and less obtrusive features. The spelling of "Pattani"/ "Patani" and the use of "Thai Muslims"/"Malay Muslims"/"Muslim Malays" are small, but significant, indicators. The ordeal of Pattani can therefore be told as a story of ethnic struggle, religious resurgence, as well as administrative success or failure. It can sometimes be told by combining many stories into one.

These are stories in the sense that ultimately heroes and villains can be identified. In the process of depicting the good and the bad, the possibility of maintaining or changing existing social order tends to follow. Thus, the classical notion of politics emerges. In this sense, academic works on the Malay Muslims in southern Thailand then constitute the present political stories of Pattani.

CHAPTER 3

Kru-ze: A Theatre for Renegotiating Muslim Identity

INTRODUCTION

The majority of people who inhabit the four southernmost provinces of Thailand, Pattani, Yala, Narathiwat, and Satun, are Malay Muslims. Their homeland was incorporated into the modern Thai nation-state after the policy of administrative centralization, known as the *thesaphiban* system, was introduced by King Rama V (1868–1910) in 1906.[1] With the Anglo-Siamese Treaty signed in March 1909, the present Malaysia Thailand border was established and Malay Muslims became citizens of the new Thai nation-state.[2]

The Pattani area of southern Thailand has always been associated with separatist violence.[3] Towards the end of the 1980s, however, violence in these provinces appeared to be subsiding.[4] Conflict, nevertheless, continues to erupt. One of the most revealing conflicts involving the Muslims recently took place in Pattani in 1990. It concerned an ancient Pattani mosque by the name of "Kru-ze" which was officially declared a historical site by the Thai government in 1935. The Muslims have sought to reclaim the mosque. Mass demonstrations were held and fiery speeches were made by Muslim speakers. The leaders of the demonstration were later charged with *lèse-majesté* and labeled secessionists. Some of them fled the country and a few were later apprehended. Government officials have cast this incident as another episode of Shi'i instigation. A strong theme of foreign involvement has been stressed. The author will argue that the official explanation of the event is inadequate and will attempt to re-examine the recent protests at the Kru-ze mosque as a theatre where Muslims tried to renegotiate their identity as minority group in Thai society.

60

This paper begins with a brief description of the geographical and architectural traits of the mosque. A brief description on the protest events and the official explanation given by the government follows. Finally, a new perspective on the event as a theatre of conflict where Muslims renegotiate their identity under changing local and regional circumstances will be analyzed.

KRU-ZE, THE MOSQUE

The *problématique* of Kru-ze can be easily detected. Its geographical, architectural, and temporal aspects are all enigmatic. One source indicates that the old mosque is located by the Pattani-Narathiwat road, at village no. 2, Kru-ze, 6 kilometers from the city of Pattani in Tambon Tanjong Lulo.[5] Another points out that it is 7 kilometers from the city.[6] A journalist, on the other hand, quoting the Fine Arts Department as his source, maintained that it is located 12 kilometers from the center of Muang district.[7]

The unfinished brick building is 15.1 meters wide and 29.6 meters long. Its height from the floor to its beam is 6.5 meters. A source maintains that its round columns with pointed-arch and rounded-arch gates and windows are of European Gothic-like design.[8] But the data book published by the Office of the Educational District points out that the design is Middle Eastern.[9] A Muslim lawyer wrote in a local Muslim newspaper that the design of the mosque is Persian.[10] The official data book gives conflicting construction dates for the Kru-ze mosque. Under the section "historical site," it maintains that "the mosque was built before B.E. 2328 (1785)."[11] But under the section "religious site," this very same book points out that Kru-ze mosque was built around B.E. 2121–36 (1578–93) in the reign of King Naresuan the Great."[12] On the other hand, Anant Wattananikorn, former educational commissioner of Yarang, Pattani, suggests that based on the *Sejarah Pattani*, the mosque was built in A.H. (Hijrah Era) 1142 or B.E. 2265 (1722).[13] A Muslim writer disagrees that the mosque was built in B.E. 2265 on the ground that the Hijrah year follows the lunar calendar. Therefore, each Hijrah year has only around 354 days, 11–12 days less than a common calendar year. If Kru-ze was built in A.H. 1142, then it must have been built in the year B.E. 2271 or 2272 (1728 or 1729).[14] He also makes reference to data given by the Archaeological Division, Department of Fine Arts, Ministry of Education that the mosque was built towards the end of the Ayudhaya period around B.E. 2199–2231 (1656–88). But he questions the validity of this date as he could not find any evidence to substantiate it. If the Archaeological Division based its estimation on the type of bricks used, some of which were from the latter period of the Ayudhaya era and some of which were similar to those from the Tawarawadi period, then the conclusion that the mosque was built towards the end of the Ayudhaya period is still debatable.[15] As a matter of fact, one can only surmise from these data that the bricks, possibly brought from somewhere else, could be older than the mosque.

Here it is not possible to provide definite answers to all the debatable problems mentioned above. Suffice it to suggest that these problematic geographical/archaeological aspects pale in significance when compared with the politics of the mosque which have gained great visibility in recent years.

KRU-ZE: POLITICAL EVENTS FROM THE OFFICIAL PERSPECTIVE

Recent activities centered around Kru-ze began in 1987 when a group of Muslims from Yala invited others to perform prayers at the mosque on those dates marking significant occasions in Islam. From 13 to 15 July 1989, some 150 Muslims organized prayers at Kru-ze and forbade non-Muslims to enter the mosque. The Maulid-in-Nabi (Prophet Muhammad's birthday celebration) was organized at Kru-ze on 13 October 1989, and attracted some 300 Muslim participants. The number of participants increased threefold, reaching approximately 1,000 Muslim participants, when an anti-*shirk* (those who fell from religion) week was organized on 26–27 January 1990. More than ten days later, on 9–10 February 1990, the organizers held "a week for the oppressed." Some 700 to 1,000 Muslims joined in the activities which included a march in front of the mosque. One month later (16–17 March 1990), an anti-satan week was organized, which attracted 600 to 700 participants. One week after that, another protest was organized. Approximately 700 to 900 Muslims joined the protest against any attempt to renovate the mosque using government funds. On 12–13 April 1990 some 800 to 1,000 Muslims joined in the "Badr war commemoration week" (the war fought by the Prophet on 17th Ramadan, A.H. 2). A week later more than a thousand Muslims joined in the "Al-Kuds commemoration week" (the now occupied Bait al-

Makdis in Jerusalem). On 20 April 1990, there was a peaceful demonstration in the city of Pattani. That same month, on *Hari Raya* (*Eid-ul-Fitr* or the end of the fasting month celebration), some 300 Muslims offered prayer at the mosque. On 11–12 May 1990, some 3,000 Muslims attended the *Dawah-Ansar Muhadjirun* (remembering the Prophet's helpers in Madina and those who "led the way" by following the Prophet from Mecca) activities. Finally some 3,000 Muslims participated in the "remembering the *ulama*" activities on 2–3 June 1990. At this event some of the leading organizers were said to have made speeches detrimental to the monarchy and some policemen reportedly were assaulted. This led to the arrest of a number of the demonstration organizers.[16]

An official of the National Intelligence Office who is himself in charge of research on Islamic revolutionary movements in Thai society collected information on the above-mentioned activities. His primary sources of information included documents from the National Intelligence Office and the National Security Council.[17] This official has labeled the organizers of these activities as "the Shi'a core group." In the author's opinion, his thesis, which was submitted to the Army Defense College, adequately reflects the official position.

After the events of 2–3 June 1990, the government issued warrants against two of the organizers charging them with *lèse-majesté*. It also charged two other organizers with attacking officers of the law. Border Patrol Police and soldiers were sent in to guard the area surrounding the mosque as a deterrent against "Shi'i gatherings." The police searched the home of the accused and confiscated documents for the prosecution. On 10 July 1990, 11 charges were filed against eight of the leaders of the Kru-ze group including the four persons earlier charged. Among other things, they were accused of having committed *lèse-majesté*, instigating a mob, and violating security laws. A Muslim lawyer remarked later that if the accused were found guilty of all these charges, they could face death sentences or up to 200 years in jail.[18] By 31 December 1990, three of the accused had been arrested. The court began hearing the case on 16 January 1991.[19] Sorayuth Sakulnasantisart, the alleged leader of the demonstration who fled the country right after the incident was arrested by Malaysian authorities on 12 July 1991 and later handed over to the Thai authorities.[20]

From the official perspective, the demonstrations at Kru-ze had pressured the government to compromise at first. The Thai government, however, could no longer pull its punches and tolerate these demonstrations once government officials were attacked, the monarchical institution was criticized, and organizers began to advocate the establishment of the Islamic Republic of Pattani.[21] In an interview with a Muslim newspaper in Thailand after the Kru-ze incident, the Governor of Pattani, Chamnong Kumrak, stated that he believed that the demonstration at the mosque had moved beyond the religious sphere, and that the people who attended the activities at Kru-ze were unaware of the real motives of the organizers. He also voices his feelings of suspicion against "the outsiders," especially those from Bangkok and *Yala*.[22]

The official view maintains that it was the "Shi'a core group" with the assistance of foreign elements who should be held responsible for the Kru-ze problem. In fact, some officials strongly believe that this group has been assisted by the cultural wing of the Iranian embassy in Bangkok. Therefore, the root cause of the Kru-ze incident can be traced back to Iranian influence.[23] Although clearly a non-Muslim country, these officials believe that Iran considers Thailand as a part of the Islamic world due to the existence of Muslim minorities in the country.[24] However, the Iranian Ambassador to Thailand, Mehdi Sazegara, has categorically denied that his country was involved in the Muslims' rallies at Kru-ze.[25]

Due to the nature of the Kru-ze problem, it is difficult to assess the evidence given to support the official claim. Clandestine operations are hard to verify. But there are two basic points that should be critically examined. First, the government believes that it was the Shi'a core group which initiated the demonstrations at Kru-ze. If such is the case, why were there so many Muslims at the gathering? A resident of Kru-ze told a journalist that the people who came to the mosque were not locals but Shi'i Muslims from Yala, Satun, and Nakorn Si Thammarat provinces.[26] But the Shi'i constitutes only a small minority of the total Muslim population in Thailand. According to the official count of 2,632 mosques nation-wide, there are only 32 Shi'a mosques, a dozen of which are in Bangkok.[27] It has been estimated that there are 183 households.[28] This would mean that there are 46,848 Shi'i of all ages in Thailand. The *Nation* estimated that there were 6,000 Muslims at the rally,[29] while *Matichon*, a Thai-language daily, put the number between 6,000 and 7,000.[30] On the other hand, the *Islamic Guidance Post* reported that there were more than 50,000 Muslims, and that most of these participants were Sunni.[31] Using the attendance figures given by the *Nation* and *Matichon*, if all those present at the Kru-ze demonstration in June 1990 were Shi'a and not Sunni Muslims as some believed, it would mean that 12 to 14 per cent of the total Shi'a population from all over the country came to Pattani. Further, it is clear that the number of people attending the demonstration quoted by the *Islamic Guidance Post* exceeds the estimated number of Shi'i in the country. It is therefore highly likely that a significant number of Muslims who attended the Kru-ze rally were Sunni. Even the Pattani governor believed that a large number of Muslims attending the rally were Sunni. He insisted that there is no Shi'i in his province.[32]

The Shi'a element worries the Thai authorities and their associates. In 1988 some southern government officials were concerned that the Shi'a element would create disunity among Muslims in Thailand which would, in turn, adversely impact national security.[33] As early as 1987, a Satun Muslim leader publicly urged Muslims in Thailand not to co-operate with the Shi'i.[34] If the Shi'a group is responsible for the Kru-ze demonstrations, then their success in mobilizing so many Sunni Muslims at these rallies needs to be examined. On the other hand, if the Shi'i group was not responsible, then the Muslims' enthusiastic response to the rallies at Kru-ze still needs to be explained.

Second, reasons regarding why the Kru-ze case could be problematized are conspicuously absent from the officially embraced thesis submitted to the Army Defense College. Perhaps, the nature of security-related discourse dictates that structural explanations and meanings of the incident are of no importance compared with questions specifically delving into who did what and their motives. In order to understand why many Sunni Muslims joined in the Kru-ze protest and why they decided to do so at this particular moment in time, the whole incident needs to be viewed from a totally different perspective. The author would argue that it is important to contextualize the Kru-ze incident, taking into account the changing character of the myth of Kru-ze as it relates to local factors as well as the transnational influence of the Islamic resurgence.

THE MYTHS OF KRU-ZE

In front of the Kru-ze mosque lies an equally ancient tomb. It is the tomb of Lim Kun Yew, a Chinese saint. The myth of Kru-ze is inseparable from the story of Lim Kun Yew, a Chinese girl who came to Pattani to persuade her brother, Lim Tho Khiem, who had earlier embraced Islam to leave the faith and return to their mother in China. At that time Lim Tho Khiem was involved in the construction of the Kru-ze mosque. Having failed to convince her brother to leave the faith and return to China, Lim Kun Yew committed suicide under a cashew nut tree nearby the mosque. Before taking her life, however, she issued a curse that the construction of the mosque would never be completed. She was buried in front of the mosque. Touched by her sincerity and commitment to the religion of her ancestors, the Chinese of Pattani thought of her as a goddess. They made an idol in her image from the wood of the tree where she hanged herself and established a shrine called Leng Ju Kiang. Located in the center of the city of Pattani, the shrine or *Toh Pe Kong* ("temple" in the Hokkien dialect) is widely respected among the Chinese. Every year in February or March, there is a festival to commemorate the goddess. Legend has it that the mosque remains unfinished as a result of the curse. Every time someone tried to complete it, it was said that there had been anger in the sky and that lightning has struck the mosque.[35]

It is interesting to note that the degree to which this legend has been problematized varies from source to source. The official data book and the Institute of Taksin Khadi Suksa's encyclopaedia of southern cultures report the legend in no uncertain terms. Thus the authoritative version of the Kru-ze myth has been transferred to the popular imagination. The other sources, however, choose to problematize it. Prapon, for example, cited another legend which maintained that Lim Kun Yew did not take her own life because she could not persuade her own brother to leave Islam and Pattani. Instead, this legend maintains that there was a rebellion in Pattani and that she fought bravely alongside her brother against the rebels. In the end when she was surrounded by the rebels, she valiantly used her sword to take her own life. Prapon, nevertheless, turns to the legend of the curse when it comes to furnishing an explanation for the unfinished mosque.[36] For his part, Anant makes reference to the legend of the curse based on the Pattani chronicle. But Anant raised some doubts about the veracity of this story, pointing out that the beam of the mosque showed no sign of being struck by lightning. Along these lines, he also notes that there is no crack on the wall of the mosque and that its 6 meter height does not seem lightning-prone.[37]

On the other hand, Abdullah, the Muslim who discussed the year when Kru-ze was built, offered an alternative explanation to the curse legend. He pointed out that 57 years after it was built, King Rama I sent his troop to conquer Pattani. Following the tradition of war in those days, the conqueror destroyed much in Pattani. The Kru-ze mosque was burnt around the same time that the cannon, Phya Tani, was brought from Pattani to Bangkok. But since the mosque was a brick structure, it was only partially destroyed by the fire.[38]

As mentioned above, the myth of Kru-ze is inseparable from the story of Lim Kun Yew. This story of the Chinese goddess is, in turn, connected with the exploits of Lim Tho Khiem, who is believed to be her brother. The name Lim Tho Khiem appeared in the *Sejarah Kerajaan Melayu Patani* only in connection with the manufacture of a large cannon.[39] According to the *Hikayat Patani*, the cannon was cast by a man from Rum called Abdussamad.[40] Teeuw and Wyatt have also discussed the story of the casting of the Patani cannon, making use of Ibrahim Syukri's writing. They believed that Ibrahim Syukri followed a Thai Chronicle of Pattani written by Phraya Wichiankhiri (Chom na Songkhla) at the end of the nineteenth century.[41] The name Lim Tho Khiem, however, also appeared in a Chinese source, Hsu Yun-ta'jao's *Pai ta nien shih* published in Singapore in 1946, which Teeuw and Wyatt referred to. They suggested that Lim Tho Khiem was a historical figure by the name of Lim Tao-chi'en. He was a Teochew pirate active off the China coast and South China Sea during the sixteenth century. He settled in Pattani after 1578 and was offered the hand of the daughter of Pattani's ruler. Subsequently he became a Muslim with the name Tok Kayan.[42]

In relating the story of the casting of the cannon of Pattani during the reign of Raja Biru, Ibrahim Syukri also included the tale of Lim Tho Khiem's sister who followed him from China and committed suicide after she failed to persuade her brother to leave Islam and return to their homeland. According to Teeuw and Wyatt, the casting of the Pattani cannon took place near Kampung Kersik,[43] also called Gresik or "sand, gravel beach."[44] However, the curse of Kru-ze issued by Lim Kun Yew against the mosque was nowhere to be found in both texts.

In fact, Lim Kun Yew has always been a widely respected Chinese sea goddess. Chinese seamen believe that she can protect those who live by the sea. There are thousands of Lim Kun Yew's shrines all over the world. In Taiwan alone, there are more than 800 shrines. In 1990 the People's Republic of China organized an international conference to commemorate the 1,030 years of the goddess with participants from the United States, Canada, Australia, Japan, and South Korea.[45] It seems that her mythical existence was known and respected among the Chinese long before the time of the casting of the Pattani cannon. As a result, her fame is not derived from her death on the sandy beach of Pattani although the Chinese genealogist Lao Shuan Hua wrote in Thai that she died a heroine defending the land of Pattani.[46]

The curse of Kru-ze did not figure prominently in the myth of Lim Kun Yew outside Thailand. Even in Thailand, the Kru-ze curse had not been emphasized. The Chinese in Pattani could choose to believe in the myth of her suicide and the curse of the mosque while the Malays could choose to believe in the alternative myth that Lim Kun Yew sacrificed her life to protect the land of Pattani. Apart from the curse, the legend of Kru-ze itself had been used as a theatre where the identities of the Malays and the Chinese were negotiated.

KRU-ZE AS A THEATRE TO RENEGOTIATE MUSLIM IDENTITY

It can be argued that the rallies held in 1990 did not constitute the first time that Kru-ze had become a theatre for identity negotiation. In the past it had been used as such a theatre for another group of ethnic actors. In fact, the "past" in this case is linked to the beginning of the myth of Lim Kun Yew itself.

Immediately after Ibrahim Syukri described the manufacture of the Patani cannon in the reign of Raja Biru and the myth of the suicide of Lim Kun Yew, he noted:

> This Lim Kun Yew was known as a woman of firm resolve who did not wish to turn her back on the religion of her ancestors and she killed herself because her elder brother had dishonored this religion. All of the Chinese strongly agreed with her, and her death is eternally remembered as a holy sacrifice. ... The Malays of Patani called the statue of Lim Kun Yew *Toh Pe Kong Mek* and the image has been kept in the *Toh Pe Kong* in Patani until this very day.[47]

Apart from Ibrahim's non-hostile tone towards Lim Kun Yew, there are two points to be noted. First, Pattani's position as one of the best harbors on the east coast of the Malay peninsula[48] helps account for the large

Chinese population there during the sixteenth and seventeenth centuries.[49] Skinner quoted the Dutch Resident at Pattani in 1616 who maintained that the Chinese far outnumbered the natives. A Chinese source written in 1617 also notes that there were so many Chinese that "their toes followed one another's heels."[50] These Chinese had worshiped Lim Kun Yew of Lin Ku-Niang who tried in vain to persuade her brother to return home as a "symbol of fervent Chinese patriotism."[51] The case of Lim Tho Khiem who decided to settle down in Pattani, married into a Muslim family and converted to Islam was possibly one among many. Immigrant Chinese had to forsake their traditions as well as part of their identities in order to gain and preserve their economic opportunities. In this sense, the sacrifice made by Lim Kun Yew can be read as an admonition to the Chinese, especially Chinese males who traveled to foreign lands in search of wealth, not to forget who they were.[52] Their decision to make an image of Lim Kun Yew which has been prayed to as a revered holy idol[53] and the creation of *Toh Pe Kong* can be read as the Chinese community's attempt to renegotiate Chinese identity with the native Malay Muslims. Lim Kun Yew failed in her mission to bring her brother back to the Chinese way and committed suicide as a way to communicate to others the significance of retaining Chinese identity. For the local Chinese who chose not to go back to China, they had found a way to retain their Chinese identity through the construction of *Toh Pe Kong* in her honor as well as carrying on the myths and performing the rituals at her shrine.

Second, the reaction of the Malay Muslims to the making of the idol of Lim Kun Yew and the creation of the shrine was also worth noting. They seemed to quietly accept the existence of the shrine. Given the Malay Muslims' history of repeated attempts to regain their identity with rebellions and uprising against their northern conqueror,[54] it is possible that they sympathize with the meaning of the shrine of Lim Kun Yew as a symbol of a return to traditions and patriotism. While the symbolic quality of the shrine as an affirmation of Chinese identity can be accepted by the Malay Muslims, Lim Kun Yew's curse of the mosque is a direct challenge to the constitution of their Muslim identity. This challenge, however, had been tolerated in the past when the curse was merely a whisper within the local Chinese community. All this began to change when the curse began to be pronounced more loudly in recent years.

THE CURSE OF KRU-ZE AS COMMODITY

As mentioned above, the Kru-ze mosque first became a theatre of modern day political conflict in 1987.[55] The year 1987 also marked the first time that Thailand officially launched its highly successful "Visit Thailand Year" in order to generate revenue from the tourism industry. In 1987 the country earned some 50 billion baht (approximately US$ 1.96 billion) from 3.48 million foreign visitors—a 23.7 per cent increase in international tourism arrivals from the previous year.[56] It was also the year that Malaysians and Singaporeans ranked first and third, respectively, on the list of tourists who visited Thailand.[57]

There seems to be a connection between the rally at Kru-ze and the rise of the tourism industry in the country. A Thai anthropologist, Pornchai Trakulwaranond, suggests that the Kru-ze issue is a result of a promotion of culturally insensitive tourism which led to a breakdown of the ethnic balance within a community.[58]

In the past, the curse of Lim Kun Yew was told only within the small Chinese community and the Muslim majority could relegate the myth to the realm of insignificance. Provincial authorities, who are predominantly non-Muslims, saw in the shrine of Lim Kun Yew a cultural commodity that could be packaged and sold to tourists. As a matter of fact, in drawing up a master plan for tourism in Pattani, Chamnong Khumrak, the governor of the province not only referred to the shrine of Lim Kun Yew as a prime tourist spot, but mentioned the procession of "Chao Mae Lim Ko Niew" (goddess Lim Kun Yew) alongside the festival of Hari Raya as reflecting ways of life of the southern people.[59] Such an official promotion transformed the annual rite in honor of Lim Kun Yew from a once small-scale event into a spectacular fanfare with grand processions, a fire-walking ceremony, and fancy celebrations. Consequently, Chinese visitors from Malaysia and Singapore have come in increasing numbers to Pattani to pay their respects to the goddess, especially during the Chinese New Year festival.[60]

Because of the physical proximity between the mosque and the tomb of Lim Kun Yew, the curse has become louder as growing numbers of Chinese and Thai tourists come to visit the goddess to pay their respects. According to Pornchai, since 1985 the curse of Kru-ze has been included in the leaflets advertising the shrine of Lim Kun Yew as a tourist attraction.[61] As a result, the legend which was once an oral tradition has turned into a written myth. The transformation of the curse from an oral myth popular among a Chinese minority into a written document effectively relegates the Muslim oral version of the death of Lim Kun Yew, which does not include the story of the curse of the Kru-ze mosque, to marginal significance.

The legend of Lim Kun Yew in the age of tourism is visibly inseparable from the curse of the mosque. Some validation of the myth is needed in order to better convince the tourists that the commodity they are paying to visit is genuine. The official recognition of the Kru-ze mosque provides the legend of the curse with such validation.

According to the *Royal Thai Government Gazette*, the Department of Fine Arts, Ministry of Education, proclaimed Kru-ze to be a historical site on 25 February 1935.[62] On 26 August 1983, almost half a century later, the Department of Fine Arts declared that the 4.2 acre area surrounding the mosque was also a part of the said historical site. Structures are declared historical sites on the basis of their age or design or other historical evidence. Such sites purportedly make a valuable contribution to the arts, history, or archaeology.[63] Once declared, no one can repair or change anything at the historical site unless the Director General of the Department of Fine Arts gives permission.[64] In addition, according to the Ministry of Education Order no.1, those who visit the registered historical site are not allowed to do thing that would depreciate or damage such site.[65] In short, the rules which govern a historical site make it difficult for the site to be used for normal functions. In the case of the Kru-ze mosque, the Muslims can still use it for prayers but by virtue of being a historical site, it is a public place open to all and sundry visitors. In addition, its roof cannot be completed or repaired unless permission is granted by the Thai authorities. This lack of repair renders it difficult to use the mosque for prayers during the rainy season, among other things.

More importantly, the "historical" value added to the mosque by the Thai Department of Fine Arts has had a spin-off "veracity" effect on the goddess' shrine. Now that the mosque is officially "historical," the myth surrounding the mosque, especially the curse of Lim Kun Yew, have been given a more concrete validation. Due to its related mythical value, a tour operator who guides visitors to the Lim Kun Yew shrine can simply point to the unfinished Kru-ze mosque which has been declared a historical site certified by the Department of Fine Arts itself to validate the curse of the Chinese goddess against the mosque. In other words, the social construction of the curse of Kru-ze as a commodity becomes possible through tourism advertising leaflets which are, in turn, supported by the sign in front of the mosque official designating it a historical site. As more tourists come to visit the goddess' shrine, the social reproduction of the curse become more intense.

The commoditization of the curse of Kru-ze[66] coincided with a new demand for identity affirmation among the Chinese in the region, especially those from neighboring Malaysia. It is therefore instructive to briefly examine the issue of Chinese tourists who visit the shrine of Lim Kun Yew.

CHINESE TOURISTS

From 1981 to 1988 Malaysian tourists ranked first in terms of foreign visitors coming to Thailand.[67] It was therefore possible to assume that a large number of Chinese tourists who visited the shrine of Lim Kun Yew in Pattani came from Malaysia, not to mention the geographical proximity and convenient transportation between the two countries. They would pay their respects to the Chinese goddess and read the leaflets advertising the shrine together with the curse of the Kru-ze mosque. Although they are Chinese, these people are in many ways different from their ancestors who came to this land centuries ago in search of wealth. The context from which they came was mainly responsible for such a difference.

Malaysia in the late 1980s was a country that had to live with the memory of the May 1969 ethnic violence which redressed the then imminent political power shift into the hands of the Chinese back to those of the native Malays.[68] The rise of the Islamic resurgence in recent years, and the much publicized and analyzed *dakwah* (an Islamic call to faith) groups in particular,[69] has prompted the Malaysian Government to adopt Islamization measures and related policies that were viewed with growing apprehension by non-Muslims. For example, in the early 1980s, non-Muslims resented the fact that the allocation of land for churches and temples has been declining.[70] Given the fact that religious differences in Malaysia coincide with ethnic distinctions, religious mobilization of non-Muslims in response to the perceived Islamic encroachments on their spheres of activity represents another form of ethnic alignment.[71] A result of such ethnic mobilization was that the non-Malay ethnic expressions have been channeled into the religious arena.[72] Viewed from this perspective, the Malaysian Chinese were discontented with the political/ethnic effect of the Islamic resurgence in their country. If they felt that their identity can be strengthened through the affirmation of religious belief, then their visit to the shrine of Lim Kun Yew assumed a cathartic meaning where the goddess' curse of the Kru-ze mosque plays a vital role. For it is in Pattani, the one-time cradle of Islam, now merely a province in non-Islamic Thailand, where the Chinese whose identities were compromised elsewhere could see an Islamic place of worship which was cursed by a Chinese woman whose sacrifice and commitment to her Chinese tradition earned her the status of a goddess. Perhaps a little solace could be gained when their identities become strengthened.

At the same time, the commoditization of the curse and its social reproduction among foreign visitors and others involved in the tourism industry in the province were taking place in a changing Pattani characterized by worsening economic conditions among the Muslims.

PATTANI'S ECONOMY

The Pattani that the tourists visit is a poor province. According to the National Statistical Office, the per capita income of the four southernmost provinces in 1990 was 12,839 baht (US$513.6) compared with the national figure of 40,125 baht (US$1,605). The annual per capita income of Pattani itself was 7,975 baht (US$319).[73] According to Uthai Dulyakasem, the economy of the 14 southern provinces including Pattani is in the hands of six Sino-Thai or Thai-Chinese families. They own a number of businesses including mining, rubber plantation, fishery, and real estate businesses. As against this, the Malay Muslims remain poor. Most of them engage in farming, traditional fishing or work as wage laborers in rubber plantations.[74]

It is important to understand that the worsening economic situation among local Malay Muslims has been taking place in a social context influenced by the Islamic resurgence. While economic deprivation may be reducing Muslim's material self-confidence, the religious resurgence might serve as a platform of action to regain and strengthen their cultural confidence.

THE INFLUENCE OF THE ISLAMIC RESURGENCE

The existence of a transnational phenomenon where the Muslims "return" to their faith and act out the effects of those returns, most visible in the form of dress codes for men and women, cannot be denied.[75] The Islamic resurgence has not only made itself felt on Muslim majority countries like Indonesia and Malaysia, but on other non-Muslim countries in the Association of Southeast Asian Nations (ASEAN).[76] It is the impact of the Islamic resurgence in Malaysia, however, that seems to have been most directly experienced by the Malay Muslims of southern Thailand.[77]

Although not unproblematic, the term "Islamic resurgence" connotes a view from within the Muslim community which underscores the growing impact of Islam among them. In addition, it suggests a phenomenon which has taken place before, and consequently it connects the present with the past. The term also embodies the notion of a challenge and even a threat to those who adhere to other beliefs.[78]

Following Muzaffar's notion, the demonstration at Kru-ze could be seen as an expression of the Islamic resurgence. From the official point of view, the rally was obviously considered a threat to national security.[79] But for the Muslims, the meaning of the phenomenon can be construed was apprehended. It can be argued that the way in which Kru-ze is perceived by the Muslims is principally informed by religious sentiment which links them not only to the past of Islam but perhaps to the past glory of Patani.[80]

From a kaleidoscopic perspective, "Kru-ze" means different things to the various groups of people involved. For the Thai authorities, it means a historical site while for those who reap tourism benefits it is a tourist attraction. For the Chinese tourists, it can provide validation of the curse of a Chinese against a non-Chinese place of worship, which came into being as a result of a heroic attempt at identity preservation. For the Muslims, Kru-ze means none of these things. In an age of Islamic resurgence when an awareness of the Muslim identity is emphasized, Kru-ze simply means a mosque.

According to verse 18 of chapter 9 in *Al-Qur'an*, a mosque is a house of God and the one who should visit it is he/she who believes "in God and the Last Day, and is constant in prayer, spends in charity, and stands in awe of none but God."[81] For the Muslims then, a mosque has a sense of sacredness because it is a place where one prostrates to Allah during a most important Islamic ritual, prayers (*salat*). It goes without saying that God in Islam embodies absolute power of the universe; God is the Creator of all things, living and non-living, and consequently is superior to all creations. In fact the leader of the June 1990 rally at Kru-ze, Sorayuth Skulnasantisart, asserted in 1989 that the Muslims were bitter about the circulation of "the untruthful" explanation that the mosque remained unfinished because of curse issued by a human being.[82] Many Muslims felt that it was necessary for Kru-ze to revert to its original status as a mosque, in order to silence the belief in the curse which was an affront to Islam.[83]

The Muslims who rallied at Kru-ze in June 1990 also made two important demands. First, they wanted the authorities to officially revoke the Kru-ze mosque's status as a historical site.[84] Second, on 20 April 1990 some Muslims marched into the city of Pattani to demand that the authorities removed the nearby shrine of Lim Kun Yew on the ground that it was improperly located.[85]

Taken together, the rally at Kru-ze and the two demands made constitute an effort to renegotiate Muslim identity with Thai society as a whole, the Thai authorities in particular, and the Chinese community in Pattani. The rally in 1990 did capture the Thai media attention.[86] The demand to revoke the historical site designation was specifically directed at the government on the religious ground that once a mosque is built, it will forever remain a place of worship and should not be under the supervision of non-Muslims. But the demand to remove the Chinese shrine, though addressed at the local authorities, had a direct effect on the Chinese community as a whole.

The Muslims' belief in the omnipotence of God is unconditional; therefore the myth of the curse needs to be denounced. The act of denouncing the curse by performing prayers at the Kru-ze mosque can also be seen as an attempt to reassert Muslim identity by using religious belief substantiated by standard religious practices to counter the prevalent myth. Some Muslims believed that in praying at Kru-ze, the curse has already been nullified.[87] The fact remains, however, that the legendary curse was not directed against praying at the site but at the attempt to complete the construction of the mosque. Hence, many Muslims feel that there is a need to revoke the mosque's historical status so that Muslims can undertake its repair and completion, thereby directly challenging and disproving the curse. Muslims have not only challenged its official status designation by questioning the inconclusive information used to declare Kru-ze a historical site,[88] but by affirming the religious meaning of the place in rejection of the government's official designation. The Muslims' strategy of renegotiation also includes a questioning of the legality of the nearby Lim Kun Yew tomb on the ground that the Kru-ze mosque and its surrounding 4 acres had been officially declared a historical site. Because of the tomb, the Kru-ze mosque is left with only 1.6 acres. In this sense, according to a Muslim lawyer, the tomb which is not declared a historical site is violating the law governing historical sites in Thailand.[89] Hence in making a demand on the government to remove the goddess' shrine, the Muslims can be seen as trying to expand the cultural space of their own identity by contracting the Chinese space.

Seen in this light, Kru-ze becomes a theatre whereby Muslim identity was renegotiated because the former constitution of their identity was no longer tenable due to changing circumstances. Such a process of identity renegotiation of a minority Muslim group does transcend sectarian division and therefore a large number of Sunni Muslims could be mobilized to engage in rallies at the unfinished mosque in Kru-ze.

CONCLUSION: THE POLITICS OF IDENTITY RENEGOTIATION

The Thai Government's apprehension of the Kru-ze incident is basically based upon a politics of local actors and foreign influence. The successful mobilization of ordinary Muslims to the rallies could be explained away by highlighting the organizational skills of the organizers or their supporters. From an alternative perspective, Muslims participating at Kru-ze were engaging in a complex process of identity renegotiation as a result of changing circumstances. The promotion of the tourism industry in Pattani led to a transformation of the Lim Kun Yew shrine as a prime tourist attraction. The commoditization of the curse of the Kru-ze mosque, validated by the unfinished Kru-ze mosque which is an official historical site, added to the mythical value of the goddess' shrine. The curse became more prominent at a time when local Malay Muslims were in poverty while the economy of Pattani was in the hands of a few Chinese-Thai families. The current transnational influence of the Islamic resurgence also contributes to a need for the Malay Muslim to reaffirm their identity under these circumstances. This, in turn, resulted in the rallies which can be seen as an attempt to acquire a broadening cultural space by using religious beliefs and practices.

There are a number of critical lessons that need to be considered in analyzing Kru-ze. First, to understand why popular participation could be successfully mobilized in this case, a new perspective based on the politics of identity renegotiation is necessary. Second, the process of identity negotiation involves the uses of elusive resources such as myth, a curse, and religious beliefs. It can be seen that myth and a curse can be commoditized for the benefit of a modern project such as the tourism industry. But the extent to which a religious belief continues to be a match to myth is uncertain. The emphasis on religious belief has its own limitations. For example, if the Muslims decide to rebuild the mosque in defiance of the goddess' curse and the roof accidentally collapses, does it mean that they have to give up their faith? Is it possible to advance a broadened concept of Islamic faith to include the curse of Lim Kun Yew as a part of God's design? Third, the process of identity negotiation is dynamic. It involves negotiations and renegotiations by different groups of ethnic actors across time in their attempts to chart or expand their cultural space while sometimes trying to contract that of others. Like the unfinished mosque itself, it will continue to be a shaping and reshaping of cultural spaces in an ongoing process of identity renegotiation in the relationship between the Malay Muslims and other ethnic counterparts in the Thai nation-state. Conflicts of contending cultural spaces may continue to result. This would, in turn, mean that although the theatres may change, the politics of identity renegotiation would continue to be more relevant to an understanding of a Muslim minority's relation to changing circumstances than the official politics of conspiratorial actors and clandestine foreign intervention.

CHAPTER 4

Hijab and Moments of Legitimation: Islamic Resurgence in Thai Society

INTRODUCTION

In early 1988 there was an extraordinary debate concerning Muslims in Thailand. As a result of the so-called *hijab* crisis, daily papers carried numerous articles and letter from Muslims and non-Muslims alike exchanging views on the issue of Muslim dress. Responding to my letter arguing against a columnist's piece that had suggested that *hijab* dress is more of Arab culture than Islamic code,[1] a foreign reader wrote to the *Bangkok Post*:

> The various dresses of these people (Muslims) are determined by their disparate cultures. This is not to say that the new radical elements of Islam worldwide are not trying to change this; these fanatics are trying to make dress an Islamic issue.... When Islamic people [sic] use Islam itself in an attempt to have their own way regarding dress, they are taking unfair advantage of the Thai government by escalating their "cause" from a simple cultural matter to a religious crisis.[2]

Another angry letter from a Thai reader asks, "Do schoolchildren and students in Islamic countries demand to dress according to Buddhist, Christian, Sikh, Jewish, etc., religions?"[3] It is important to note that for Muslims, dressing is an Islamic issue; "these fanatics" may be symptomatic of a people who need to reassert their own identity; and wearing *hijab* in this case at this time is no "simple cultural matter." The second letter, despite its angry tone, raise question concerning the relationship between a dominant religious group and a religious minority and the way in which the latter is treated by the former. These letters are examples of the kind of debate generate by the *hijab* crisis of December 1987 to March 1988.

This essay examines the way Muslims in Thailand express their Muslim identity in a society in which the majority of people are Buddhists and in which Buddhist rhetoric and symbolism are use extensively by the Thai state. It seeks to construe the dilemma of legitimation when the Muslims appeal to religion as a form of legitimation that supersedes that of the state. The *hijab* crisis is chosen as a case study trough which a pattern of relationship between the Muslims and Thai society, amidst the wave of Islamic resurgence that contributes to a new moment of legitimations, can be constructed.

I begin with a discussion on the problematic nature of "Islamic resurgence" and its possible impact on Muslims in Thailand. Then, reasons for choosing the *hijab* crisis as a case study will be suggested and a detail account of this event presented. As this event has generated a lively debate that touches upon important issue concerning Muslims in a Buddhist country, the nature of this public debate will be discussed. Finally, problem of legitimation resulting from this *hijab* crisis will be analyzed.

ISLAMIC RESURGENCE

The notion of "Islamic resurgence" is problematic. Two other notions commonly used in the same vein are "revivalism" and "reassertion." The former clearly indicates idea of returning to the past and perhaps "a desire to revive what is antiquated."[4] The latter term is more complicated. Arguably, "reassertion" does not convey the idea of a challenge to existing social arrangements. "It does not even come close to suggesting that dominant paradigms are being questioned. It merely connotes insistence, insistence upon one's cause, one's position. It is essentially a positive statement."[5] For Muslims, however, the notion of "reassertion" has one clear advantage: it is a religious concept. The history of Islam can be characterized as a movement of resistance (*al-muqu-wamah*) and reassertion (*al-takid*). The latter notion finds its sanctity in the original conception of Islam, for the Prophet Muhammad was obliged to practice resistance as a prerequisite for asserting the doctrine of *tawhid* (unity of God) and its corollaries.[6]

Some scholars use the terms "resurgence," "revivalism," and "reassertion" interchangeably without taking into account their fine differences.[7] Chandra Muzaffar[8] has pointed out three reasons for

THE LIFE OF THIS WORLD

THE LIFE OF THIS WORLD

choosing "resurgence" over other term such as "reassertion" or "revivalism." First, it is a view from within the Muslim community itself and highlights the growing impact of the religion among its adherents. Second, it suggests a phenomenon that has happened before and thereby connect present events with the past. Third, the term embodies the notion of a challenge and perhaps more importantly, even a threat to those who adhere to other world views.

Muzaffar also argues that Islamic resurgence as a social phenomenon began more than two hundred years ago. It is normally associated with names such as Muhammad ibn 'Abd al-Wahhab of eighteenthcentury Saudi Arabia (the founder of the Wahhabi movement), Jamal al-Din al-Afaghani in the nineteenth century, Sayyid Muhammad bin Ali al-Sanusi of nineteenthcentury Algeria (the founder of the Sanusiyyah movement), Zia Gokalp of early twentiethcentury Turkey, Mulla Hadi Sabziwari of eighteenthcentury Iran, and Shah Wali Allah Dihawi of eighteenthcentury India.[9] But it is also possible to argue that Islamic resurgence is a recurring phenomenon. Piscatori, for example, asserts that throughout Islamic history there have been those who have thought of themselves as *mujaddid* (renewers) of Islam. He writes:

> One thinks of the agitation surrounding the Hashimiyya in the eighth century; the Carmathians in the tenth; the Fatimids in the tenth and eleven centuries; the Naqshbandiyya, particularly Ahmad Sirhindi, in the late sixteenth and early seventeenth centuries; Ibn 'Abd al-Wahhab of Arabia in the eighteenth; Uthman dan Fodio of western Africa in the early nineteenth; the followers of al-Afghani, 'Abduh, and Rida, often referred to as the Salafiyya, in the late nineteenth century; and the Muslim Brotherhood in this century.[10]

Examining the examples of Imam Husain, Umar bin Abdul Aziz, Al-Ghazzali, Ibn Taymiyya, Imam Shamil of Russia, and many of the others mentioned above, one can also argue that it is naive and misleading to say that the present wave of Islamic resurgence is a strange phenomenon. Because it emerges out of the recurring conflict between Islam and *jahiliya* (pagan practice or practice resulting from the age of ignorance), Islamic resurgence can be seen as a continuous process throughout the different phases of Muslim history.

In general, Islamic resurgence has been inspired by the following factors: disillusionment with Western civilization as a whole among a new Muslim generation; the failings of social systems based on capitalism or socialism; the lifestyle of secular élites in Muslim states; the desire for power among a segment of an expanding middle class that cannot be accommodated politically because of the prevalence of unelected rulers and limited institutions in Muslim societies: the search for psychological security among new urban migrants; the urban environment resulting from, among other things, the process of development, which has strained the social and political fabric, effecting a turn to traditional symbols and rites as solace; the economic strength of certain Muslim states resulting from their oil wealth; the defeat of Egypt, Syria, and Jordan in the 1967 war with Israel, which resulted in a sense of inferiority based on technological rather than theological inadequacy; a sense of confidence about the future in the wake of the 1973 Egyptian victory over Israel; the success of the 1979 Iranian revolution against one of the most powerful armies in the world (and one backed by major Western powers); and the dawn of the fifteenth century of the Muslim calendar.[11]

These factors have given rise to Islamic resurgence, which assumes two broad forms. One is to fall back upon Islamic tradition as much as possible, believing that any change would be for the worse. The only solution is to hold fast to Islamic tradition and legacy either by withdrawal from the processes of Westernization or preservation of the Muslim legacy in culture, knowledge, and institutions. The other form emphasizes that the preservation of the past is inadequate. A creative, positive response to the Western challenge, an attempt to understand its nature and offer an alternative, is needed. Islamic resurgence must prepare for an all-out confrontation with the challenging powers and offer Islam as the alternative basis for culture and civilization. This kind of response, as seen in the lives and works of al-Afghani, Iqbal, and Shariati among others, has been described as *tajdid* (renewal and reconstruction), a perennial phenomenon in Islamic history.[12] These Muslim resurgents can be referred to as neither "traditionalists" nor as "fundamentalists" in the generally understood sense of dogma and petrification because they do not simply hold the Islamic principles as they are "frozen in time in their historical applicability."[13]

Despite this broad structural explanation of Islamic resurgence, however, it would be misleading to overemphasize similarities among widely separated phenomena. In fact, one of the most salient features of contemporary Islamic resurgence is that it manifests local features, sectarian differences, and indigenous accents.[14] Islamic resurgence, like other social phenomena, needs to be contextualized if the relationship between Muslims and the society they reside in is to be meaningfully analyzed. Because contexts differ, the nature of Islamic resurgence in various societies will vary accordingly. In a context wherein Muslims constitute a numerical majority, the portrait of Islamic resurgence will inevitably differ from that sketched in places where they are a minority. Ethnic and religious components also contribute to different features of Islamic resurgence. Therefore, an understanding of Islamic resurgence in Thai society, wherein Muslims constitute a clear minority in a culture vastly different from their own, will shed light on the strategies that the resurgents and the Thai state utilize in coping with each other. Such a process has crystallized in the recent *hijab* crisis in Yala in southern Thailand.

SIGNIFICANCE OF THE *HIJAB* CASE

In several cases, patterns of relationships between the Muslims and the Thai state have required readjustment. Chief among them were incidents of school burning in the four southernmost provinces from March 1987 until the end of that year.[15] In another case, a government report stated that 18 Muslim youths trained in terrorist activities by Libya were returning to carry out terrorist acts in the southern provinces.[16] A Narathiwat deputy governor published and distributed a book on Islam that many Muslims considered blasphemous.[17] A time bomb was planted at the large Buddha statue in Narathiwat on 24 March 1987, to be detonated at 1:00 pm, but the authorities successfully defused the 30 pound TNT bomb three minutes before it was to explode.[18] Cases like these were either isolated or lacked a clear religious overtone. Violence, for example, does not occur in everyday life and can be considered an aberration rather than the norm. In this sense these cases can be seen as lacking the strength to generate serious questions about the normal pattern of relationships between Muslims and the Thai state.

The Yala *hijab* case is different. It concerns dress, which is a normal everyday activity. Like many other common human actions, besides depending on economic and climatic conditions, dress is a function of accepted social values and dominant world views. A change in dress can sometimes reflect a genuine change in basic social values. It is not accidental that pictures of Muslim women in their *hijab* or words about *hijab* tend to grace the front pages of publications dealing with Islamic resurgence.[19] Muzaffar[20] points out that the rapid diffusion of what is regarded as Islamic attire among a significant segment of the Muslim female population in Malaysia, especially in urban areas, is the most obvious sign of Islamic resurgence in that country.

Islamic resurgence in Malaysia is by no means monolithic. In fact, it reflects different levels of belief, commitment, and lifestyle. The turn toward Islam occurred through contact and exposure to Islamic ideals, "oftentimes plus pressure from those already in the *dakwah* (to call or to preach) movement."[21] In other words, peer pressure can play a significant role in convincing a female Muslim student in Malaysia to change her attire. Therefore, while wearing *hijab* is "the most obvious sign of Islamic resurgence," it cannot be used to assess the extent of religious commitment of those who wear it. In Malaysia, changing into "Islamic attire" is but an outward manifestation; it may not honestly reflect conscious Islamic resurgence, unlike *hijab* in Thai society.

Because they are a minority in Thai society, Muslims in Thailand sometimes try to live the way Thais of other religious persuasions do. Many emphasize similarities rather than differences between Muslims and non-Muslims. Because there are few Muslims at Yala Teachers' Training College, peer pressure is not significant enough to influence female students to put on *hijab*; in fact, to differ from the majority of students is to invite difficulties. Female students who put on *hijab* have had to face numerous obstacles including opposition from fellow students and school authorities. Unlike the Malaysian case, their change of attire does express a strong determination reflecting genuine commitment. In this sense, because Muslims are a minority living in an alien culture, wearing *hijab* in southern Thailand is a better indicator of Islamic resurgence than it might be in other societies.

The high visibility of wearing *hijab* is also significant. Especially when this attire appears in a situation governed by clear regulations, such as a college which normally has its own uniform, it can be read as a direct challenge to existing rules. When these rules are espoused by an institution of higher learning supported by official policy, the student's decision to change their attire effectively calls into question the existing rules as well as the institutions behind them. As a result, the dynamism of relationship adjustment between the Muslims and the Thai state becomes crystallized when one analyzes cases such as this. When the Muslims decided to demonstrate in support of the students' decision, the political nature of the *hijab* case, which cannot be separated from the original cultural issue, became apparent.

As mentioned above, the *hijab* crisis received unusual attention from the press. Muslims and non-Muslims alike participated in this public debate. Thai decision makers as well as lower-ranking official aired their opinions, some more openly than others. The publicity in this case resulted from an amalgamation of factors including visibility, religious overtones (considered sensitive in Thai society), and geographical significance. That this event took place in Yala, one of the four southernmost provinces of Thailand, where the Malay Muslim population is a clear majority and which borders Malaysia, must be taken into consideration. The Thai state always regards incidents in the four southernmost provinces as indicative of a sensitive security problem.[22]

The Malay Muslims of southern Thailand tend to take pride in Malaysia as the epicenter of Islam and view events there positively. Malaysian based *tabligh* (propagation) groups have ventured into Thailand in the last decade or so to participate in mass meeting organized by their counterparts in Thailand. The impact of Islamic development in Malaysia is also far greater among this group of Muslims in Thailand because they appear identical in dress to, and display other outward religious symbols prevalent among, their neighbors in Malaysia.[23] Despite the impact of Malaysian religious awakening on the Malay Muslims in Southern Thailand, the religious content of the *hijab* issue enables Muslims from all corners of Thai society to consider it more than "another southern problem." This is another reason why the *hijab* issue can be better used to understand Islamic resurgence than other cases such as the planting of a bomb at the basement of the Buddha image in Narathiwat. A discussion of the latter is usually overshadowed by conditions specific to the southern problem such as the historical background of the area, poverty, and separatist movements with their international linkages.[24]

HIJAB CRISIS: AN EVENT

In 1986 a school in Nonthaburi laid off a Muslim teacher because she came to work after the end-of-year examination dressed in accordance with Islamic teachings: she wore a blouse with long sleeves, an ankle-length skirt, and a head covering. The school fired her after issuing an order on 6 May 1986 claiming that she disturbed the "normality" of the school. The woman said that her dressing in accordance with Islamic tradition should be considered an attempt to preserve morality and civilization. She saw no reason for her dismissal.[25]

A similar incident took place in Pattani on 2 June 1986. A Muslim civil servant dressed modestly with her head covered walked into the government house in Pattani to report to work. The governor urged her not to dress in an Islamic way. He told her that he had been serving in the province for ten years, during which he had seen numerous religious people, and that there was no need to cover her head. If she were allowed to dress as she desired, other government officials would want to follow suit. She was eventually transferred to Bangkok.[26] These cases show that the bureaucracy had been serious in its response to *hijab* for sometime, so when a few female students in Yala decided to put on their *hijab*, the reactions of the Yala college officials were not unexpected.[27]

On 11 December 1987 a group of female Muslim students at Yala Teachers' Training College conveyed a message to the college administration concerning their intention to dress in accordance with their religious beliefs. Three days later, three of the students walked into their respective classes in their *hijab* dresses, only to be met with strong reaction from the administration. Some Muslim lecturers pointed out that their dresses were not in keeping with college regulations. Other lecturers threatened that if they did not wear college uniforms they would have to find a new place to study. A week later, 12 Muslim students gave up their college uniforms and went to study in their *hijab*. Some lecturers began to ignore them, while others criticized them severely. On 23 December, the college administration announced that some students were intentionally violating college uniform regulations and that therefore the college would be unable to accommodate their demands. Moreover, they claimed, the action of these students was a result of outside intervention. The vice-rector in charge of student affairs met with the Muslim students. He asked them to bring their parents to the college and announced that they would be suspended.

The next day, a pamphlet with the following anonymous message was issued:

> Every religion teaches people to be good, to sacrifice for the benefit of society and not to disrupt peace in society, nor create disunity.... Because you misuse education, it amounts to an attempt to sabotage this society. The effects of your actions will definitely be felt in the future! You have lived peacefully for a long time with no problem, haven't you? What kind of a joke are you thinking so that it bothered you now? So much fantasy. We strongly believe that this kind of

idea does not belong to students of Yala Teachers' Training College. It is the idea of those who are uneducated, barbaric, and irrational.

The Muslims, of course, were furious. Meanwhile, the offending students were barred from their classrooms.

During the first week of 1988, a student in *hijab* tried to attend her classical dance and drama class. Her teacher, apparently annoyed by her dress, asked her to leave the classroom. She sadly complied. Later that day, Ms. Fatima Kaewdamrongchai attended another class. When students who had not previously taken a test were asked to identity themselves, she did so promptly but received no attention. The test questions were distributed to everyone but her. She remained in class until the end of the test. On the same day, 4 January, all students in *hijab* were simultaneously asked to leave their classrooms. They were also barred from using the college library. One of the librarians reported having received "an order from someone in high position" to do so. Another young woman tried in vain to lead a normal student life. When asked to leave her classroom, she requested that she be allowed to study "right outside" her class. The teacher refused and said that "it is would be an objectionable scene" Other lecturers reprimanded the student in *hijab*, accusing them of trying to achieve notoriety by wearing such dress. "If you don't want to study," they said, "then leave so that everything will be over." As a result of these pressures, some of the students decided to ask for leaves of absence. On the morning of 7 January, students found six prayer mats, one ordinary mat, and one *telekong* (dress worn by Muslim women during their prayers) near the college dog house. All the Muslim students, both female and male, were furious. They decided to boycott classes altogether as a sign of protest. On the next day, a Friday, they continued to boycott all classes and gathered in their group room, which also served as a prayer room. Other students were taken aback when they heard the sound of a powerful *takbir* three times. After collectively saying *"Allahu akbar"* (God is great), they performed their Friday prayer together.

During the protest, students tried to approach politicians and concerned government agencies for solutions. From Den Tomina, a Pattani member of parliament, they received a copy of an order issued by the minister of education, Mr. Marut Bunnag, asking the Teacher' Training College to accommodate the Muslim students' demand.

On Monday, 11 January, non-Muslim students protested that order. The next day, some students came to class in Thai classical and *likae* dress, colorful costumes worn for traditional performing arts. The protesters demanded that the ministerial order be lifted. Meanwhile, some lecturers continued to consider wearing *hijab* dress a violation of college regulations in spite of the ministerial order.

As if the issue were not complicated enough, the media reported that Mr. Sawai Pattano, then deputy minister of the interior, publicly voiced his disagreement with Minister Marut's accommodating order. He argued that Minister Marut was wrong because compliance with the Muslims' demand violated regulations, which should be applied to all without exception, in addition to creating a breach of national unity.

At the college the non-Muslim protesters insisted that those wearing *hijab* put on uniforms like all the others. The Southern Border Province Administration Center (SBPAC) offered a compromise, urging that *hijab* be worn only on Friday, the *jumma-at* (congregational prayer) day. Muslim students refused this proposal, arguing that there was no religious justification for them to wear *hijab* only on Friday. To do so might be considered *bid'a* (deviant behavior).

The college administration then tried to enforce its regulations step by step. First, the student would be allowed to wear *hijab* for a few more days. Then there would be three official warnings to those who refused to comply with college regulations. After this, students' parents would be called in. Finally, students would be asked not to come to college.

By then Muslims in Bangkok had begun to intervene; many issued protest letters to concerned organizations. On 27 January 1988, the National Security Council deliberated the issue and decided not to allow those who wore *hijab* to go to classes. At a press conference four days later, seven Muslim organizations, including the Muslim Lawyers Association, Muslim Students Association of Thailand, and Muslim Youth Association of Thailand, voiced their support for those who wanted to uphold Islamic principles in Yala. Some groups sent a letter to General Prem Tinsulanonda, then prime minister, urging the government to reconsider its stern position. Meanwhile, the Office of the Chularajmontri (*Shaikh-ul-Islam*),[28] complaining that the SBPAC no longer sought their advice, protested the way the situation was handled. Acting on reports that there was going to be a huge protest in the south, the police and the military were ordered to block the Muslims from Bangkok and the southern province who planned to join the Yala protest.

On 11 February more than ten thousand Muslims protested in front of the Yala central mosque. One day later, the crowd was informed that "agents" of the Thai state—the secretary of the Ministry of Education, a representative of the national Security Council, and the governor of Yala—agreed to relax the regulations, allowing the students to wear *hijab* at least until the end of their examinations. The protesting crowd dispersed.

However, on 15 February, when Muslim students in *hijab* came to the college, they were forbidden to enter the campus. College officials explained that this was for their own safety because some student groups were very upset and might do something drastic. In addition, they said, they had not yet officially received word from higher authorities about the relaxation of regulations. Female Muslim students were barred from appearing on campus; a special examination would be arranged for them on 12 and 13 March. The students did not accept these conditions. When they returned the next day, they were barred from all classes.

On 18 February, 13 Buddhists student representatives from the consortium of Southern Teachers' Training Colleges presented a letter to the minister of education urging him to uphold regulations and order the Muslim women to put on student uniforms before sitting for the examination nation on 22 February

When examination day came, all female Muslim students were asked to take the test in a separate room. They requested permission to sit in the same room as their non-Muslim friends, arguing that "this is not South Africa and there should be no discrimination bases upon racial or any other factors." The college administration did not grant their request, so 20 male and seven female Muslim students decided to boycott the examination. This led to another mass protest beginning on 23 February. After a few days, the number of protesters in front of the Yala central mosque reached ten thousand. More letters of protest were sent to both the prime minister and the commander-in-chief of the army, General Chavalit Yongchaiyudh.

On 2 March, representatives of the Ministry of Education accepted all requests by the protesters to put the relaxation order into practice, to investigate college administrators who failed to follow the orders of the minister of education and the National Security Council, to amend uniform regulations to accommodate Islamic dress, and not to punish the students who had participated in the protest (as well as to provide them a later opportunity to sit for the examination). Upon learning that their voices had been heard by the state, the crowd dispersed. Shortly after the crisis, a deputy minister of education announced that a new

College Act was being prepared and would be considered by the parliament in May. This act would contain an injunction allowing a college to pass regulations concerning students' dress in accordance with local needs and cultures. But the parliament was dissolved. The *hijab* case is no longer a burning issue, although its potential to reemerge remains.

The *hijab* crisis at the Yala Teachers' Training College reflects social patterns found more generally in Thai society. Muslim students constitute a minority in the college, which is governed by administrators armed with rigid regulations. A basic question is whether those regulations were formulated to take into account the existence of minority religious groups. If the answer is negative, them questions need to be raised concerning the foundation upon which those regulations stand. Several key issues haveemerged from the public debate generated by this *hijab* crisis.

PUBLIC DEBATE ON THE *HIJAB* CRISIS

The immediate debate generated by the *hijab* crisis produced two groups: those supporting the right to wear *hijab* and those opposed. Such a categorization is inadequate, however, for a proper understanding of how the *hijab* crisis at Yala Teachers' Training College reflects the nature of Islamic resurgence in the Thai polity. A better way to analyze the different opinions expressed is to examine the nature of the arguments themselves.

Some oppose *hijab* because such attire violates college regulations. The college administrators were the main exponents of this argument. A vice-rector in charge of student affairs pointed out that the regulations of Teachers' Training Colleges are important. If students want to dress differently, then regulations would have to be amended first. Such amendment must follow official procedures.[29] One columnist insisted that Muslim students must unconditionally follow regulations. "If they don't want to follow [regulations], they should not come to study. It has nothing to do with religion."[30] This kind of argument, though simplistic, is usually effective in relegating the issue to the domain of bureaucratic procedures, which the ordinary citizen normally dares not enter.

Another argument opposing the wearing of *hijab* is based upon politics. Mr. Taveesak Srisuwan, a representative of Buddhist students from Sahavidhayaalai Taksin, of the Consortium of Southern Teachers' Training Colleges (consisting of teachers' training colleges in the provinces of Yala, Songkhla, Phuket, Nakorn Srithammarat, and Surat Thani), went to Bangkok in February 1988 to persuade the minister of education to uphold the regulations. He threatened that if the minister failed to accept his group's suggestion, they too would protest. He argued that the problem of *hijab* dress had already spread to primary schools; left unchecked, it would spread to secondary schools as well as vocational colleges, igniting separatist problems. He also emphasized that southern politicians were involved, as well as a shadowy group calling themselves "Mujahiddeen who wanted to see the four southern provinces transformed into the Republic of Pattani."[31] Another "analysis" published in a weekly magazine pointed a finger at intervention from a Muslim country that "operated through its cultural office in Thailand." The article argued that this outside force was using propaganda and sabotage to spread its ideology.[32]

Two basic assumptions seem to characterize this political argument. First, politicians are manipulating already explosive conditions for their own benefit. Second, a secessionist group may want to manipulate the situation, posing a serious security issue. In addition, because of the transnational character of Islam, foreign intervention is always suspected. This type of security-related reasoning points to a deeper set of arguments that emphasize the benign nature of the Thai state as well as unity in Thai society.

A Muslim letter writer suggested that *hijab* should be abandoned and students should return to their uniforms. He argued that religion need not interfere with accepted social practice. Dressing in accordance with religious teaching, though morally correct, should be exercised with care by taking into account the specific local cultural context. Besides, the Thai state has guaranteed "more than enough" extra rights to the Muslims. He cited as examples, religious holidays when Muslim officials are normally permitted to take up to five days off and the quota system for Muslims students in the four southern provinces who enroll in colleges and universities.[33] Another Muslim argued that *hijab* dress originated in the desert and therefore is not proper for Thai society. Muslim students should quit their protest because of the security threat posed to Thailand by Laos in the Rom Klao incident.[34]

M.R. Kukrit Pramoj, a former prime minister and influential newspaper publisher and columnist, unequivocally promoted the theme of unity in relation to the *hijab* crisis. He disagreed with students wearing *hijab* because, he asserted, while Islam is a matter of personal faith, everyone in the country is a Thai. From time immemorial, Muslims in Thailand have been dressing like Thais. He said, "It is a pity that this dress issue will create disunity among the Thais who love one another."[35]

This type of reasoning ignores two basic questions. First, what exactly is the meaning of "Thai-ness"? Is this "Thai-ness" defined by the Thai state? This relates directly to the second basic question: is Thai society as monolithic as many have been led to believe?

Other perspectives on the *hijab* case, especially those that support the Muslims' position, employ a different kind of reasoning from those that make bureaucratic regulations or national unity the fundamental premises of the argument. Some writers simply point to the facts that people are different, that their religious convictions are protected by the constitution, and that as long as wearing *hijab* does not create any problem for Thai society, they should be allowed such religious freedom.[36] Others try to answer the two questions above.

Two prominent academics, taking the nature of Thai society seriously into account, have drawn on deeper reasons for their positions. Chalardchai Ramitanon, an anthropologist from Chiangmai University, points out that religious holiness stems from the use of a symbolic system supported by the faith of the religious community. Religions have several functions: they provide norms for societies, legitimize existing power, and endow people's lives with meaning, among other things. He states succinctly that in a society consisting of peoples of different religious persuasions, it is difficult to create a unified nation, particularly when the state interprets the notion of nation or country by association it fundamentally with a particular religion. The possibility of conflict is thereby enhanced. He writes: "Being Buddhists is no proof of being Thais. The Burmese and Sri Lankans are Buddhists but they are not Thais."[37] Acknowledging differences in religions and citing the authority of history to support the point that in the past quarrels about religious symbols have easily led to battles as well as to the founding of new countries. Professor Nidhi Eiosriwong, a noted historian, asked: "Will our country disintegrate because Muslim girls who go to schools or colleges dress differently?" He argued forcefully that to push a people to choose between their religious loyalty and their love of the nation is the most unwise thing a state can do. A state with some degree of wisdom would try with all its might to avoid creating such a dilemma.[38]

These two academics help elucidate the fact that Thai state tends to ignore basic differences in Thai society. The sociological basis of their argument is helpful to understanding the complexities of Thai society. When serious attention is paid to the sociology of religion, both the limits and contributions of Buddhism as a pillar of the Thai state become apparent. In this sense these professors argue that the foundation of the Thai state, which many claim to be Buddhism, is not broad enough to accommodate the Muslims in Thailand. Meanwhile, the Muslims' commitment to their religion can effectively call into question the thesis of a unified Thai political community.

The line of reasoning of the Muslims who participated in the public debate in support of the young women who were wearing *hijab* is basically religious. Religious reasoning in this case helps to clarify the kind of sociological reasoning mentioned above. The secretary-general of the Shaikh-ul-Islam Office began his article in a Thai daily newspaper by pointing out that covering a woman's head is a cultural symbol of Muslim women's dress code, not, as many suspect, a symbol of Iranian women. He then cited an oft-quoted verse from the Holy Qur'an which reads:

> And say to the believing women
> That they should lower
> Their gaze and guard
> Their modesty; that they
> Should not display their
> Beauty and ornaments except
> What (must ordinarily) appear
> Thereof; that they should
> Draw their veils over
> Their bosoms and not display
> Their beauty.
> (Al-Qur'an XXIV:31)

Using this verse, he pointed out that those who tried to characterize *hijab* as mere tradition were abusing Islamic principles. Islamic dress does not undermine other people's culture, does not violate anybody's rights, does not jeopardize national security or the educational system. Arguing that Islamic injunctions on dress would instead serve as a protection from such evils as rape and fornication, he concluded that those who opposed an Islamic dress code were directly opposing Islam itself.[39] While Phra Khru Thavorn Stakom, a Buddhist monk, claimed that the *hijab* crisis was the result of foreign intervention, especially by Shiites, determined to threaten the Buddhists in the society,[40] another Buddhist-oriented writer posed a much more fundamental question. "Pagadhamma," a senior *Matichon* columnist, pointed out that the *hijab* crisis was generated by "people who cannot appreciate *dhamma* [teaching, the way] and *dhamma* that cannot reach people." This columnist argued that the state had to understand fundamental *dhamma*, namely, the diversity that exists within any given political community. Regulations formulated without taking into account diverse groups of people who belong to different religious persuasions are not based on *dhamma:*

> It is important not to tolerate any violation of legitimate rights simply because of official regulations implemented by governing bureaucrats who believed that such a singular norm is appropriate, connotes "Thainess" and will protect it. They forget that there are other Thais who belong to other religions with different norms. It is as if they were determined to press the Muslims to choose between their nation and their religion, although there is absolutely no necessity to make that drastic choice.[41]

Although the columnist's exposition seems to be similar to the sociological reasoning of the academics cited above, the reasoning here is basically religious. By pointing out that fundamental *dhamma* accurately reflecting social reality is ignored, the columnist seems to question the claim that Buddhism is a basis for the Thai state. More straight-forwardly, Pagadhamma questions whether the "Buddhist Thai" group who protested against Muslim students wearing *hijab* are real Buddhists; if they are, they should meditate on the "Four Noble Truths" and show compassion to all. Based on Buddhist-oriented wisdom and compassion, they should not attach too much significance to how people dress and should be able to appreciate those who dress differently. An ultimate question for "Buddhist Thais" should be "In what way does their dressing differently from us affect the extent to which we are Buddhists?"[42] In other words, attachment to a specific uniform sanctioned by the state does not enhance the quality of being a "Buddhist," whereas coming to terms with diverse and changing social realities by using compassion and intellect does.

The debate generated by the *hijab* crisis is political. Two kinds of politics based upon two different kinds of reasoning —distinguished by their capability to correspond to diversified social reality—can be identified. They are "bureaucratic reasoning" and "sociological reasoning." I would argue that as a result of its institutional character and rules governing its practice, the former tends to resist change and is less capable of corresponding to the dynamism of social reality. The strength of "bureaucratic reasoning" is drawn from regulations enunciated chiefly for governing and security purposes. These regulations, in turn, are implemented by bureaucrats who suspect the governed.[43] When facing problems, those influenced by bureaucratic reasoning have resorted to solutions that include enforcing regulations without exceptions, punishing violators, blaming outsiders for the perceived disruption of social order, even appointing a special committee to pass judgment on Muslim students' dress codes, as suggested by a Muslim member of parliament.[44] The *hijab* crisis in Yala is a fruit of such petrification of social reality.

"Sociological reasoning," in contrast, is based upon the sociological character of a given society. It is sensitive to differences among peoples in the society and therefore amenable to critical appraisal of both the bureaucrats who sometimes blindly follow petrified regulations and the foundation on which such regulations rest. Chalardchai Ramitanon's piece and that of the secretary-general of the Shaikh-ul-Islam reflect this kind of reasoning. Unlike bureaucratic reasoning, wherein rules and regulations are of utmost importance, sociological reasoning can and must include local voices on the issues. In the *hijab* crisis, voices of the young Muslim women at Yala Teachers' Training College who chose to brave the controversy indicate that at the fundamental level the incompatibility between these two kinds of politics points to the problems of legitimation:

> In the past, the relationship between the teachers and myself was good, but when I put on my *hijab*, they stopped talking to me. They said: "If you want to dress like this, then go to live in your own country. This is not your country. This is Thailand with the Thai dress code. Go to where you belong!"

When asked whether family pressures were present, another answered:

> There are some. The first day I put on my *hijab*, my brother warned me not to do it because they might think that I am radical.... Then he asked whether I was worried that my action would jeopardize the position [of] my other brother who is a soldier in the Thai army because he happened to be my guarantor when I was admitted to the College. I did not know what to do. That night I could only cry. Then I told my mother that if I were expelled from the college, do not feel sad. If I follow their regulations and graduate with a bachelor's degree, are you certain that Allah Almighty would have blessed me when I had lived in accordance with His Way?... I cannot knowingly follow them and ignore Allah's Truth.[45]

One of the Muslim girls who, in her *hijab*, attended a rally in front of Government House in Bangkok in support of the Yala Muslim students, spelled out the case from a Muslim point of view. She said:

> Thanks be to Allah for giving us a chance to participate in this protest. It is clear what a Muslim should do in this case. The *kafir* [nonbelievers] refused to let the Muslims practice their religious duties. They are not opposing us but we regard them as opposing Allah.[46]

From these young women's point of view, the *hijab* crisis arose from the fact that the Muslims are now conscious of Islam and want to follow its tenets to the best of their abilities in a state chiefly constituted by nonbelievers. Their reaffirmed sense of religiosity within the larger context of Islamic resurgence portrays the limitation of the Thai state's legitimacy. It is therefore important to analyze the dynamics of legitimation reflected from the interaction between the Muslims and the Thai state.

MOMENTS OF LEGITIMATION

A Buddhist philosopher explained that according to the Buddha, *dhamma* is to used like a raft to cross over to the safety of *nibbana* (nirvana) but not to carry as a burden, identifying oneself with it and becoming obsessed with a sectarian identity. *Dhamma* is universal, and the religious community or *samanabrahmana* is an essential ingredient of society because it turns people away from evil. As a result, a Buddhist can neither disparage nor discriminate against a follower of another religion without violating the fundamental principles of the Buddhist doctrine. Thus, he concludes: "Within a polity governed by Buddhist principles, the problem of minority rights should not exist at all."[47]

The Thai state is sometimes characterized as a political manifestation of all Buddhist values and ideals based upon Buddhist cosmology. Its rulers are "the very essence and best exponents of Buddhist teachings. The blessings that permeate the land flow from the *baramee* (charisma) of the highest ruling institutions, which are the earthly images of the ideal Buddha himself."[48] If such is the case, how can the problems of religious minority rights in Thai society, such as the *hijab* crisis, be explained? A common answer is to point to "the gap between the ideals cognitively acknowledged and how individuals and groups professing these ideals behave in actual life situations."[49] Perhaps a more enlightening question is not to measure Buddhist society against a set of principles derived from the canon of Buddhism but to examine the way in which Buddhism of its doctrines are partially used in a state that claims Buddhism as one of its revered pillars.

In a study attempting to investigate the interactions of the *sangha* (order of monks) with politics in a situation of sociopolitical change, Somboon Suksamran argues that Buddhism "has long served as one of the most important sources of political legitimation for political rulers." In fact, because of the kind of influence Buddhism has over Thai society in its various dimensions, political rulers "may make use of religious ideas and the *sangha* to legitimate their rule and to facilitate social control."[50]

In the *hijab* crisis, young Muslim women claimed legitimacy for their Islamic dress by citing God's commandment. One problem with a state's using Buddhism not as principle, but merely as legitimation to subordinate sectarian identity to marginal importance is its possible inability to incorporate differences among its citizens. Although the Muslims are Thai citizens, the basis for legitimation of the Thai state with its emphasis on Buddhist rhetoric cannot accommodate their totally different cosmology based on Islam. Realizing this, in times of heightened conflict the Thai state shifts emphasis from its religious-oriented legitimation to rules and regulations. In other words, if the state's basis of legitimacy is dysfunctional, the state will resort to the authority of rules and regulations to govern the citizens' behavior, because in the realm of impersonal regulations differences of identity cease to be of much importance. To rely on Jürgen Habermas's wisdom, the *hijab* crisis embodies a case wherein "supplies of legitimation can compensate for deficits in rationality and extensions of organizational rationality can compensate for those deficits that do appear."[51]

A legitimation deficit makes it impossible to maintain or establish by administrative means "effective normative structures" to the extent required.[52] Facing a protest by Muslims who based their case on a different type of legitimation, the legitimation basis of the Thai state proved inadequate. To maintain social control under such circumstances, the state used official regulations based upon bureaucratic reasoning. Such reasoning becomes rationality produced and maintained by the bureaucracy for its own sake. This is what Habermas called "organizational rationality," maintaining that "while organizational rationality spread, cultural traditions are undermined and weakened."[53] In this case, however, "organizational rationality" seems unable to compensate for the legitimation deficits and to weaken the Muslims' cultural traditions, as theoretically anticipated.

A more fruitful approach to the "minority problem" posed by Muslims in Thai society begins with the recognition that Thai society is not monolithic.[54] Benedict Anderson has pointed out that the state of old Siam was defined by its center, not its boundaries. Thus different peoples such as the Muslims could be loyal to the monarch yet keep their cultural (read religious) and ethnic identities undisturbed. Elites in the Bangkok area suffered from "historic failures in dealing with the 'minorities' (especially 'indigenous minorities'), indeed in ever really comprehending the problems posed by this group."[55] In fact, it can be argued that the nation-building phase of Thai society is not yet over. The process is long and quite difficult among the Muslims, especially those Malay Muslims in the border provinces, because of their distinctive culture (language, religion) and history.[56] But stating that there are different groups of people in Thailand with different principles of legitimation, although necessary, is not sufficient to explain why the *hijab* crisis erupted at this particular time. One of M. R. Kukrit Pramoj's questions during the height of the *hijab* crisis was "Why do Muslim women begin to put on their *hijab* now although Islam was born more than a thousand years ago?"[57] The question, in spite of its rhetorical tone, points to the fact that mere differences of legitimation cannot fully account for the eruption of such a crisis. It is therefore important to examine the "moment" when such legitimation is exercised.

Legitimation processes can be separated into two phases or "moments," establishing a referent against which actions can be vindicated. In the first moment legitimation is based upon the authority of the referent itself. The legitimation referent is treated as not problematic and thus becomes an "extra-discursive non-practice-related entity."[58] For example, some groups of people claim to be who they are on the basis of a sacred text or a unique history. Such a basis serves the purpose of legitimating their existence. It is not necessary for many of them to know exactly what the text or that history is about. But if this kind of legitimation referent is criticized or desecrated, many adherents will do what they can to "protect" it. In this sense, the referent is not included in their discussion.

The second moment of legitimation deals with the commentary or set of commentaries on the referent. "Even if the referent is taken to be authoritative in principle, its features emerge in a commentary on those features."[59] Here I would argue that one of the best forms of commentary on the referent is to put the principles enunciated by the referent into practice. In so doing, the referent needs to be discussed. Some social conditions must serve as prerequisites for bringing the referent back into the discussion. The revitalization of Islam is just a major condition to question the gap between the sacredness of the text as referent and the importance of practices in accordance with the teachings embodied in the text. Once the principles are being practice, legitimation will consequently be strengthened. With a newly strengthened legitimation, a minority group can challenge the dominant legitimation. In other words, legitimation of the dominant group will be seriously challenged when the religious minority group arrives at their second moment of legitimation.

For a long time, Muslims in Thai society lived in the first moment, using Islam only as a referent to identify who they were. Muslims "practice" their religion: the majority of them do not eat pork; many pray five times a day. But these practices assume the form of ritual, while the referent itself becomes "extra-discursive." Religious discussions have rarely sought to question the teachings contained in the referent. In the past, religious conflicts among Muslims in Thai society were not about issues such as the evil of usury or the tragedy of Muslims in faraway lands such as Afghanistan or Palestine, but about the procedure of prayers. In this first moment of legitimating Islam's sociopolitical message, which emphasizes the reunification of religion and public action by asserting the Muslim identity, was not clearly evident. If at times their "practices" as Muslims came into conflict with accepted behavior in Thai society, they compromised. Although many were aware of the Islamic dress code, they continued to wear uniforms sanctioned by their different institutions. The legitimation deficit of the Thai state did not manifest itself, and not only because it was compensated for by organizational rationality. The fact that organizational rationality prevailed meant also that the legitimation basis of groups such as the Muslims was not strong enough.

With the tide of Islamic resurgence sweeping the world, however, Muslims in Thailand have begun to practice their religion in a new moment of legitimation. In this moment, Islamic principles are articulated,[60] and many Muslims assert their identity by practicing the newly found principles. The meanings of Islamic resurgence become crystallized not with such phenomena as the success of the Iranian revolution, but when ordinary Muslims unify principles and practices of Islam in their lives against the background of a society largely ignorant of their conviction and somewhat frightened by the seriousness with which they take their religion. In the second moment of legitimation for the Muslim minority, the true meanings of Islamic resurgence emerge, and its potential is tested.

CONCLUSION

In the *hijab* crisis in Yala a religious minority reacted to a state legitimized by Buddhism. Dress codes may be considered trivial by some, but for Muslims they are a religious matter. When a columnist in a daily paper wrote that "there is no need to heed any god. Living in Thai society, one has to follow the Thai social order regardless of religious denominations."[61] It was evident that the problem was deeper than a mere questioning of college regulations. The debate generated by the *hijab* crisis elucidates two kinds of politics resulting from bureaucratic of sociological reasoning. The Thai state, legitimized by Buddhism, relies upon bureaucratic reasoning or organizational rationality when there is a deficit of legitimation. This kind of legitimation substitute would have sufficed if the Muslims in the Thai polity had not arrived at the second moment of their Islamic legitimation. Contrary to the first moment of legitimation, when practices according to Islamic teachings may be easily compromised, the second moment gives rise to assertive practices in accordance with Islamic principles. In this movement, Islamic ceases to be but a referent to outside discourses and comes alive in the daily practices and discourses on those practices of the Muslims.

An emphasis on moments of legitimation does not mean that the leadership of the protest, the psychohistory of the Muslim students who decided to wear *hijab*, the geopolitics of Yala as one of the four southernmost provinces, intracollege politics, or government policies are unimportant. In fact, some analysts might choose to view this incident by using gender analysis as a framework and argue that *hijab* must be viewed in relation to the desire of ethnic groups to reassert their autonomy through a gendered discourse. Because "masculinization" represents a claim to full humanity, the minority group assert themselves by insisting on female conformity to a restrictive dress code.[62] To look at Islamic resurgence from the framework of gender analysis would necessitate an examination of Muslim male/female relationships in addition to the masculinization attempt mentioned above. The process of Muslims' identity reassertion also involves males. More and more Muslim men wear beards, for example. Many Muslimsæboth male and femaleæno longer greet one another with traditional Thai salutations but by the Islamic *salaam*. Here I am addressing the significance of *hijab* at a different level and emphasizing the relationship between the Muslims and Thai society through contrasting sets of legitimation.

Analysis of the significance of Islamic resurgence in the Thai polity reveals the foundation of political actions underscoring different sets of legitimation as well as changing moments of legitimation. Such an analysis sheds meaningful light on the foundational strengths and weaknesses of Muslims in both Thai society and the Thai state.

In *Religion as Critique*, Robert John Ackerman[63] suggests that major religions always retain the potential to develop a social critique. To provide this possibility, a religion can never be reduced to mechanically understood dogma because in that form it would lose touch with changing social reality. This assertion seems incompatible with the case of the Muslim minority in Thai society because in the *hijab* crisis, the Muslims seem to have returned to dogma and altered their daily practices in accordance with Islamic principles. Did they lose touch with social reality? An answer is not easily forthcoming because there may be more than one social reality. They may have lost touch with social reality as defined by the Thai state, but that is not the only reality. By clinging to dogma, religion becomes for Muslims a critique not of itself, but of its alien social context. By presenting a different set of legitimation, the Muslims effectively call into question the dominant legitimation used by the Thai state with Buddhism and bureaucratic rationality as its core.

PART III

Negotiating Muslim Lives in Bangkok: Minority in the National Center

CHAPTER 5

Bangkok Muslims and the Tourist Trade

INTRODUCTION

The biggest contributor to the high growth rates of the Thai economy in recent years is tourism.[1] In 1987, there were 3.48 million visitors to Thailand and through them the country earned some 50 billion baht (approximately US$1.96 billion).[2] These figures exceeded the official projections for 1987 which had put the tourist arrival at 2.83 million and the earnings at 42 billion baht.

Contemporary discussion on Thailand's tourist trade concentrates on the socio-economic factors behind the country's remarkable success in attracting foreigners and the social impact of tourism. The people involved in this industry are not given due attention in such discussions.

This study chooses to focus on the Muslims who constitute a sizeable minority group in the heterogeneous Thai society,[3] and seeks to portray their roles in Thailand's booming tourist trade. By virtue of their faith, the Muslims in the tourist trade seem to face a high degree of ethical dilemma. It is this conflict and how they live through it which constitute the subject matter of this study. Bangkok is chosen not only because it remains the most important gateway for international arrivals, but also because the tourism industry in a big city can sharpen the kind of conflict "devout" Muslims will encounter. Wherever possible, the portraits of problems and conflicts will be "described" from the point of view of the "actors" themselves. Documentary research is supplemented by intensive interviews with these social actors.

This study begins with a general picture of tourism in Thailand and its contribution, both positive and negative, to Thai society. It then

* The author gratefully acknowledges helpful comments from Dr. Preeda Prapertchob and a stimulating discussion with Dr. Yos Santasombat and Professor Erik Cohen during the preparation of this paper.

raises the question of the role of Bangkok Muslims in this tourist trade. In the process, facts and figures about Muslims in Bangkok and their economic role in Thai society are discussed. The lives of Bangkok Muslims in the tourist trade and the pattern of conflict resulting from their identity as Muslims engaged in the tourist trade are also highlighted. This study concludes by raising some fundamental questions on the compatibility of Islam as a religion and a way of life with the modern world characterized by capitalism, which is basically responsible for the lives of paradox many Bangkok Muslims lead.

TOURISM IN THAILAND: A GENERAL PORTRAIT

The success story of the tourism industry in Thailand cannot be construed independently of the global trends in tourism. The World Tourism Organization reports that there were 215 million international tourists in 1973. Seven years later, there were 285.5 million tourists, an increase of 32 per cent. More importantly, there have been more and more tourists coming to Asia and the Pacific. In 1977, this region played host to some 8.3 million international tourists. In 1980, there was an 80 per cent increase in this figure, as there were 15 million tourists visiting the region.[4]

Thailand has much to offer its visitors: magnificent beaches, natural beauty, superb architecture, rich collections of arts, excellent cuisine, and good tourist facilities at affordable prices. In 1957, there were 44,375 visitors from overseas. Within 23 years, there has been a more than 4,000 per cent increase in the number of foreign visitors. During the Vietnam War period, there were American troops coming to Thailand for recreational purposes. The number of R & R personnel peaked in 1969, with some 70,000 American soldiers, Number of visitors from neighboring countries also increased by 738 per cent from 1963 to 1980 (Table 5-1).

From 1981 to 1986, there has been a continuous increase in the number of tourists coming to Thailand, except for 1983 when there was a 1.2 per cent decrease. International tourist arrivals to Thailand increased by 15.6 per cent in 1986 and by 23.6 per cent in 1987 (Table 5-2).

Tourists from Asia possess a major market share, with Malaysians heading the list and the Japanese trailing behind since 1981. From 1981 to 1983, tourists from the United Kingdom and the United States ranked third and fourth in terms of market share, but this began to change in 1984 when the Americans and the Singaporeans became the third and fourth largest groups of tourists coming to Thailand. In 1986 and 1987, Singapore came third and the United States dropped to fourth.[5]

The figures provided in Table 5-3 are significant because tourism revenue is a result of three basic factors: number of tourists, their average length of stay in the country and their daily expenditure.

TABLE 5-1   Number of visitors to Thailand, 1957–80

Year	Visitors From Overseas	Visitors from Neighboring Countries	Total	R&R Personnel	Total
1957	44,375	—	44,375	—	44,375
1958	55,210	—	55,210	—	55,210
1959	61,527	—	61,517	—	61,517
1960	81,340	—	81,340	—	81,340
1961	107,754	—	107,754	—	107,754
1962	130,809	—	130,809	—	130,809
1963	134,271	60,805	195,076	—	195,076
1964	158,588	53,336	211,924	—	211,924
1965	189,620	35,405	225,025	—	225,025
1966	207,111	78,006	285,117	33,000	318,117
1967	244,283	91,562	335,845	54,000	389,845
1968	297,856	79,406	377,262	69,070	446,332
1969	378,315	91,469	469,784	70,737	540,521
1970	485,366	143,305	628,671	44,287	672,958
1971	465,992	172,746	638,738	26,614	665,352
1972	594,348	226,410	820,758	7,707	828,465
1973	763,189	274,548	1,037,737	1,447	1,039,184
1974	806,447	300,945	1,107,392	3,530	1,110,922
1975	850,459	329,616	1,180,075	—	1,180,075
1976	877,528	220,914	1,098,442	—	1,098,442
1977	923,046	297,626	1,220,672	—	1,220,672
1978	1,122,518	331,321	1,453,839	21,525	1,475,364
1979	1,230,820	360,635	1,591,455	—	1,591,455
1980	1,348,919	509,882	1,858,801	—	1,858,801

SOURCE   Constance M. Wilson, *Thailand: A Handbook of Historical Statistics*. (Boston, Mass.: G.K. Hall, 1983), p. 233.

TABLE 5-2 Number of tourists coming to Thailand, 1981–88

Year	International Tourist Arrivals
1981	2,015,615
1982	2,218,429
1983	2,191,003
1984	2,346,709
1985	2,438,270
1986	2,818,092
1987	3,482,958
1988	4,300,000

SOURCES *Annual Statistical Report on Tourism in Thailand 1985, 1986; 1988*
Mid-year Economic Review and 1988 Year-End Economic Review.

TABLE 5-3 Revenue from international tourism, 1981–88

Year	No. of Tourists	Average Length of Stay (Days) Person/Day (Baht)	Average Expenditure	Revenue (Million Baht)
1981	2,015,615	4.96	2,146	21,455
1982	2,218,429	4.79	2,248.11	23,879
1983	2,191,003	4.91	2,328.56	25,050
1984	2,346,709	5.47	2,128	27,317
1985	2,438,270	5.58	2,334.92	31,767.86
1986	2,818,092	5.93	2,233	37,321
1987	3,482,958	6.06	2,370	50,024*
1988	4,300,000	6.10	2,478	65,000*

* Figures for 1987 are from *1988 Mid-Year Economic Review*, and for 1988 are estimates
from *1988 Year-End Economic Review, Bangkok Post Supplement* (December 1988). These
figures, though accurate, are not as precise as those obtained from the Tourism
Authority of Thailand. In addition, total revenue for 1987 and average expenditures per
day per person for 1988 are based on my own calculation.
SOURCES Wuthithep Intapanya and Chamlong Atikul, *Economic Consequences of
Tourism Industry in Thailand*, pp. 16, 20, 24, 28; *Annual Statistical Report on Tourism in
Thailand* 1985, pp. 56–57; *Annual Statistical Report on Tourism in Thailand 1986*, pp. 10, 12,
58; *1988 Mid-Year Economic Review*, pp. 9, 36; and *1988 Year-End Economic Review*, p. 11.

In the past, rice used to be Thailand's major export which brought in more revenue than other products. Now this is not the case because revenue from tourism has superseded those from other major exports since 1982 (Table 5-4).

The Thai Government anticipated that revenue from tourism would reach 90,000 million baht with approximately 4.8 million tourists in 1989.[6] It is thus interesting to briefly note who these tourists are.

TABLE 5-4 Comparison of revenue from internationaltourism and other major exports of Thailand, 1981-87 (in million baht)

Rank	1981	1982	1983	1984	1985	1986	1987
1	Rice	Tourism	Tourism	Tourism	Tourism	Tourism	Tourism
	26,367	23,879	25,050	27,317	31,768	37,321	48,500
2	Tourism	Rice	Rice	Rice	Textile	Textile	Textile
	21,455	22,505	20,157	25,932	23,578	31,268	35,899
3	Tapioca	Tapioca	Tapioca	Textile	Rice	Rice	Rice
	16,446	19,869	15,387	19,155	22,524	20,315	22,668
4	Textile	Textile	Textile	Tapioca	Tapioca	Tapioca	Tapioca
	12,531	14,049	14,351	16,600	14,969	19,086	20,719

SOURCES Sources for data from 1981 to 1986 and tourism revenue in 1987 are the same as in Table 5.3. But for other export goods in 1987, see *1988 Mid-Year Economic Review*, p. 13.

In 1986, about 63 per cent of all the tourists coming to Thailand came independently. Male tourists made up approximately 68 per cent of the total. A little more than half of them were in the age bracket of 25 to 44. More than 80 per cent of the visitors came to Thailand for travel and holiday reasons. In terms of occupation, 20.89 per cent were administrators and managers, 17.22 per cent were laborers, production and service workers, and 14.63 per cent were professionals. First time tourists accounted for 46.58 per cent of the total international tourists to Thailand. More than 90 per cent of the tourists found accommodation in Thailand's hotels while some 5 per cent stayed at their friends' places, youth hostels or guesthouses.[7]

TABLE 5-5   Revenue from Middle Eastern tourists, 1984–86

Year	No. of Arrivals	% of Total Tourists	Average Length of Stay (days)	Average Expenditures per person/day (baht)
1984	127,081	5.41	7.06	4,055
1985	127,441	5.22	9.26	4,222.86
1986	113,004	4.00	7.58	2,759.54

SOURCES   *Annual Statistical Report on Tourism in Thailand* 1985, p. 56 *and Annual Statistical Report on Tourism in Thailand* 1986, pp. 56–57.

It is also interesting to note that tourists from Saudi Arabia constituted only 0.85 per cent to 1.46 per cent of the total international tourists during 1981–83. Between 1984 and 1986, Middle Eastern tourists account for 4 to 5 per cent of the total. In 1983, visitors from the Middle East ranked first as the biggest spenders (4,855 baht per day) per person, double the overall average (2,328 baht per day). In addition, while the average length of stay for international tourists in Thailand was less than five days in 1983, an average Middle Eastern tourists stayed in Thailand for 7.93 days. An average Saudi Arabian tourist, in particular, stayed in Thailand more than nine day at a time.[8]

Middle Eastern tourists are highlighted here because the majority of them are Muslims and they tend to spend more than any other group of tourists. In addition, they have been staying in Thailand longer than most other groups. Moreover, it is widely know that their behavior as tourists in Thailand does not reflect the tenets of Islam. However, due to deteriorating economic conditions in the Middle East, the numbers, length of stay and amount of expenditure of these tourists have been declining (Table 5-5).

LITERATURE ON TOURISM IN THAILAND: PROS AND CONS

Many of the studies on tourists have concentrated on forecasting either the number of tourists visiting Thailand[9] or the revenue from tourism vis-à-vis the four main exports of country.[10] One study found that for the period 1963–80, tourists' income and political instability emerge as the most important factors affecting tourist arrivals, and that the prices of goods and services in the host country did not have any significant influence.[11]

A different set of the studies has concentrated on the impact of tourism on the Thai economy. Focusing on the multiplier effect of tourists' expenditures and the balance of payment during 1962–75, a study has concluded that tourism was quite beneficial to the Thai economy.[12] Another study has indicated that a decrease in the flow of foreign tourists can cause a considerable loss of revenue and employment. It has shown that a decrease of 1 foreign tourist will result in income loss of 9,400.04 baht and employment decline of 0.11 persons. It was found that the service sector was most vulnerable to this danger followed by manufacturing and transport/communication sectors respectively.[13] Another study has cautioned that focusing on revenue earned from tourism may be misleading as it may lead to more imports while tourism itself cannot provide a strong basis for national development.[14]

It cannot be denied that it is because of tourism that arts, crafts and classical dance are preserved and revived,[15] but at the same time there is the danger of local values of adherence to familial ties and social discipline giving way to money culture.[16] It is argued that tourism served merely as a catalyst in the proliferation of crimes and prostitution but is not its cause. The development of tourism in Chiengmai has resulted in the decline of the local people's participation in religious activities and festivals. There is also evidence of the northern languages being affected. However, changes in diet patterns, dress styles and traditional values seem to result more from media exposure and proximity to the urban areas than directly from tourism.[17] One study points out that, more often than not, the Thai authorities tend to overemphasize the economic impact of tourism at the risk of overlooking the adverse impact on spiritual values and traditional virtues.[18] Another study has shown that tourism tends to impact negatively on nature (e.g., deforestation and pollution), architecture (e.g., ignorant destruction of traditional architecture), local cultures (e.g., standardization of art forms and commercialization of traditions) and on the very lives of those residing in tourist locations (e.g., migration and prostitution).[19]

Since contrived adventure, fake liberty and unauthentic romanticism constitute the ideal of modern tourism, there tends to be a confrontation between tourism culture and local culture. An inevitable result is that local culture has to adapt itself to suit the rhythm of tourism culture

THE LIFE OF THIS WORLD

backed by wealth and bureaucratic power. Such adaptation for the sake of commercial value tends to bring about the destruction of traditional values which are integral to the Thai way of life.[20]

In most of the literature under review, only scant attention has been paid to religion. One study made reference to "unIslamic" activities such as the selling of prohibited food and beverages, Ram-Wong (Thai popular folk dance) with dancing girls provocatively dressed and some forms of gambling in the annual fairs organized in the province of Pattani in conjunction with the Eid-ul-Fitr celebrations. This fair, which has become a tourist object, can be considered an affront to the Muslim's cultural identity. This has widened the rift between the Muslims and the non-Muslim bureaucrats who lack cultural sensitivity and knowledge.[21]

As a Thai Roman Catholic Cardinal in Thailand has pointed out, modern tourism is basically for pleasure and vacation unlike traveling in the Bible such as Abraham's voyage, Moses's exodus, or Jesus's journey. Tourists do not travel in order to share what they have or to learn from others. The result is exploitation and cultural destruction. He concludes: "Forms of travel aiming at victory, exploitation or cheap women do not have a right to exist. Any country which chooses to promote such activities is betraying its own people."[22]

It is clear from the above discussion that Islam has not come up as a point of focus in studies related to tourism. The voice of the Muslims with respect to tourism from a religious perspective has not entered public discourse.[23] It is therefore interesting to discuss how the Muslims stand in relation to the fast moving world of tourism industry especially in Bangkok where approximately 70 per cent of all visitors to Thailand pass through.[24] However, it is instructive to first briefly sketch the role of Muslims in the Thai economy.

MUSLIMS IN THAILAND: FIGURES, FACTS AND ECONOMY

Based on information about Thailand published by the Ministry of Foreign Affairs, Muslims account for 4.05 per cent of the population of the country. However, according to the National Statistical Office, the number of Muslims in Thailand had declined from 2.24 million in 1984 to 2.01 million in 1985. Common wisdom suggests that this decline is plainly impossible. According to an independent estimate. There were approximately 2.6 million Muslims in Thailand in 1986.[25] A Muslim academician notes that there are approximately 2.2 million Muslims in a country of 52 million.[26]

There are 2,573 mosques in Thailand, and it has been estimated that there are 183 Muslim households per mosque and eight members per household.[27] The Muslim population, according to this calculation, numbers 3.77 million. A member of the Islamic Council of Bangkok recently indicated that Muslims in Thailand number 5.2 million. This figure is based upon the number of mosques, which was just at 2,600 and a rough estimate of 2,000 Muslims per mosque.[28]

All these estimates suffer from some weaknesses. The official figure of slightly more than 2 million Muslims in Thailand does not seem to take into account the fact that family planning is least effective among the Muslims. For the purpose of this study, an estimate of eight members per household may be questionable in the case of Bangkok Muslims, while a flat estimation of 2,000 Muslims per mosque seems rather unrealistic. All this is mentioned to suggest the following: first, it is still difficult to prove or disprove most of these figures. Second, if it is already difficult to provide an exact figure of the number of Muslims in Thailand, obviously other data concerning this particular group of people will not be easily forthcoming. Be that as it may, it is something argued that the number of Muslim population in Thailand is not a matter of statistics alone. It depends of whose figures one is using. It is safe to suggest that official figures or figures from institutions close to Thai officialdom will always be lower than figures given by Muslim writers, especially those who do not consider themselves a part of the Thai official domain for the obvious political reason. In this sense, the number of Muslim population in Thailand is basically political.

The economic role of Muslims in Thailand began during the Ayudhaya period when Persian, Malay, Indian, Arab, and Cambodian Muslims interacted with the Siamese for commercial purposes. Because of their wealth, they began to gain political power, which in turn was used to secure more wealth for themselves and other Muslims, as evident during the reign of King Narai.[29]

During the first three decades of the Chakkri dynasty, Muslims around Bangkok were not very active in their business because many paid more attention to agriculture. But after the Bowring Treaty in 1855, they concentrated more on business. Those who were well established excelled as exporters and importers. Those who were not, traveled to four corners of the land as retailers taking with them all kinds of clothes, salt, sugar, and onions. On their way back, their boats were loaded with rice, black pepper, fruits, teak, and sometimes cattle. As middlemen, their business became quite profitable. It is believed that many Muslims in Bangkok had always been fairly well-to-do. Those who lived in the center of Bangkok excelled in the field of commerce, while those who dwelled in the suburbs possessed large pieces of land for farming. Later, they also enjoyed the fruits of rising land prices.[30]

Although Muslims in Thailand have been the focus of attention among academics and journalists alike for quite some time, most of the literature on them seems to focus on politics, especially problems in the South.[31] In a recent article on Islam and Development in ASEAN, economic development was mentioned only in the context of ethnicity and state relationship.[32] It deems safe to conclude that very little has been done with respect to the economy of Muslims in Thailand in general and those in Bangkok in particular.

Surin Pitsuwan has pointed out that, through commercial pursuits, Muslim merchants of Indian of South Asian extraction in Bangkok are among the wealthiest Thai nationals.[33] However, Preeda Prapertchob has observed that Bangkok Muslims are not that well to do, adding that a large number of Muslims still live in slum areas.[34] Muslim residents of Ban Krua, descendants of the early Cambodian Muslims had sold their land and spent their money without moderation, ending up as have-nots. To be sure, exceptions do exist.

As a people, Bangkok Muslims are not dissimilar to other residents of the capital city. There are those poorer ones who constitute the majority of Bangkok Muslims. There are rich Muslims engaging in commercial pursuits of all sorts. In their own ways, they live and work as part of the fast moving city.

There are approximately 276,520 Muslims in Bangkok, a city of 6 million people, accounting for 4.6 per cent of the total.[35] It is interesting to ask how many are involved in the lucrative tourist business in Thailand at present. But more significant than mere numbers are the ways in which the Muslims of the tourist trade conduct their lives. The portrait that emerges from a description of the process of claiming to be Muslims on the one hand and working in the tourist trade in a modern non-Muslims city may perhaps shed a meaningful light on the destiny of Muslims in a rapidly changing economy.

MYRIADS OF MUSLIMS IN THE TOURIST TRADE

According to the International Union of Official Travel, tourists are "temporary visitors staying at least twenty-four hours in the country visited and the purpose of whose journey can be classified under one of the following headings: (a) leisure (recreation, holiday, health, study, religion and sport); (b) business (family mission, meeting)."[36] Be that as it may, an ordinary tourist has to have a place to stay, food to eat, transportation facilities to move from place to place, some form of entertainment to relax themselves and some souvenirs to take home. In order to construe the economic locus of a people in relation to the tourist trade, it may be wise to approach it from the actual expenditure of the tourists while in the host country.

Except for shopping and local tour/transportation, tourists' expenditures in Thailand seem to follow an identifiable pattern. They spend most on accommodation, which accounts for a little more than a quarter of total expenditure. In 1986, there were 97 hotels with 22,576 rooms in Bangkok alone. Accommodation in these hotels can cost anywhere from some 500 baht a room per day to more than 3,000 baht for a night in a standard room of a five-star hotel. Food and drink amount to one-fifth, while entertainment takes up approximately one-tenth of the total expenditures (Table 5-6). The share of shopping had fallen in 1986–87.[37]

If modern tourism can be considered as "commercialized hospitality,"[38] the pattern of tourists' expenditures can be used as points of contact between the tourists and the local people where the latter's self understanding, whether a Muslim or not, will be manifested. However, not all these points of contact are relevant to this study of Muslims in Bangkok and the tourist trade. For example, of all the existing 97 hotels in Bangkok, none is owned by a Muslim. Although there are approximately 190 small-sized guesthouses, (some of them using Arabic names advertising *halal* Indian/Pakistani food and decent accommodation), the owners of some of these establishments turn out to be Christian Indians of Sikhs. As such, it may be more fruitful to focus on points of contact other than in the field of accommodation.

TABLE 5-6 Distribution (in percentage) of tourist consumption expenditure, 1984–86

Type of Expenditures	1984	1985	1986
Accommodation	28.12	25.62	26.63
Food and Drink	20.53	19.14	16.93
Entertainment	10.43	11.64	10.02
Shopping	30.16	33.66	27.39
Local Transport/Tour	8.48	7.82	15.59
Miscellaneous	2.28	2.12	3.44
Total	100.00	100.00	100.00

SOURCE *Annual Statistical Report on Tourism in Thailand* 1986, p. 58.

Before discussing the lives of Muslims in Bangkok and the tourist trade, a note on some problems encountered in the process of conducting research is called for so that the data presented here can be better construed. In the course of this research, government institutions, the official Muslim institution (i.e., the Shaikhul Islam Office) and a local business paper were approached for relevant data without success. It seems that either they are not interested in systematic collection of data because of a lack of understanding of its significance or they are too unorganized to handle this task. In addition, there is no way to identify a Muslim tour company, restaurant, or souvenir establishment if Arabic names are not used. Even when such names are used, the owners may not be Bangkok Muslim. As a result, unless one knows from other sources of information, names like Put-taan Tour or Plublueng Restaurant do not reveal their Muslim identities. Such difficulty in identifying Muslim in the tourist trade together with a rather small number of Muslim in Bangkok curtailed the scope of this survey. More importantly, intensive interviews and candid dialogues with some of those involved in the tourist trade can better cope with the basic question crucial to this research, i.e., the Islamic ethical constraint that Muslim face or overcome in their tourist trade. It was through these dialogues that we were able to gain an insight into the ethical dilemma and tensions that confront the "actors" in the arena.

The form of presentation which will follow will be narrative. Data reported will come from both observation and dialogues.

Wherever possible, the stories will be told from the subjects' perspectives in order that "their" process of overcoming the tension of being a Muslim on the one hand, and involvement in the tourist trade on the other can be highlighted.

MUSLIM RESTAURANTS: DIFFERING SHADES

There are several Muslim restaurants in Bangkok. The *Muslim Telephone Directory* published in 1987 listed 32 of them. The list is not complete, however. An average Muslim restaurant is no more than a small shop with five to six tables. Many are close to mosques surrounded by Muslim communities in the neighborhood. Most of them are not directly linked to the tourist trade. Therefore only restaurants that are either famous or close to a hotel have been targeted for interviews. Fame is important in this case, because tour groups will sometimes drop by to experience particular dishes even if the restaurant is far from a hotel.

"Remote" Restaurants

There is only one Muslim restaurant in Bangkok whose name is a combination of a Japanese dish and a fabled Indian Muslim Queen. The restaurant is in Nonthaburi, North of Bangkok. Because of its location, the chance is slim for a tourist to just walk in. It is beautifully built, clean and well kept. There are 16 tables which can accommodate up to 82 customers at a time. The owner, a Muslim butcher from Ayudhaya, invested about 5 million baht in this two-year-old restaurant. It is making around 3,000 baht a day.

There have been few foreign guests. Those who did come were brought here on purpose. Most of them were business people. Many of them were Saudis, Malaysians, and Bangladeshis. There have been no tour group coming to this restaurant. "Some tour agents approached us but we did not take it because they wanted us to charge the tourists more. We could not do that. We do our business with *ikhlas* (sincerity)," so said the proprietor.

When asked about his staff, the proprietor said, "We do not use a Muslim cook. We serve Thai and Chinese/Japanese-styled food. Muslim cooks only know how to cook *biryani* and there is no need for that here. In addition, we cannot afford to have all Muslim waitresses because the Muslims have too many relatives. They always find reasons to leave their

115

work for a day or two. That is not good for business. I spent two years working in a famous Chinese noodle restaurant in downtown Bangkok and those experiences were extremely useful. I can only summarize it this way: For the Thais, when they are rich from business, they quit. For the Muslims, they do business just to survive. For the Chinese, they will always try to improve their businesses. Yet, we are proud to prove that Muslims can do business too."

There are two clear signs in the wall: "No beer or liquor allowed in this restaurant" and "If you wish to pray, please go upstairs." One can find a bathroom for ablution and a nice room for prayer there. "This restaurant is an 'on-the-way mosque.' There are people who will just come here for prayers and they leave without eating." It was easy to sense a trace of quiet religious content in his last remark.

Although far from the tourist district, "J Fried Chicken" occasionally entertained tour groups. Most of the tourists who visited the restaurant were from Malaysia. They came in groups of 30 at a time. "They added us on their list of restaurants simply to allow the tourists to taste Muslim food at least once. I don't think that they are doing it for religious reasons," the female proprietor remarked.

The restaurant is not new. It first opened for business in the Phra Kanong area 30 years ago, and has been in Klong Tan since 1983. There are 18 four-seat tables with one two-seat table. At its peak, the restaurant can make around 10,000 baht per day, while the lowest take per day is 3,000 baht. All the workers including the cook in this restaurant are Muslims. "Because they are clean," reasoned the owner.

Three highly visible signs reveal the character of this restaurant. The first is "Liquor and beer are not available here. Please do not bring them in. Thank You." The second is a huge picture of the Baitullah (the Grand Mosque in Mecca). The third is presumably the restaurant's motto taken from the Hadith, "Earn your living as if you are immortal. Do your Ibadat as if you will die tomorrow." This restaurant made its choice known clearly. Unfortunately, it ran out of business recently.

In contrast, two other famous restaurants seem to manifest their Muslim color less visibly. "E" is a famous restaurant in the Thonburi area, approximately 5 to 10 minutes from Sanam Luang and the Grand Palace. It specializes in Northeastern dishes popular among those who love to drink. There are 27 four-seat tables and can accommodate up to 112 customers. One of the managers mentioned that in the previous month there were three small tour groups, ten at a time, which came to this restaurant. Most of the tourists were from Malaysia. With six waitresses and non-Muslim cooks, the restaurant earns from 10,000 to 30,000 baht a month. Liquor and beer are served.

There is noting to indicate that this is a Muslim restaurant except for a frame of Qur'anic verses hanging decoratively on the wall and the conspicuous absence of pork dishes on the menu. Two of the four shareholders of this restaurant are Muslims. One of them is a very popular television personality and budding business tycoon.[39] "We do not advertise this place as a Muslim restaurant. But in the beginning, we started it because it was so difficult for the Muslims to find a good place to eat. So we do have the Muslim in mind," the night manager concluded. To my knowledge, except for a number of Muslim food vendors with similar dishes, this is the only restaurant where Muslims can come in and taste the *halal* Northeastern dishes.

"L" is a fancy restaurant far away from the main Ramkamhaeng Road. It was established in 1984 with some 5 to 6 million baht investment. With 30 waiters and waitresses, wearing their uniforms of Thai semi-formal dresses, serving up to 250 customers a day it is making 25,000 baht daily on the average.

Liquor and beer are served liberally. Against beautiful popular Thai and international songs performed by professional singers including one Filipino, there is no sign of any "Muslimness" in that restaurant except for the absence of pork dishes on the menu.

"We did not intend to start a restaurant," said the night manager (who occasionally serves as the Imam in a local mosque in numerous religious functions). "We had to entertain soccer teams coming to play in Thailand because the owner's father is involved in professional soccer sport. Now there are few tourists coming this way."

This restaurant does not describe or advertise itself as a Muslim restaurant, although during the month of Ramadan it uses the Muslim radio programs which go on air every night as a channel for advertising. While all the food are definitely *halal* because the one who purchases the ingredients at the market is a family member, the cooks are non-Muslims. They are Chinese and non-Muslim Thais. Most of the waiters and waitresses are not Muslims either. "The Muslim workers lack perseverance," said the night manager. It seem that the business has been doing so well that this restaurant has to open even on the Eid days.

Muslim Restaurants in the Tourist Area

There are a number of Muslim Restaurants in the Silom/Suriwong areas. Three restaurants are of particular interest to the present study. They are restaurants specializing in Thai dishes, Chinese cuisines and roti-styled dishes, respectively. These restaurants share two things in common. First, they describe themselves as Muslim restaurants. Second, a sizeable number of their customers are tourists.

"D" is not a very big restaurant. With 11 tables, it can serve up to 40 guests at a time. There are four waitresses, three of them wearing Pakistani dress. While none of the waitresses cover their heads, the woman manager does. In addition to food, the restaurant also sells Muslim newspapers, cigarettes, handmade artificial flowers, prayer mats and ladies' *talakong* (prayer outfit). Qur'anic verses are hung on the wall for decorative purposes. Everything looks Islamic. However, popular songs are played in the restaurant.

The manager said, "A group of friends joined hands to start a restaurant. We wanted a place to meet after graduation from the university so we started an ice-cream parlor. Five years ago, we moved from Siam Center to Silom and started a restaurant. We decided from the very beginning that this was to be a Muslim restaurant and hence, the name of this restaurant which means 'religion' or 'way of life'. More than 70 per cent of our customers are Muslims. Many of them are tourists, mostly from Malaysia and a few from Brunei."

Tourist customers, mostly from ASEAN countries, can be classified into three groups: businessmen who frequent the place during their stay, tour groups which drop in for only a meal while in Thailand for a couple of days, and sportsmen who are participating in international tournaments in Bangkok. Occasionally. Muslim diplomats would order food from this restaurant for their national day celebrations.

50 per cent of the customers are tourists. Most of them are from the Victory and Narai hotel. "As long as the food is good and customers are treated well, we will have good business," the manager indicated. For a given month they are making 25 to 30 per cent profit, but monthly expenditure ranges from 90,000 to 100,000 baht. Although the head cook is a Muslim, assistant cooks are not. While the restaurant wants to hire Muslims to work, it was difficult because "the Muslims are not interested in this kind of job."

When asked about business constraints, the manager and her husband who joined in the conversation later gave the following details.

"It is not easy to operate a Muslim restaurant. We have to understand that we cannot get rich by being a restaurant operator because we cannot think only of profit. We are serving the Muslims who need us. It is even difficult if we want to close the restaurant for a day because our customers may not be able to find other dining places. It is indeed a sin to do so. Problems facing us are numerous. For example, Muslims from South Asia would not eat squids and some other "scaleless" fish. When some ordered American fried rice and two slices of sausages were served with that dish, they would not eat it. It was useless to explain to them that the sausages served here are made from *halal* beef. Once a person came in and 'informed' me that oyster sauce cannot be consumed because it is mixed with lard. Then someone would prohibit the serving of Lipton tea accusing it of being mixed with gelatin. And gelatin, as you are aware of, is made from animals' bones. In the past, we used to serve jelly ice-cream. When jelly wad prohibited because of its gelatin content, we dropped it from our menu. We had to inform our customers that we had stopped making it because it had become less and less popular. It was difficult to explain the truth of the story to non-Muslim customers. But if we are serious with everything, we will lose our sanity. We have to make up our minds in the end."

Coming from a Muslim family with backgrounds in agriculture and fishery, the owner of "D" tried hard to observe religious values. However, in terms of the relationship between the restaurant and the present capitalist economic system, the owners' solution is more compromising than their practice of serving *halal* food. The manager concluded: "In the capitalist system, the Muslims have to walk a difficult path. It is not possible to avoid all the sins in a society where the Muslims constitute but a portion. But even in a Muslim society, it is not that pure either."

"CJ" is a Chinese Muslim restaurant a few blocks from Narai hotel. Managed by a husband and wife team, the restaurant has ten tables and can serve up to 40 customers. The husband, who is also a cook, came from Yunan in mainland China while the wife is a Chinese Thai. They started this restaurant some thirty years ago. Most of the customers are local Muslims hungry for the taste of authentic Chinese food. Foreign customers constitute only 5 per cent of the total because "people in this restaurant do not speak English … But there are some Chinese Muslim tourists coming from Hong Kong. There are not many of them, however."

With drawings from Islamic history depicting Muslim seafarers in the past and Qur'anic verses hanging on the wall, this restaurant is currently the only one of its kind serving *halal* and authentic Chinese food in Bangkok. Most of the waitresses and the present cook are not Muslims. Similar to other restaurants, the owner's reason was: "The Muslims are lazy. They cannot match the Thai or Chinese Waitresses."

"CJ" faces a number of problems. The sale of Chinese Muslim food has been dropping. Each month "CJ" has to spend some 25,000 baht while profit is nominal. One of the reasons for this is, according to the owner, the decline of faith among the Muslims themselves. The customers are no longer as strict as those in the past. They do not feel that it is necessary to eat in a Muslim restaurant. In addition, when the husband stopped serving liquor and beer to customers, his business suffered a significant decline.

His wife tried to reintroduce beer by arguing that it was strictly business. In addition, even most Muslims ordered and drank beer. She was also "informed" that beer is different from other kinds of liquor because it is milder and therefore it is easier for a Muslim restaurant to "tolerate" this kind of drink.

"B" is a unique restaurant in Bangkok. It is a really small restaurant with only five tables and cannot accommodate more than 20 customers at a time. It specializes in *roti* with sugar or curry. Many of its customers are either Westerners or Bangladeshis because it is quite close to various guesthouses in the Banglampoo area. More than three-quarters of the total customers are Muslims. Due to the nature of food this restaurant serves, the best time for its business is early morning serving breakfast.

"B" is clearly a Muslim restaurant. It does not serve beer or liquor. It started more than 45 years ago as a food stall near Thammasat University. The owner still retains his old stall which is doing better than "B" because of its location. The lack of manpower also contributes to the restaurant's problems. The owner tried to hire Muslim workers whenever possible.

Muslim Restaurants: Non-Thai Owners

There are Muslim restaurants whose owners are not Bangkok Muslims because they are not Thais. One of these is Bagh, a restaurant serving Arabic and Indian/Pakistani food. It opens from breakfast time until 3 am Its peculiar dining hours can be explained by its location which is close to Grace Hotel where many Arab tourists choose as their lodging place for "entertainment" reasons. The restaurant, however, can be considered a strict Muslim restaurant. Liquor and beer are not served. All four waitresses dress politely. All the meat used in this restaurant is *halal*. It has been here for more than four years. For the capacity to accommodate about 50 customers, the owner, an Iraqi, has to pay a very high rent of above 50,000 baht a month.

"S" is perhaps the most Islamic of all restaurants in Bangkok. Signs of Islam are everywhere. It can serve up to 30 customers at a time. Most of its customers are Indians or Pakistanis. Despite the fact that the cook is a Northeastern Thai, it specializes in Pakistani and North Indian cuisine. Laundry service is also available in this "restaurant." The owner is a Pakistani from Karachi.

Taken together, the preceding sections present a diverse pattern of Muslim restaurant businesses operating in a modern capitalist system. Some are able to practice their faith better than others especially in terms of services made available to their customers. Aspects of services such as serving liquor, dresses of the waitresses, omission of some kinds of food, or conspicuous display of their "Muslimness" are matters of choice for the Muslim proprietors. However, with regard to those aspects of business which deal with a larger economic system, especially banking, they seem to have no control. Suffice it to say here on this issue, that the smaller the business, the easier the adoption of Islamic values.

ENTERTAINMENT: EXTREME ENVIRONMENT

If there is be an economic locus where participating Muslims are facing an environment that is basically contrary to the tenets of Islam, it is the field of entertainment. It goes without saying that the kind of entertainment which Bangkok is famous (of rather infamous) for is the exploitation of women. However, in describing the lives of Muslims participating in tourist-related entertainment, activities other than sexual entertainment will also be included, namely Thai classical dance performances for tourists. It is important to note here that unlike the discussion concerning Muslim restaurants (since I cannot find a single Muslim owner of this kind of business) the focus will be on the lives of those Muslims who earn their living from tourist-related entertainment.

The Case of a Thai Classical Dancer

"J" is an attractive 37-years-old ex-Buddhist woman now happily married into a devout Muslim family. She is no longer a Thai classical dancer, but at present she teaches classical dancing at a local college. When asked whether performing arts is acceptable for a Muslim woman, she answered that her husband was not pleased with it. She decided to quit when she had a baby. To her, dancing was for fun and it had nothing to do with religion.

Thai classical dancing has to follow rituals based upon Hindu traditions. The classical dancers can only perform their dances after going through a ceremony paying homage to the Hindu deities. The ceremony requires the dancer to present a water bowl, a cone of banana leaf, money (16 baht), and some flowers to the teacher who will then place different classical dancing masks on the student's head.

"J" has been through all this although she underwent this ceremony before she became a Muslim. Though now a Muslim, everytime before she begins to dance she will still pay her respect to her teachers and the shining head gear she is about to wear by pressing both palms of her hands together in a respectful manner. She believes that all this has nothing to do with religion, given her intention to pay her respect to her teachers.

Muslim Girls in the Pleasure Business

An authoritative study on prostitutes maintained that there were 500,000 to one million women engaging in the sex industry all over Thailand. In Bangkok alone, their number is estimated at about 200,000 to 300,000.[40] Child prostitutes number around 20,000.[41] Prostitution is closely related to the tourism industry because foreigners constitute about half of their clients, especially in massage parlors.[42] Given such figures, one cannot help but wonder about the role of "Muslim" prostitutes in Thailand in general and in Bangkok in particular.

It seems that Muslims are perhaps most unlikely to participate in this unholy business. A survey research on Bangkok masseuses conducted in 1979 found that from 1,000 service girls in 13 massage parlors in the city, only 0.81 per cent had claimed to be Muslims.[43] It appears that there are quite a few "Muslim" girls working in a-go-go bars and cocktail lounges, places considered havens for prostitutes.

In an a-go-go bar, girls have to dance on the counter wearing very little to attract male customers. Ms A is one of them. She said she was 16 years old and had been in this business for more than a year.

She had this to say:

> I believed in heaven and hell because I have listened to a famous tape by a Buddhist colonel who was dead and came back to life and revealed all about afterlife. Yes, I consider myself a Muslim although I do not know how to pray. But I do not eat pork. I am sure I will go to hell when I die.

Ms S and Ms N have been friends for a long time. They went to Assala-fiya school together when they were younger. S is from Thonburi while N's family lives in the *kampong* of Maebaeng Mosque. While the father of S is a convert, both N's parents are Muslims. Both S and N have "studied" the Qur'an but found it difficult and incomprehensible. Both of them had fasted occasionally during the month of Ramadan in the past but now they have stopped this practice. N said she was making up to 30,000 baht a month, and spent it all on gambling.

S was unsure about her identity. She went with friends to Buddhist temples and sometimes paid respect to the monks. She knew what she was doing is sinful but,

> I am not sure what will happen after death. Perhaps, we will all forget what has happened in the past. When we are brought back to life, we will no longer remember our past lives. Therefore, it may not be too painful.

While Sainub works in an a-go-go bar, Naya works in one of those where profane shows are performed nightly. Describing her first pork eating experience, she said

> I felt as though my tongue was swollen. But I thought pork was tasty so the next day I tried again. You see, when you are with friends, you have to eat whatever is available. You do not have much choice. After eating pork for some time, I felt bad about it. So I decided to refrain from eating another kind of meat as a compensation. I stopped eating beef as a substitute for pork. However, it did not last long.
>
> I try not to think about Islam. At the bar there are a Buddha image and "Grandpa and Grandma" (animistic objects depicting sexual acts)

dolls which every nude performer has to pay homage to before beginning her act. I also do it. Once in a while I visit my folks and that's where I think about religion. My mother taught me to make merit by killing a lizard everyday. And I try to do so to lessen my sin. When I die, I want to be buried in an Islamic way because I consider myself a Muslim. I also think that the Muslim funeral is the best because it saves a lot of money and trouble.[44]

What I found in this brief encounter with these "Muslim" girls contradicts what an American anthropologist has suggested more than three decades ago that tourism-oriented prostitution in Thailand is incompletely commercialized.[45] The relationship between the girls and their clients is based on a clear understanding on both sides and sexual services are exchanged for money.[46] From the data obtained, it seems that the girls' identities as "Muslims" are subsumed under the new rules of the social environment. In fact, their "Muslimness" has already been undermined from the dynamics of diverse factors including family background, first sexual experience, friends and economic conditions. It is indeed amazing to see how they continue to call themselves "Muslims" and acknowledge their sin in such an unholy environment.

THE TRAVEL BUSINESS: AGENCY AND PERSONNEL

There seems to be a number of Muslims working in the travel business. Upon closer examination, most of the Thai Muslims are salary earners employed by airline and travel agencies. But rarely do they own the business themselves. In Bangkok, there are only two significant travel agencies owned by Thai citizens who are Muslim. One of them, "A1-K" is owned by a naturalized Thai citizen originally from Northern India. Most of the others are small agencies owned by Muslims who are Indian citizens. They start their businesses by sharing them with Thai citizens. For them, the travel business simply serves as a parallel with another more lucrative, business, namely foreign money exchanges. Even a relatively large travel agency such as "A1-K" did not occupy the main thrust of its owner's large business empire. Mr. K himself told me that, "I started the A1-K travel agency for my own convenience because our people have to travel so much." When asked about the kind of profit his travel agency is yielding, he said, "It is negligible." From other sources of information, I understand that the travel wing of the A1-K business is not that significant.

"BL," another travel agency, began its business without any proper office space in 1974. At that time, Mr. A was working with the East Asiatic Company. One day at a social gathering, the Pakistani Ambassador to Thailand asked whether there was any Muslim travel agency in Bangkok? The reply was negative. He then suggested that Mr. A should start one, promising to give whatever assistance he could muster. With 50,000 baht, Mr. A started the business with his wife, who was then working with Pakistan International Airlines. The business began to take off when the Americans left Indochina in 1975. Together with PIA, "BL" succeeded in securing contracts to transport refugees to Paris. Later on, with the emergence of the job market in the Middle East, "BL" continued to expand. Now located in Suriwong in a moderately spacious apartment, it has 11 full-time staff, one-half of whom are Muslims. Except for the workers going to the Middle East, 90 per cent of its customers, mostly Pakistanis and Bangladeshis, are Muslims. Another significant sector of his business is to serve people going for Hajj and Umrah. Each year these pilgrims account for some 10 million baht of business which amounts to some 40 per cent of the total business volume. It shows that "BL" is a travel agency dealing with some 25 million baht a year.

When asked about the secret of his success, Mr. A answered in one word: *Iman* (faith). He said,

> Our name is very clean in terms of honesty. The prices of the tickets are reasonable and we try to help our customers in every way we can. Do you believe that I, as a managing director of this business, would go to an embassy and wait two hours for a Muslim consul and persuade him to grant visas to my clients? Even if you give me 10,000 baht, I will not waste my time like that. But I am doing it for Allah.

> I am not at a disadvantage being a Muslim businessman. Of course, there are the usual constraints in terms of social functions. For example, we cannot drink liquor with friends in the business, nor eat or enjoy ourselves as they do. I understand that if you are a minority in some countries, there will be a lot of obstacles for your business. But here in Thailand, things are fine for us and we can certainly compete with any travel agency of the same size and capital in Bangkok.

> In Thailand the only problem seems to be the authorities' lack of knowledge about Islam. While Muslims who go to Hajj are exempted from paying travel tax in the amount of 1,000 baht because it is

considered a religious function, those who go for Umrah have to pay. Yet, Buddhists going to the Birthplace of the Buddha (which is not a religious requirement) are exempted from paying travel tax.

As a Muslim businessman, there are times when these two identities (being a Muslim and a businessman) clash. Each year, there are several cases of Muslim customers running out of money. As a businessman, such is not my problem. But as a Muslim, I sometimes lend a helping hand.

Another problem relates to the economic system we are in. There is no way that a travel business or any modern business in a non-Muslim society can avoid *riba* or band interest. Even the *ulama* themselves are far from conclusive in their judgments. The guideline I am using is whether in so doing I am causing problem to others. If we take usury from people we are exploiting them and this is not acceptable. But taking bank interest does not seem to cause problems to anyone. If we really want to avoid using credit, then we have to have plenty of cash to engage in travel business which is not possible. My only solution is to seek repentance from God in whatever we do."

As in other cases, I asked about his Muslim staff. He expresses an intention to find good Muslims to work for his agency. But "the Muslims are slower and lazier. The Chinese are the best workers, They work as though this business is theirs." With his remark, one cannot help but wonder where the good quality Muslim workers are. One answer is that there are many but they work for international airlines.

Ms V is the chief of the ticketing division of a Northern European Airline. She does not have any problem concerning her Muslim identity. When people in the business know that she is a Muslim, they treat her accordingly. Soft drinks will be available instead of wine whereas dish other than pork-related food will be provided. It is up to her to choose *halal* food as opportunity avails itself. *Riba* does not present a problem to her, because "we simply pass the money from our clients to the cashier. We don't have to deal with the banks directly."

She also pointed out that there were four Muslim staff in the same company. In her division alone, there were two. Whenever there was an Eid holiday, there would be a problem because both of them had to be absent on the same day. This has sparked some dissension among her non-Muslim colleagues who sometimes pointed to Islam as the cause of disruption of normal life in the office.

When asked whether it was right. From an Islamic point of view, for a Muslim mother of three to work with men in such a secular environment, she answered: "We have got to survive. I have three children and they have to be brought up as best as possible. Working like this, however, religiously improper it may be, is indeed an unavoidable economic necessity."

"S" is an air hostess who has been working on international flights with Thai International for nine years. She became a Muslim after getting married to a Muslim pilot. Now, she is a working mother with two lovely children living with her husband's family.

She described her life as a Muslim hostess on the plane,

> In terms of my own eating, there is no problem. People know that I am very strict and I can simply get by with just bread and butter. But sometimes you have to serve pork dishes and wine to passengers on board. I consider it my duty to do so although I would prefer not to violate any Islamic precept. Some passengers may try to take advantage of the hostess. The Arabs are the worst when they are drunk . The hostess' uniform is plain and modest enough but you will have to be careful. What choice do I have? It is my career.

Her husband, a pilot with the same airline, did not think there was any serious problem as a Muslim that could not be overcome. Apart from the usual food and drink constraints which affect one's social function in a non-Muslim society, there are problems of performing obligatory duties. For example, a pilot's prayers, or for that matter an air hostess', may not be performed on the plane. He or she has to do the compensating prayers later. However, a pilot cannot fly with an empty stomach according to international airline regulations. This rule certainly affects fasting during Ramadan. Again, the pilot said he did not have a choice.

"D" is a 40 year old area manager of a Thai International office based in the Indian subcontinent. In his case, being a Muslim was an advantage.

> Whenever there is a position vacancy in Muslim countries, either in the Middle East or South Asia, Muslim staff will be thought of by the management first. They believe that we are able to do a better job than non-Muslims. So in this company of more than 10,000 staff, there are three Muslim country or area managers. However, it will be difficult for Muslims to reach the very top such as the position of a vice president. One of the reasons for this is the VP of this airline

has to perform a lot of rituals, most of which are not acceptable to Islam. We know it and they know it too.

In the airline service, there is a sizeable number of Muslim workers. For many women working in this tourist-related business, the question of whether they should even work in the first place is never raised. To raise a "good" family in a city such as Bangkok, one needs a stable job, and working with airlines is certainly an attractive proposition.

SOUVENIRS: BRONZE AND BRASS

One of the most famous souvenirs from Thailand is a set of bronze spoons, forks, and knives. In the country, there are only five factories making bronze tableware and one of them is owned by a Muslim family.

"SB" started its business some 30 years ago when a Muslim who was then working with an international airline saw the opportunity of selling Thai souvenirs to the Japanese tourists. He began by selling everything that was Thai, such as silk and gems, focusing solely on tourists. He then decided to venture into production, emphasizing the Thai character of the products and the uniqueness of handmade goods.

At present, Thailand is the only country in the world selling bronze tableware. Every piece in "SB" is handmade. There are some 40 workers mostly farmers from the Central plain and Northeast whose skills in producing bronze items come from their family tradition. Most of the products are for export and produced on orders. Sale volume for a month is between 1 to 1.2 million baht. Walk-in customers contribute to some 20 per cent of total sales. Most of the products are sold to prestigious hotels in Bangkok or exported to Europe and North America.

These beautiful spoons and forks have three Thai patterns, two of them are Indra's three-headed elephant and a Hindu/Thai god. In "SB," there are other bronze and brass animal statues of women also available.

I asked the daughter of SB owners whether producing souvenirs using images of Hindu deities or naked figures was appropriate for a Muslim business. She said it had nothing to do with religion. What she was doing, according to her, was strictly business, i.e., producing and selling bronze and brass sets based upon Thai culture. Bronze sets were seen as uniquely Thai, whose patterns were determined by market tastes.

PATTERNS OF OVERCOMING TENSION

In the study of tourism in general, there seems to be a tendency to overgeneralize, depicting a stereotyped model of participants in the tourist trade. A tourism researcher concludes that "Too much was imputed to the participants in the touristic process, tourists, entrepreneurs, and hosts alike; but their perceptions, evaluation and the bearing of these on their behavior were too little investigated."[47] It is therefore imperative to analyze the patterns of how Muslim participants in the tourist trade perceive themselves within the web of tension characterized by religious beliefs and economic realities.

It is important to note first that the notion of "Muslim" itself is not unproblematic. The nude bar girl who pays homage to objects is a case in point. It is easy to argue that in so doing she ceases to be a Muslim. However, her self-understanding is such that she regards herself as a Muslim. Therefore, rather than passing judgment on the "Muslimness" of the subjects based upon their behavior, their self-understanding is considered more relevant to this study.

Based upon the data collected, the following patterns of coming to terms with being Bangkok Muslims, on the one hand, and being practitioners in the tourist trade, on the other, emerges.

If tensions exist in the realm of private lives, then the kind of compromise which results tends to cluster around minor social behavior. Compromise in the area of eating and drinking seems to be most common among participants who do not own the business but simply work either in the tour business or entertainment parlors. The degree to which they compromise their faith will depend on other factors influencing their lives such as background knowledge about Islam and family life. Those who come from secure homes tend to be in a better position to acquire more knowledge about Islam as well as better social positions which will, in turn, give them more confidence in their identities as Muslims. But the Muslim girls in the entertainment business hail from questionable family backgrounds which cannot provide them with a secure life and basic religious knowledge. Their confidence as Muslims easily gives way to the conventional night life enjoyed by their new-found friends. When this situation occurs in a context where money is the arbiter of living. It is not unusual for their "Muslimness" to fade into oblivion.

Where tensions exist in the economic sphere, two minor patterns can be discerned. First, for some, the tourist trade is nothing more than a business. For a business in the capitalist system, the prime objective is maximization of profit. Those who aim for profit will not choose to concern themselves with religious injunctions more than necessary. Hence, some Muslim restaurants which serve liquor liberally do exist. There are also some Muslim restaurants which proudly exhibit their Muslim character. True to their choice, religious injunctions in matters of food and drinks will be strictly observed. But despite being religious, quite a few Muslim tourist-related business owners do not want to tolerate the ineffectiveness of Muslim workers. This shows the extent to which they try to subscribe to the principle of Muslim Brotherhood.

Muslim tourist business existing in Thailand's present economic system seem to have no choice but to succumb to the omnipotent capitalist system. In the domain of credit, it would be extremely difficult to avoid bank interest. The result is that the Muslim businessmen are forced by circumstances to make compromises of some sort.

There are also those who do not see any relation whatsoever between their work in the tourist business and Islam as their religion. The most common justification for ignoring religious injunctions in these cases is the assertion that whatever they do has nothing to do with religion.

FACTORS EXPLAINING PATTERNS OF SELF-EXPLANATION

In discussing some juristic aspects of Muslim living as minorities in non-Muslim states, a Muslim writer has suggested three guidelines. First, whatever is *haram* (forbidden) in Muslim states remains equally unlawful for Muslim in non-Muslim states. Second, whatever is *halal* (permissible) for Muslims where they are the majority remains equally lawful for Muslims in non-Muslims states. Third, the principles of *darurah* (necessity) would come into effect in the event of extreme compulsion.[48] These guidelines are not without problems, however.

The question of what is *halal* and *haram* is sometimes unclear. For example, there are a number of Muslim women working in the tourist business, Are their lives as career women, not to mention their dresses, *halal*? According to the very popular guide for the Muslim woman by Shaykh Muhammad Mutawalli al-Sha'rawi, the editor of *Minbar al-Islam* published in Egypt, the woman's place is in her home. He argues that when a woman stays at home she contributes through her labor far more to the economy of the family than when she works outside and has to pay for the expenses which accompany such a lifestyle. It is acceptable for a woman to work with her husband. But if she leaves home to work elsewhere, it is most problematic. He concludes that, "such a course is acceptable only if there exists a true and established need for them to do so."[49] Although al-Sharawi's position can be reasonably argued against,[50] it is important, precisely because of its rigidity, which encapsulates a current stream of conservative Muslim thought. If this position is taken as final, then all the Muslim women working outside their homes without "a true and established need" are engaging in *haram* activities, not to mention the rather clear-cut *haram* cases such as prostitution.

In fact, one of the most important principles of Shari'ah about *halal* and *haram* is the *asl* or the basis of things created by Allah and the benefits derived from them which are useful for mankind. In other words, this principle points to what a Muslim author calls, "the natural permissibility of things."[51] This principle is based upon the following verse of Al-Qur'an, among others:

> Do you not see how Allah has subjected to you all that the heavens and the earth contain and lavished on you both His visible and unseen favors?[52]

It can indeed be argued that, as in other kinds of law, the number of prohibited things is smaller than those left out which are then considered permissible. Whatever is not mentioned as *haram* is consequently permissible. Prophet Muhammad (Peace be upon him) himself has said:

> Allah has prescribed certain obligations for you, so do not neglect them; He has defined certain limits, so do not transgress them; He has prohibited certain things, so do not do them; and He has kept silent concerning other things out of mercy for you and not because of forgetfulness, so do not ask questions concerning them.[53]

Another problem facing the above guidelines is the meaning of *darurah* or necessity. Many of the Bangkok Muslims in the tourist trade portrayed above look upon themselves as sinners. Some of them are even certain that they will go to hell after death. But they continue to work in the bars or engage in business transactions with commercial banks, and argue that they do so out of necessity and that they have no choice. The question then is what constitutes "necessity" which is acceptable to the canons of Islam.

In discussing women and word, A1-Sha'raw points out that Islam's assessment of need involves the need itself and the rating of the need, among other things. To sustain life is a necessity, but it is luxury if a four-room apartment equipped with a refrigerator are "needed." He argues that, "Society lost its equilibrium when man forgot his natural worth and aspired to aspire to live beyond his level, which compelled him to steal or accept bribes or cheat."[54]

As is normally the case, the Qur'an is less specific than the *ulama*'s exegesis. A verse in Surah Al-Baqera reads:

> But whoever is constrained to eat any of these (forbidden food), not intending to sin or transgress, incurs no guilt. Allah is forgiving and merciful. [55]

For a situation to be considered "necessity," some conditions must be met. First, the person becomes so destitute due to either poverty or sickness that would endanger his life or his family's. Second, the person has absolutely no intention to break Islamic Law. Third, even under such circumstances, he does not partake of the unlawful more than necessary.[56] For example, facing starvation, one should only take a few morsels of *haram* food and not behave as a glutton.

If the Islamic guidelines suggested above are accepted, it seems that many Bangkok Muslims have transgressed the conditions of acceptable necessity judging from the kind of income some of them earned. It is important to note that what is needed here is not condemnation but explanation. It is always easier for some in a privileged profession, such as university academicians, to avoid things that are *haram* than those in other professions, especially tourist trade, in Bangkok. It is obvious that the former group are relatively cleaner not necessarily because they are "better" Muslims but presumably because their line of work seems less susceptible to the domain of *haram* things.

Three interrelated factors stand out as variables capable of significantly explaining the tensions discussed above. They are personal background, the city life, and the powerful capitalist system.

The extent to which a Muslim will maintain his or her posture as a sincere Muslim in the tourist trade depends largely on the Islamic knowledge one gains from his or her family background. One's knowledge about Islam as a way of life is largely shaped by the kind of family one has. A family where one of the parents is not a Muslim is clearly in a high risk category. A broken home will not be conducive to the process of Islamic upbringing of young children. A poor Muslim family may be hard pressed to make compromises because of economic necessity, while a rich Muslim family may easily fall prey to *haram* life-styles due to its social status. In a society where Islam is not understood as a way of life but as a religion of rituals, it is possible for a worldly educated person to separate Islam from his or her economic activities.

A modern city avails itself to the kind of life that seems to relegate religion to a marginal sphere, Approximately 13 per cent of the country's population live in the capital city. As a gateway to international tourists, temptations abound in Bangkok. Some tourists who had gone overboard were apprehended by the police. The files of the Bangkok Tourist Police shows that during the first six months in 1988, there were 126 arrests involving Muslim tourists. About 40 per cent of them were apprehended because they had caused social disturbance,[57] presumably due to drunkenness. Temptations are not confined to tourists only. The Bangkok city life is not conducive for the Muslim community. The community life of the Muslims is being eroded because of the advent of the nuclear family and the search for better living conditions. There are Muslim families that have become part of the city's slums. This transformation is accompanied by numerous social problems, drug addiction, sexual abuse and crime. Middle-class students are sent to good secular schools, usually quite a distance from their homes. By the time they return home, they are too tired to pay attention to Islamic lessons, if available. Their parents too suffer from fatigue resulting from work tensions and Bangkok traffic. It is obvious that all these do not contribute positively to the strengthening of Muslim family life. It is evident that for some Muslims, security in life is not sought in the holy setting of their homes but from friends in the streets to whom Islam may mean next to nothing.

Although it is still debatable whether Islam opposes capitalism *in toto* given its strong support for trade as well as its respect for private property, the Shari'ah is more explicit in its denunciation of exploitation, hoarding, usury, cheating, theft and unlawful dispossession.[58] In this sense, Islam is not congruent with capitalism where maximization of profit constitutes its main pillar and interest nurtured by the ubiquitous banking system serves as its artery. Tourist-related business, or for that matter any kind of business operating in the city (with the possible exception of small-scale self sufficient units) has little choice but to come to terms with the prevailing economic system. Does this mean that the Muslim cannot do business in a capitalist system without compromising their faith? One author points out that some *ulama* are of the opinion that there is no harm in giving (receiving) interest to (from) non-Muslims or non-Muslim banks. He is quick to add that the ideal thing for Muslim minorities living in non-Muslim states is to organize and support Islamic banking. But if such facilities are not available, there will be no harm "if business is transacted with interest involved in it on the basis of *darurah*."[59]

Perhaps it is safe to assert that doing business, especially tourist-related business, in a capitalist system much to be desired from an Islamic point of view. But realistically, what is expected from a Muslim minority living in a non-Muslim country? Is the notion of *hijrah* still applicable in today's world firmly divided by the idea of the modern nation-state? It is therefore understandable why many Bangkok Muslims consider themselves sinners and seek repentance only from Allah, the most Forgiving, the Most Merciful.

CONCLUSION: COMMERCIALIZATION OF HOSPITALITY AND COMPROMISE OF A FAITH?

In the celebrated book *Islam and Capitalism*, Maxime Rodinson concluded two decades ago that the power of the capitalist economy has reduced other modes of production to secondary roles. None can stand up to the competition of a capitalist economy, especially inside a capitalist socio-economic formation. Although Rodinson recognized the specificity of Islam as a religion as well as that of the Muslim world, he emphasized that it was not exceptional.[60] If this is true, it means that in a world characterized by capitalism, Muslims do not have much choice but to lose themselves to the tide of this powerful economic system.

According to the late Faruqi, from an Islamic point of view, man is definable in terms of his economic pursuits. To him, man is *homo economicus* but he rejected the idea that man is subject to economic laws which dominate his activity, Faruqi maintained that the economic pattern to which man subjects his life is deliberately chosen.[61]

The case of Bangkok Muslims has to be understood in the context of Thai society as a social reality. In the capital city, Islam is relegated to a marginal position. In fact, religion itself seems to have become somewhat irrelevant. Many things that happen in Bangkok in the name of tourism is as unacceptable in Buddhism as it is in Islam. The corruption of life in such a surrounding blurs the line drawn between religions. Although the meaninglessness of modern life for a minority group in the midst of Islamic resurgence may propel the Muslims to search for meaning in the security of a more holistic life of a Muslim community, it is relatively easier for those privileged to be distanced from the center of capitalism.

I would argue that the tourist-related business is now at the center of capitalism. It is where the power of capitalism is at its zenith, because tourism itself is "commercialized hospitality," among other things.[62] The tourism process can be conceptualized as a commercialization of the traditional guest-host relationship in which strangers were given a temporary existence based much less on human relationship than on monetary values. It is capitalism *par excellence* when even a smile and gentle courtesy can be bought. It proves conclusively the undeniable power of capital manifested in the form of money. The effect on participants of tourist-related business is the degeneration of decent human relations based on sincerity. If even sincerity is undermined in the process, how can a Muslim live fully in accordance with Islam and "choose the economic pattern" he or she may have once desired?

In conclusion, it seems that Bangkok Muslims participating in the tourist-related business are facing an extremely difficult situation. They are at a critical point where Islamic values are being undermined because of the secular city life. This is exacerbated by the fact that they constitute a religious minority in a non-Muslim state whose residences are scattered all over Bangkok because of historical circumstances. They are facing an uphill battle because tourism as a business, in the process of over-commercialization, highlights the power of capitalism, especially its dehumanizing effects on the participants.

In the century that saw the birth of the Prophet, the Syrian Monophysite Bishope Jacob of Sarong described a scene when Satan was lamenting its collapse of authority as a result of the recent disappearance of paganism. But finally the Devil exclaims, "I do not mind if the priest uses the interest he draws from his money to buy an axe with which to smash the temples of the gods! The love of gold is a greater idol than any idol of a god…"[63] In Bangkok. While some Muslims are trying to lead their lives in accordance with Islamic teachings, many who are participating in tourist-related businesses are now facing this greater idol which, in some ways, contributes to the compromising of their faith.

6

Spiritualizing Real Estate, Commoditizing Pilgrimage: Globalization and Islamic Responses in Asia-Pacific?

INTRODUCTION

Kwame Anthony Appiah and Henry Louis Gates Jr., noted Afro-American professors at Harvard University, wrote, in the introduction of a remarkable volume, *The Dictionary of Global Culture*, that, "we all participate, albeit from different cultural positions, in a global system of culture. That culture is increasingly less dominated by the West..."[1] Several questions can be raised concerning this participation in a global culture. For example, what characterizes such a global system of culture? Moreover, in the process of participating in that global culture, what kind of changes take place as a result of "our" participation from different culture positions? Is "the West" less influential as a dominant force of that culture? And, who are the "we" that is being talked about?

Using Appiah and Gates' formulation as an academic lever to address the problem of globalization and religious responses, in this paper, the "we" means the Muslims of Thailand, and perhaps of Southeast Asia by extension. "Global culture" means, primarily, the capitalist economy and the construction of images through the advertisement that accompany it. "Participation from different cultural positions" means participation from Islamic traditions existing in Asia-Pacific at the very end of the twentieth century.

This essay is an attempt to elucidate possible inherent contradictions when modern economy is spiritualized using religious injunctions and idioms, while religion is being commodified when utilized as an appendix to business transactions. The essay begins with a brief discussion of the notion of globalization with a strong emphasis on its culture components to be use here. Then a real estate advertisement, where the *Haj* (Islamic pilgrimage to Mecca) is used to attract potential Muslim buyers, will be critically analyzed. Finally, inherent contradictions between a modern globalized economy and a resurgent Islamic spirituality will be discussed and the possibility of such a phenomenon emerging among Asia-Pacific Muslims

GLOBALIZATION: THE MODERN ECONOMY AND ITS CULTURAL COMPONENTS

The present global condition can be characterized by the fact that the relations between local and distant social events become stretched to the extent that the nodes of connection between different social contexts or regions can be networked across the world as a whole. According to Anthony Giddens, globalization in this sense is "the intensifications of worldwide social relations which link distant localities in such a way and vice versa."[2] But these linkages at world level are not novel. They have existed in the past, for example, between the Muslim world and the West through international trade and economic exchange.[3]

In fact, "the modern world system" is said to have originated in Western Europe between 1450 to 1640, and is often called "the long sixteenth century." The need for labor, raw materials and markets fuelled the expansion of trade and culminated in European colonization of much of the world, justified by its own religious ideology. However, only in the twentieth century has such a "world" system become truly global.[4] This truly globalized world economy is primarily a result of the closer interconnectedness of the world of money, electronic and otherwise, the speed of communication and transportation made possible by modern technology. While proponents of globalization rejoice, for example, at the Asian economic miracle that has increasingly become part of this globalized economy,[5] its critics argue that globalization has entailed both an expropriation of producers who have to submit to systemic demand and domestication, or consumers who have to compromise or, in some cases, alter their tastes and customs.[6] This is possible because globalization relies on "authoritative intervention structures, acting on a global scale," which include the "directoire" of the "G7" (now G8), the IMF's structural adjustment norms and the "regulating action"[7] of the World Bank and GATT (now WTO) among others. These structures and supporting institutions are primarily informed by a more fundamental aspect of globalization, namely, culture globalization.[8]

The role of culture in relation to globalization is also complicated by the expansion of culture images and fashion across borders.[9] But this does not necessarily signal the emergence of a homogenization of global culture, because the ways in which cultural contacts take shape between global products produced by hegemonic global centers and local receptions are naturally heterogeneous.[10] What seems to be happening is that the cultural realm is becoming not so much globalized as "glocalized" (a combination of global and local). In other words, while the logic of globalized economy dictates the rules of business transactions, and the power of image-making perverts the Cartesian notion of the self into "I am what I buy,"[11] the "being" that bought the products from a global center (e.g., watching American movies) is shaped, among other things, by his/her own historical/ cultural legacy, the adaptation of the products through the use of local contents such as dubbing, translation, local criticisms or even censorship, and not the cultural contents of the products alone. A more interesting question immediately arises: how is the new identity of a buyer formed?

This identity formation is shaped, on the one hand, by the global rules of business transactions, such as telecommunications or real estate businesses at work in a local context, and, on the other, by local beliefs and values energized by the global resurgence of ideas such as Islam or ecological consciousness. To understand the process of such a formation, the analysis will focus on a real estate advertisement in a Thai language newspaper.

THE ADVERTISEMENT:
REAL ESTATE AND PILGRIMAGE

Islamic Guidance Post is a unique newspaper in Thailand. It is a Muslim newspaper. Its owners and the majority of its readers are Muslims, a significant minority in the country. Published in Thai, using a tabloid format, this monthly newspaper features news related to Muslims both at home and abroad. A cursory glance at the headlines of its recent issue reads: "Muslim leaders warn: state religion will cause problem;" "Boy Scouts are allowed to wear trousers;" and "Background of Indonesian Election Revealed."[12] I have argued elsewhere that the dominant worldview of the *Islamic Guidance Post* is its firm commitment to Islam, which, in turn, is influenced by the tide of Islamic resurgence, the ethno history of Muslims of diverse ethnic origins in Thailand, and the proximity between the Malay dominated area in Southern Thailand, where the majority of Muslims in Thailand live, and Malaysia,[13] Recently, the editor-in-chief of *Islamic Guidance Post* informed me that the majority of its readers are in the Malay-dominated southernmost provinces of Pattani, Yala, Narathiwat and Satun. He also indicated that for the first time in many years, the newspaper is able to stand financially secure due to both subscriptions and advertisements.

In Thailand, newspapers obtain about 80 per cent of their revenue from advertisements. From 1991 to 1995, newspaper advertising revenue increased 15 per cent annually. Reflecting a sharp downturn in the Thai economy, total newspaper advertising revenue began to decline last year, and continues to do so this year. From January to May 1996, total newspaper advertising spending, of all types of business, was 4.8 billion baht (US $192 million). For the same period in 1997, it was only 4.3 billion baht (US $172 million), a 9.16 per cent decrease. It is interesting to note that, compared to other businesses, housing projects/real estate are spending much less on newspaper advertising, from 1.2 billion baht (US $48 million) during the period January–May 1996 down to only 682 million baht during the same period in 1997 due to their serious economic problems. This is a reduction of more than 46 per cent of real estate newspaper advertising expenditures.[14] The near bankruptcy of real estate in Thailand—a result of oversupply of highly-priced real estate projects combined with bad loans authorized through unprofessional judgments and poor planning—is in no small measure responsible for the economic pathology facing the country at present. If real estate business is among the worst hit by current economic woes, Muslim real estate business should not be an exception. Consequently, it will have to increase its sales using new and sound marketing strategies.

A full page advertisement for "P.V." in Bang Boatnong, Nonthaburi, reads like any other real estate advertisement.[15] It has a text, a map and pictures of houses complete with luxurious cars in the garages. Interested buyers can choose to buy only land or a plot complete with a house. With four types of seemingly good designs, a house, with land ranging from 200 to 240 square meters, costs anywhere from 1.7 to 2.3 million baht (US $68,000–$92,000). The whole project covers approximately 16.8 acres of land. The area is said to be flood-free with clean air, comfortable living conditions, complete with health park and recreation center. This advertisement is no different from other real estate advertisements anywhere in the world; it is a blend of the modern economy and local conditions. The modern economy suggests that the price has to be reasonable and the place has to be comfortable if the product is to attract buyers. The local situation dictates that "this housing project" should be free from chronic problems facing other estates, for example floods or pollution currently plaguing Bangkok and its environs.

But the text of this advertisement is unusual. The differences lie in its decidedly religious overtones. Aiming at potential buyers who are Muslims, the world "Muslim" appears five times in the text, while "Islamic doctrine" is used once. More importantly, there are three features of this advertisement that are aimed at the religiosity (á la Geertz) of its Muslim readers.

First, it points out twice that the project is close to a Muslim community. This is essential since Muslim religious practices which encompass all aspects of daily life, from eating *halal* (permissible) food to burying the dead, are mainly communal. This seemingly trivial feature becomes more important when the minority status of Muslims in Thailand is taken into account.

Second, the advertisement says that Muslims, who desire to have a new house, can pay monthly installment payments to cover the principal over a period of 48 months. This monthly payment will be made in accordance with Islamic doctrine. In other words it will be interest free. This is also important because, according to a number of Muslim writers, the Qur'an (II: 278–79) categorically prohibits interest and forbids any claim in excess of the sum lent. As a result, lending in Islam becomes a charitable activity.[16] Interest is forbidden because it transfers wealth from the poor to the rich, thereby widening the inequality gap. In addition, it creates an idle class of people whose income comes from accumulation of wealth. Even consumption-related interest, as in the case of buying houses, violates the basic function for which God has created wealth, which envisages that the needy be supported by those with surplus wealth.[17]

Third, the advertisement of this real estate project twice states that every Muslim, who makes a deposit for a plot of land with a house, will be given "a right" to perform *Haj* the following year. In fact, the most prominent statement in this advertisement, printed in large bold letters, is this "right to perform *Haj* next year." *Haj*, or the pilgrimage to Mecca, is one of the five pillars of Islam. It is an obligatory act which every Muslim must undertake at least once in a lifetime when sufficient means are available, and those who depend on the pilgrim are well taken care of.[18] There were 22,000 Muslims from Thailand who went on the *Haj* in 1996. In 1997, the comparable number was 27,000 pilgrims, a 23 per cent increase. Each Muslim has to pay approximately 50,000 baht (US $2,000) for the pilgrimage, which covers travel, lodging, food and other expenses.[19]

A Muslim is therefore faced with a dilemma, an obligatory act, and a financial burden. The "P.V." real estate project offers a perfect solution: Buy a house with a plot of land from this real estate company, which is also owned and run by Muslims, and a believer's financial burden for one of the most sacred obligatory acts will be taken care of. In addition to owning a house, a Muslim can rest assured that the house he/she buys is close to a Muslim community, the payment is in accordance with Islamic injunctions, and the possibility of pilgrimage for the buyer is somewhat assured.

The local approach of utilizing *Haj* as a strong motivation to attract Muslims to buy land and house is nothing short of ingenious. If "I am what I buy," then by engaging in this business transaction, a Muslim's identity as Muslim seems to be strongly reaffirmed. The question at this point is whether such ingenuity embodies an inherent contradiction which needs to be elucidated.

SPIRITUALIZING REAL ESTATE, COMMODITIZING PILGRIMAGE: BASIC CONTRADICTION?

Most of the people who have been to the *Haj* confessed to their relatives and friends when they returned that they cried a lot. These almost global tears reflected the impact of the profound symbolic meaning of the rituals. To travel to Mecca, to circumambulate the *Ka'ba* signifies the human journey back to the Center, the point of origin to purify the hearts of the created. The historic power of the rituals performed by millions of people

141

across time, combined with the immanence of Divine Grace felt in every breath of prayer and supplication does crystallize the Muslim mind for the spirituality of the *Haj*.

The complex meaning of the *Haj* is certainly beyond the scope this essay.[20] Nevertheless, the learned Imam Ghazali's (1058–1111) discussion of the significance of internal actions of *Haj* in his *Ihya Ulam-Id-Din* is particularly pertinent to the present analysis. He wrote that to embark on the pilgrimage means "to pay compensation to the oppressed and to make sincere repentance to God from all sins." He also suggested that the pilgrims return home and therefore should leave one's "last words" (wasiat) to his/her children in writing. Most importantly, perhaps, the pilgrim must think of the pilgrimage as "the journey for the next world."[21] The two-piece unsewn white Ihram cloth that men put on while performing *Haj* is not unlike the white shroud used to cover human bodies at the time of death. In fact, some Muslims keep these two pieces of cloth to be used as shrouds after their death. Following Ghazali's lead, the pilgrimage is in a sense a practice in death. A believer should die to his/her own self and desires so that he/she can follow God's Will without any impediment in this world.

The first contradiction arises when *Haj* is used as a commodity. Though the cost of the pilgrimage is common knowledge, the advertisement chooses to present the *Haj* as a commodity without a price tag. It has been transformed into a "free gift." But this *Haj* is only free for those Muslims with enough money to buy houses from the company. In this sense, this "free" *Haj* does not qualify as a charitable act on behalf of the company since it is used as an incentive for potential buyers. Another contradiction presents itself when *Haj*, understood as death to worldly desires, is annexed to the purchase of real estate, which signifies a desire to own property. To own land and a house means to settle down, to plant one's social roots in the earth, to care and feel responsible for those in one's household. Moreover, this purchase is carried out through monthly installments at least over a period of four years. In spite of the fact that it is interest free, this long-term financial commitment and the purchase itself are antithetical to the Meccan pilgrimage as an act of liberation from worldly desires. Perhaps the only way to neutralize this contradiction is not to invoke the inner meanings of *Haj* and to treat *Haj* simply as a traveling ritual.

As mentioned above, in addition to the text of the advertisement, there are four pictures of four different houses, each with a car in its garage. The presence of these cars in the advertisement signifies that owning cars is natural for owners of houses such as these. But since cars are sold separately, Muslim buyers have to find their own means of acquiring these luxurious vehicles. Although real estate in this project can be purchased without interest in accordance with Islamic injunctions, buying a car is different. In positioning the cars in the picture, the advertising machines attempt to "create an alternative organization of life which would serve to channel man's desires for self, for social success, for leisure away from himself and towards a commoditized acceptance of 'Civilisation'."[22] The car becomes a symbol of success that seems inseparable from property ownership. But the desire for worldly success, symbolized by cars in the garages, and the financial arrangement necessary to buy a car, normally through a bank loan with interest in accordance with the market rate, runs against the grain of both the inner meanings of the *Haj* and the affirmation of an Islamic identity by following an Islamic code of economic conduct.

The problem at this point is how to explain the ease with which the selling of a house fits with the free gifts of *Haj*. There are at least two possible answers. First, the pilgrimage to Mecca itself has become more business-like. In 1982, there were only ten companies in the business of *Haj* arrangement. Less than a decade later, the number of these companies rose to 38 and seems to keep rising.[23] The rise in the number of *Haj* companies clearly signifies success in a business that is now worth more than 1.35 billion baht (US$ 54 million) a year.

Secondly, and more importantly, the consumption of material products in a globalized economy, such as houses, land or cars, has been transformed through advertising into the consumption of culture. The process of consumption in modern consumerism does not consist solely of the physical act of buying but also of appropriating cultural activities. In fact, Kasian Tejapira argues that:

> The most important thing being consumed by consumers under consumerism is not *the material objects of commodities but the abstract meaning* which these commodities have been made to signify by advertising.[24]

If this formulation is correct, then it would not be too difficult to spiritualize real estate with the use of *Haj* since only a short step is needed for potential buyers to move from the abstract meaning of real estate to the spirituality of the Meccan pilgrimage, which in itself consists of several physical activities endowed with profound symbolic meaning.

This "reading" of the real estate advertisement in a Muslim newspaper, that utilizes *Haj* as a free gift to attract potential Muslim buyers, suggests that, though modern economic transactions such as selling real estate can be spiritualized and the Meccan pilgrimage commoditized, contradictions are difficult to resolve. They are the result of a unique spiritual meaning of the *Haj*, the worldly quality of purchasing a house, the symbolic meaning and financial reality of buying luxurious cars. These contradictions, however, are perfectly concealed in the advertisement due to the nature of present-day *Haj* as business and consumerism, and as primarily consumption of abstraction. It remains to be seen if the phenomenon analyzed here appears elsewhere in Asia Pacific.

CONCLUSION: COEXISTENCE OF SPIRIT AND COMMODITIZATION IN ASIA PACIFIC

Is this advertisement unique to Thai society with a Muslim minority? Will it this happen elsewhere in Asia Pacific? Perhaps, judging from the present situation in Southeast Asia, I would suggest that factors that could contribute to a similar phenomenon do exist. First, real estate is big business in the booming economies of Southeast Asia. As a result, it will become more competitive. Better marketing strategies will be needed. If potential buyers are Muslims, religions will have to enter the marketing and advertising realm. Presenting *Haj* as a "free gift" has enormous potential because it is an obligatory act for all Muslims. In addition, it is expensive, and one needs to really make up one's mind to undertake the trying pilgrimage to Mecca. With the creative ways Islam is being practiced by Muslims in dynamic Southeast Asia, compared to elsewhere in the Muslim world, the widespread coexistence of a globalized economy with its advertising machines and spirituality informed by religious practices should not be difficult to imagine.

CHAPTER 7

Defending Community, Strengthening Civil Society: A Muslim Minority's Contribution to Thai Civil Society

INTRODUCTION

One of the most exhaustive academic treatments on the subject of civil society during the last decade is perhaps Jean L. Cohen and Andrew Arato's *Civil Society and Political Theory*.[1] It is interesting to note that in this 771-page volume, there is no reference to "Islam" or "Muslim" anywhere in its 26 index pages. Equally interesting, is the fact that a cursory glance at the index pages of some recent learned writings on Islam and politics such as Esposito and Voll's *Islam and Democracy*[2] and Eickelman and Piscatori's *Muslim Politics*,[3] "civil society" does not appear in there either.

In the controversial *The Clash of Civilizations and the Remaking of World Order*,[4] Huntington maintains that there has recently been a significant development of Islamic social organizations. During the last decade, it was these Islamic groups which provide health care, welfare, and educational services to the poor and ordinary people in Egypt, Jordan, the West Bank, and Indonesia. Huntington writes, "In effect, Islamic groups brought into existence in Islamic 'civil society' which paralleled, surpassed, and often supplanted in scope and activity on the frequently frail institutions of secular civil society."[5] It is, therefore, quite surprising to find that in *Conditions of Liberty: Civil Society and Its Rivals*, written by one of the most respected scholars on Muslim societies, Ernest Gellner, Islam is considered incapable of achieving civil society.[6]

There are several ways to critically appraise Gellner's thesis on Islam and civil society—his logic could be deconstructed or counter-evidence could be suggested. But, in this chapter, Gellner's thesis will be called into question by arguing that in a non-Muslim society such as Thai society, it is a Muslim minority whose participation in a public conflict, relying on their particular history and Islamic inspirations, that could help bring about a stronger civil society in the country. I will begin by first situating Gellner's thesis in a larger Orientalist discourse that fails to recognize the contribution of the Muslims to the emergence of civil society. Then the struggle of the Ban Krua Muslims, a Muslim minority community in Thai society, against the Thai state's mega project of constructing an expressway in downtown Bangkok which encroached into their residential space, will be examined. Finally, this Muslim minority's engagement in conflict, emphasizing the problematic connection between civil society and Islam, will be critically examined and its contribution to the process of strengthening the Thai civil society briefly discussed.

SITUATING GELLNER'S THESIS IN A LARGER ORIENTALIST DISCOURSE

According to Ernest Gellner, civil society is a set of diverse non-governmental institutions which is strong enough to counterbalance the state, especially in preventing it from dominating and atomizing the rest of society. As a site or space of complexity, choice, and dynamism, the existence of civil society is in contrast to political despotism. This is possible due to the fact that civil society is based on the separation of polity from economic and social life. This separation is crucial because in the absence of power wielders, there exists a spatial independence. Members of civil society can therefore act at a distance from political rulers. Consequently, they cease to be the rulers' subject and become self-transforming citizens.[7]

While Gellner's understanding of civil society is profoundly important, it has been criticized for conflating different forms of civil society together and discussing civil society in "economistic" and "masculinistic" terms. In addition, due to Gellner's neo-Popperian account of scientific progress, he "misses the elective affinity between "post-foundationalist" perspectives in philosophy and social sciences, the attitude of democratic skepticism and the horizontal diversity of forms of life that are characteristic institutional features of any civil society."[8] More importantly, his thesis that Islam is incapable of achieving civil society was said to be bordering on Orientalists' prejudice.[9] It is this point which I will now address.

Many Orientalists believe that due to the lack of independent cities, an autonomous bourgeois class, and a network of institutions mediating between the individual and the state, among other things, the social structure of Muslim society is characterized by the absence of civil society.[10] This belief is informed by a particular understanding of three related notions which constitute a civil society: separateness of society from politics, conflict between the individual and the state, and citizenship. If it is the spatial independence that separates a society from its power wielders which constitutes civil society, then Islam as a religion that emphasizes the holistic approach to all spheres of human relations, especially power relations both temporal and spiritual, could be construed as an arid ground for civil society. While the institutional arrangement that could mediate between the individual and the state is elemental to civil society, in Islam it is the relationship between a Muslim as an individual and the collectivity, that is, the *ummah* or community of believers that is of paramount importance. In fact, it could be argued that a Muslim individual derives his/her meaning from being connected to this collectivity. In this sense, Muslim society could again be seen as very different from a social platform that is conducive to a civil society. Finally, if it is the transformation from subjects to citizens that signifies civil society, then some Orientalists argue that the term "citizen" with its connotation of the right to participate in the formation and conduct of government was "totally outside the Muslim political experience, and therefore, unknown to Islamic political language."[11] The term *"madani"* which is then usually used in the place of "citizen" means something more like "statesman."[12]

Two decades ago, Edward Said had argued that Orientalism is based on a discourse of difference where the contrast between the Occident and the "exotic, erotic, strange" Orient is an expression of power relationship. The "Orient," especially the knowledge about it, is comprehensible within a network of categories and concepts defined, and therefore controlled, by the Occident.[13] The "Orient" ultimately becomes a caricature of the other, drawn on the canvas of imagination relying heavily on the shadows of the self that is the "Occident." Concepts, categories, and criteria used to determine the existence or absence of civil society in the "Orient" are not free from their contextual influence, but instead are products of a particular history of the "Occident." Moreover, the anathema between Islam and civil society in Gellner's thought could result from his deep knowledge of Muslim society itself. This is because not all groups in a Muslim society governed by Islamic injunctions could be accepted as a legitimate part of civil society in the Occidental sense of the term. Seen in this light, "the absence of civil society in Islam" or "the incapability of achieving civil society for Islam" in Gellner's line of thought is not incomprehensible.

In addition to a critique of the Orientalist discourse, I would argue that the relationship between Muslims and civil society is more problematic due to the forms of government (e.g., authoritarian or "near just society," to use John Rawls' phrase) and the reality of Muslim as minority or majority in that society, among other things. In some senses, different forms of governments elicit different responses from groups working to strengthen civil society. Demonstrations in the streets, for example, will be high-risk actions for people under a dictatorial regime, whereas they are considered a normal course of action for those governed by a constitution which guarantees their rights to organize and freedom of expression. The reality of Muslims as a minority or majority group in society would influence different directions of civil society discourses. To be a Muslim minority, working towards the expansion of the social space of civil society where people's and communal rights are respected would, in general, contribute to a free society that would better allow them to lead their lives as Muslims, which is a more basic strategic issue than engaging in a debate to choose between the "western-biased" or a more "Islamic authentic" civil society.

John Keane has suggested that nearly a third of the world's Muslims live in countries where they can never hope to become a numerical majority. For these Muslims, there are three options. First, they can turn their backs on the world and live in accordance with Sayyid Qutb's instruction that there exists an abyss between the Muslims and non-Muslims. Second, they can lead their lives as Muslims by caring little for the immediate non-Muslims around them and choose to bond themselves with Muslims elsewhere in the world as evident in the strategy of the Jemaah Tabligh. Third, within their states, Muslims minorities could live their faith and espouse the cause of tolerance and liberties for all.[14]

Facing the power of the modern project in today's world, "turning one's back" no longer seems to be an option for Muslims minorities, or anyone else for that matter. "Choosing to connect with remote communities of believers," while increasingly feasible due to technological advancement, does not answer the question of how a Muslim should live his/her daily life in a society that is largely non-Muslim. A Muslim scholar, writing on some juristic aspects of Muslim living as minorities in non-Muslim states, suggests that there are three guidelines. First, whatever is *haram* (forbidden) in Muslim states remains equally unlawful for them. Second, whatever is *halal* (permissible) for Muslim where they are the majority remains equally lawful for them. Third, the principles of *dharurah* (necessity) would come into effect in the event of extreme compulsion.[15] "Espousing the cause of liberty for all," on the other hand, is an interesting option precisely because in working "for all," it transcends the demarcation line between the Muslim minorities and the non-Muslim society. Seriously considering this option will inevitably raise questions about the ways in which Muslim minorities connect with their larger societies. To think through this option in relation to the issue of Muslims and civil society, it is perhaps instructive to examine a concrete case of a Muslim minority defending their own community against pathological development in a non-Muslim society.

BAN KRUA: A MUSLIM MINORITY'S STRUGGLE AGAINST A MEGA PROJECT[16]

Bangkok, as a city of more than seven million people, has various chronic problems. The most notorious one is perhaps traffic congestion. The diagnosis of this problem could be simple: too many people, too many cars, but not enough traffic space. According to the present Bangkok Governor, there are more than four million cars in Bangkok while there are only 2,812 km of roads of all types.[17] The solution, in line with mainstream development thinking,[18] is to build more roads. With the first National Economic Development Plan some four decades ago came a strong urge to modernize the country so much so that most canals in the city, which used to serve as transportation channels and a natural drainage system, were filled with earth to build roads. Recently, numerous mega projects such as the skytrain and underground mass transit systems sprang up in Bangkok as if the city could grow indefinitely. The expressway project is one such mega project the government planned and carried out in order to alleviate traffic problems. But to build such a mega project at a time when the city has been bursting at the seams with both rapid real estate development and demographic expansion is to risk a number of crucial problems. For example, appropriation of land already owned by Bangkok residents has become a costly endeavor on the parts of both the expressway builder and the administration. There are landowners who accept compensation, normally below market prices, without any fight. There are those, however, who would not yield so easily and have taken their cases to court for fairer treatment. But no other case of people who put up a fight against the expressway, and by extension, the development direction modern Thailand is taking without questioning, is quite like the fight of the Ban Krua Muslim community.

Some might think of Ban Krua as one of Bangkok's 843 slums. According to the National Housing Authority, these 1.1 million slum dwellers constitute 14.56 per cent of Bangkok's population.[19] So when it was suggested that one of the exits of the second stage expressway has to cut through Ban Krua community, the choice for the authorities was obvious. On the one hand, there is this slum, a living space of poor people, and on the other, a modern road project that could help ease traffic congestion for people with cars. The people of Ban Krua, however, did not yield easily. They have argued all along that they would not want to obstruct an expressway mega project which would benefit the public at large but believed that the proposed exit would only cut through their homes without being able to reduce traffic congestion as the authorities had claimed. This latter point was in fact supported by the opinion of a government-appointed neutral commission made up of several distinguished professionals. The fight of Ban Krua community has been going on for a successfully halt of the project. . It could not destroy this community, at least, not yet. But most recently, in April 2000, a deputy governor of the Expressway and Rapid Transit Authority (ETA) has stated that it was ready to proceed with land acquisition of Ban Krua where some 200 families will be affected since the handover deadline, October 2000, was drawing near.[20] On 21 December 2000, the ETA decided to hand the task of a new public hearing to the Office of the Commission for the Management of Land Traffic. The Office, however, objected to such attempt.

The question is why have they fought so hard for their community? Commenting on a columnist's remark they there are others whose land and houses were appropriated more than once under the cruel claws of these mega projects, a Ban Krua community leader responded that Ban Krua means much more than houses because of the existence of an established community where everyone knows everyone. It is this rare homely atmosphere in the midst of the city that they cherish.[21] Such a strong communal sense has its historic root because Ban Krua community is a Muslim community of Cambodian descent which was founded at the beginning of the Bangkok period some 200 years ago.[22] In a great battle between the Burmese and the Siamese in the reign of King Rama I, known by the name of "the nine-army battle," the Cham (Cambodian Muslims) volunteered to fight on the side of the King. When the Burmese were defeated, in an act of appreciation, King Rama I graciously granted a piece of land to these Cambodian Muslims where they built their homes. Thus, Ban Krua community began 200 years ago as a village of heroes who fought and died for Siam and the King. Ban Krua residents also claimed that as a Muslim community, they have built both a mosque and a cemetery which cannot be removed by virtue of their status as *waqf* property. Even if the expressway exit were to avoid both sacred grounds, a mosque without any community to sustain it with community-based social and religious activities would not mean much.

The Ban Krua community has fought the modern project using all types of nonviolent methods.[23] Sometimes they sent their letters asking for help from the government. There were times when they worked with the opposition to pressure the government in power. Internally, they organized themselves to protect their community with guards and patrol teams because as a slum, the community is susceptible to arson. In fact, there have been attempts to set houses on fire in Ban Krua, but these were put out by the residents themselves. During the past decade of defending their community, everyone has helped. Even children in the community have been trained to identify any suspicious occurrence or stranger. They have also organized cultural tours for members of the public to show their community life and indigenous Cambodian Cham cuisine and their refined silk-weaving skills, all of which help to project them as a unique community. These non-violent persuasive actions wisely tapped their cultural fountain and have helped gain much respect from non-Muslims who were welcomed into their homes in friendship.

When all these activities did not yield satisfactory results, they took to the streets. In April 1994, the community descended on the Government House, demanding to see the Prime Minister. They used all kinds of symbolic nonviolent actions to convey the message that they were serious about their fight and that they were willing to sacrifice whatever it takes to fight for their rights and for justice. For example, they called for a press conference and dug a grave in the community cemetery to show the Thai public that they were willing to lay down their lives in this fight. Prayers (*solat*) were offered before the demonstration. People put on their "Muslim" dress wearing turbans, *kapiyah*, or *hijab*. Some carried coffins covered with velvet cloth adorned with the Qur'anic verse: "Verily unto God do we belong and, verily unto Him we shall return." When they arrived in front of the Government House, they set up their makeshift community there. Compulsory prayers, five times a day, were offered in public for everyone to see. In addition, their protest letters were sent to several Muslim countries around the world.[24]

A noted non-Muslim lawyer points out that the Ban Krua struggle has three distinctive features. First, it is independent. It seeks outside alliances but does not rely on them. In fact, only moral support was emphasized. Second, the tone of the struggle has been peaceful and rational. They answered some emotionally charged remarks with studied silence. Third, the Ban Krua people were willing to negotiate with the government without losing sight of the reality of the situation and the limitation of the government. After three days, the Prime Minister came out to meet the Muslims of Ban Krua who greeted him kindly and with delight. Before he left them, they all made supplications (*doa*) asking Allah Almighty to bless him with wisdom to be able to distinguish right from wrong in order to benefit the country the most.[25]

For more than a decade now, the Ban Krua Muslims have been fighting to defend their community from development which tends to sacrifice the values of traditions, spirit, and community for the sake of dubious material gains. The fact that they have been able to halt the unnecessary expressway exit for some ten years is indeed, by itself, evidence of some success. A most salient quality of their nonviolent struggle is their resourcefulness in using Islamic religious practices and symbols to assert their identity as a Muslim community with glorious history serving Thai society valiantly in the past. They were extremely well organized with highly competent community leadership, well informed about their problems, creative in their communicative skills, and capable of constructing alliances. Most important, perhaps, is the fact that they have been able to sustain their fight all these years. This would not have been possible without perseverance nurtured by their Islamic culture and heroic history.

A number of newspaper columnists concur on the exemplary quality of the Ban Krua Muslims. They wrote that the Ban Krua Muslims' defense of their own community is "a fight of courageous people's warrior worthy of becoming future lesson." "an example for all to contemplate changes in Thai society," and "model for Thai civil society."[26] In light of the Islam-civil society problem discussed above, the Ban Krua struggle depicted in the press as "a model for Thai civil society" will be examined next.

STRENGTHENING CIVIL SOCIETY WITH PUBLIC CONFLICT ENGAGEMENT

Theoretically, I approach conflict with two basic assumptions. First, conflict is natural and can never be eradicated. The question is, therefore, how can people live with conflicts creatively and constructively? Second, conflict is not necessarily negative. In its positive manifestation, conflict could engender desirable social transformation.[27] The Ban Krua struggle is a case of a Muslim minority's engagement in conflict with the Thai authorities. The motivation for engaging in this conflict is to defend the community from what they consider as pathological development in the form of an unfair mega project. As a Muslim minority with an aspiration to sustain their community living in a larger and fast changing Thai society, they have to "live with" the impending conflict. The means the Muslim minority community have used in this case have always been creative (e.g., organizing cultural tour and indigenous food fair). The Ban Krua struggle could be considered constructive conflict within Thai society.

It is indeed possible to connect with the larger society through constructive conflict between a Muslim minority and the state. I would argue that this connection through conflict engagement by the Muslim minority is conducive to the strengthening of Thai civil society for at least four reasons.

First, participation in the conflict between the Muslim minority themselves and the state, while political, would generate an emerging independent space away from the ruling political power, which is an important feature of civil society.

Second, the individual participant in such conflict no longer remains a passive subject of the state, but an active citizen shaping his/her own interest and destiny, which is generally agreed as another condition for a civil society.

Third, engaging in conflict against a state's policy or project reflects a determination to resist domination by state power, But to engage in a conflict of this nature, the Muslim minority community needs to be mobilized as a collective entity. The individual and his/her political will to fight, though crucial, is therefore less significant than the collective action carried out in the public arena. This, in turn, is both in line with the religious importance of the *ummah* and the strategic importance of collective action carried out in public, which is crucial for the emergence of a civil society.

Fourth, if a civil society is thought to exist where free associations which are not under state power could "significantly determine or inflect the course of state policy,"[28] then the Ban Krua community's success in halting the state's megaproject for a decade amply reflects the existence of civil society.

While the ability to transform state policy through collective actions by individuals acting as citizens is an important element in the Ban Krua struggle as civil society, the other part of the problem under discussion is the Islamic component. In fact, it could be argued that these four conditions are realized because of the Islamic component of the struggle. The independent space in which the Ban Krua Muslim community operated in, away from the ruling power of the state, has been created because the community chose to reassert its identity which is founded on the Islamic religion and their ethno-history as loyal Chams who fought valiantly for Siam 200 years ago. In other words, the Muslim minority's identity in Ban Krua has been shaped both as a community of memory and faith. Being a community of memory helps connect them to a historical past that was, in turn, positively connected with a larger history of Siam/Thailand. Being a community of faith, on the other hand, helps create a strong autonomous social entity which could maintain a sufficient distance from the state's ruling power. Once their identity is affirmed, the process of their struggle involving mobilization, methods, and sustainability, was then extensively drawn from the repertoire of cultural resources that are primarily Islamic. The digging of the grave, the emphasis on the sacredness of the mosque and the cemetery, the Islamic dress code, the prayers, the Qur'anic verse, and the *doa* for the Prime Minister are evidently bases of Islamic culture. In relying on Islam as the core component of their strategy, their Muslim identity has been strengthened. I once attended a Friday prayer at the Ban Krua mosque, the *qutbah* (sermon) itself on that afternoon was about the struggle to defend the community from the state's mega project. If the Islamic component is quite crucial for the Ban Krua struggle, and this Muslim minority's conflict engagement reflects the existence of civil society, then it could be argued that Islam as a potent cultural source for conflict engagement does contribute much to the strengthening of a civil society.

CONCLUSION: STRENGTHENING THAI CIVIL SOCIETY

The message conveyed by this Muslim minority struggle is that the state's mega projects in the future cannot be carried out arbitrarily without proper support by the public. To value public support signifies, in the final analysis, the importance of legitimacy, an acceptance of the limit of state power, and the empowerment of civil society.

It goes without saying that as a result of the democratizing process during the past two decades, the Thai political space has been sufficiently expanded to be able to accommodate different demands from various groups of people. But since the struggle discussed here has been carried out by a Muslim minority affirming their identity in the process, Thai society has been forced to come face to face with three basic facts. First, Thai society is not monolithic and minorities do have voices. Second, the reality of development in the form of the state's policy of constructing mega projects needs to be confronted. Not only does this reality affect the minorities, but all members of Thai society as well. On the one hand, the Muslim minority appears to be fighting to defend their community but yet, on the other, this struggle has been carried out on behalf of all members of Thai society who are potential victims of development. There are times when a society has to choose between visible material gain and amorphous values such as the cultural existence of a people. In making an informed choice nurtured by considered empathy, civil society could grow stronger. Third, the fact that a minority could challenge, and in fact successfully resist, state policy for a decade should be a sign of hope for other free associations who are members of the majority in Thai society that they too could successfully engage in conflict with the Thai state in pursuit of participatory democracy. To be able to listen to marginal voices, making informed choices concerning structural problems, and hope for the empowerment of ordinary people could perhaps be conducive to the process of strengthening Thai civil society.

Glossary

Ayah	Refers to the verse of the Quran.
Bid'a or *Bid'ah*	An Islamic concept which refers to a religious practice which is not clearly sanctioned by authentic sources and which may constitute an illegitimate or controversial innovation.
Chularajmontri	The Thai equivalent of the Islamic institution of *Shaikh-ul-Islam* which is the broad equivalent of a *Mufti* or the Head of the Islamic religion in a particular state. The *Chularajmontri* is officially recognized as the spiritual leader of the Muslims in Thailand and the royal advisor on Islamic affairs.
Darurah	A contingency which gives the Muslims temporary immunity from full compliance of the Islamic law.
Eid	The Islamic festive occasion to celebrate the fulfillment of *Hajj* (*Eid-ul-Adha*) or the completion of the fasting ritual in the month of Ramadan (*Eid-ul-Fitr*).
Hadith	Refers to the sayings, actions and the exemplary behaviour of Prophet Muhammad which have been meticulously researched, verified and documented by the early Muslim *ulama* and which have been recognized by mainstream Islam to be an integral part of Islamic teachings, next in importance only to the Quran, the divine revelation.
Hajj	The fifth and final pillar of Islam, is the obligatory pilgrimage to Mecca incumbent on every Muslim who meets all the necessary requirements including being in good health and possessing the economic means.
Halal	An Islamic concept signifying legitimacy or conformity to Islamic law.
Haram	An Islamic concept signifying illegitimacy or violation of Islamic law.
Hijab	The modest headscarf or shawl worn by Muslim women to cover their upper body part which includes the hair, ears and neck but not the face.
Hikayat	A chronicle of kingdoms and ruling houses in Southeast Asia, with lots of historical symbolisms and which tends to glorify the ruler for whom it was written.
Ibadat	In the most general sense, the Islamic act of worship and good deed which goes beyond the rituals of prayer to embrace all acts of human kindnesses.
Iman	An Islamic term signifying genuine faith or belief which is a trait of true believers rather than superficial followers.
Jawi	Usually rendered as *Yawi* in Thai, in its original meaning, it is a Malay word which refers to the Arabic script but in the context of Thailand it has been used as a synonym for Malay. The Thais thus refer to the Malay language that is spoken in

	the Muslim-dominated provinces of southern Thailand as *Yawi* rather than Malay probably to disassociate it with the Malay language which is widely spoken in neighbouring Malaysia.
Kafir	An Islamic term which refers people who do not believe in Islam.
Khaek	A pejorative term commonly used by the Thais to refer to the Muslims, although much resented by them. The term which simply means 'guest' is also generically used to describe all 'dark-skinned' foreigners irrespective of their religious background.
Khana mae	The Thai rendering of the Malay *'kaum muda'* [young group or more appropriately, the 20th century modernist Muslim movement] to describe the modernist Muslim faction in Thailand which challenges the traditional leadership of Islam in the kingdom.
Kharijite or *Khawarij*	In Arabic, this refers to the members of the early Muslim sect who separated themselves from the main body of the Muslims and declared war on all those who disagreed with them arguing that a wrong action turns a Muslim into an unbeliever.
Kru-ze or *Kru-se*	The 16th century uncompleted historic mosque in Pattani which continues to assume a central, if somewhat controversial role in the history of Islam in Southern Thailand. On 28 April 2004, 32 alleged Muslim militants were gunned down by the Thai military as they sought shelter within this mosque, and were subsequently buried as 'martyrs' by the locals, underlining yet again the timeless political and psychological significance of this place in the history of Islam in Thailand.
Mumin	An Islamic concept which refers to the true and dedicated believer of the Islamic religion.
Pondok	A traditional Islamic boarding school in the Muslim dominated provinces of Southern Thailand which especially has a long history in Pattani.[The institution of the *pondok* is also well-established in Kelantan in Malaysia. Its Indonesian equivalent is *pesantren*].
Shahadah	Basically means to bear witness of one's acceptance of Islam.(i.e., to publicly declare before witnesses one's embrace of Islam).
Shaikh-ul-Islam	The *Mufti* or the Head of the Islamic religion in a particular state or country.
Sunnah	A concept in Islamic jurisprudence which broadly refers to the practical examples demonstrated by Prophet Muhammad as a model Muslim on how to observe Islam in its entirety in one's daily life. It is a kind of benchmark behaviour set by the Prophet for Muslims to emulate.
Surah	An Islamic term meaning chapter. There are 114 chapters in the Quran.

157

Tawhid   An Islamic term which signifies the unity of God as this is the central tenet of Islamic monotheism which underlines the oneness of God and a common humanity.

Telekong   The religious dress, usually white in colour, that Muslim women in Thailand and the Malay world put on when they perform their prayers.

Tudong   The local Malay term widely used among the Muslims in Thailand which refers to the act of covering the upper body parts of Muslim women in conformity with Islamic religious injunction. Wearing the *hijab* or modest headscarf is a form of *tudong*.

Ummah   An Islamic term used to refer to the global Muslim moral community of the faithful which transcends territorial or national divisions.

Notes

Introduction

1   See an alternative discussion of voluntary Muslim women's "re-veiling movement" in Katherine Bullock, "Challenging Media Representations of the Veil: Contemporary Muslim Women's Re-veiling Movement," *American Journal of Islamic Social Sciences*. vol. 7, no. 3 (Fall 2000): 22–53.

2   Michael Oakeshott, *Rationalism in Politics and Other Essays*. (Indianapolis: Liberty Press, 1991), p. 493.

3   *The Glorious Qur'an*. Translation and Commentary by A. Yusuf Ali. (N.P.: The Muslim Students' Association of the United States and Canada, 1977), p. 288.

4   Ibid., p. 297.

5   Sayyid Abul A'la Maududi, *Tafhim Al-Qur'an. (Towards Understanding the Qur'an [Vol.II])*. Zafar Ishaq Ansari (Trans. and Edit.) (Delhi: Markazi Maktaba Islami, 1991) , Note 20, pp. 225–226. It should be noted that Maududi translated the first sentence as: "The life of this world is nothing but a sport and a pastime,..."

6   *The Glorious Qur'an*, fn. 855, p. 297.

7   Maududi, *Tafhim Al-Qur'an [Vol.II]*, n. 20, p. 225.

8   See relevant data in Chapter 5 of this volume.

9   See Tourism Authority of Thailand's figures in http://www.tat.or.th, figures updated on January 21, 2004, accessed on March 18, 2004.

10   See relevant figures in Chapter 3 of this volume.

11   The Senate Special Commission Report: Studying Problems of the Five Southern Border Provinces, Pattani, Yala, Narathiwat, Songkhla and Satun. (Bangkok: The Thai Senate, 1999), Ch. 1, p. 10. (My calculation from the Report's data.) (In Thai)

12   Ibid., Ch. 1, p. 13.

13   *Bangkok Post*, January 5 and 6, 2004.

14   *Krungthep Thurakit* , March 7, 2004. (In Thai)

15   Data privately collected from Ministry of Interior, March 2004.

16   *Bangkok Post* , March 20, 2004.

17   Ibid., Chapter 5, p.1.

18   Piya Kitthavorn and others, *Findings for Understanding Basic Problems in Pattani, Yala, Narathiwat*. (Bangkok: Thailand Research Funds, 2002) (In Thai).

19   http://poverty.nesdb.go.th/poverty new/province/default.htm, accessed on January 9, 2004.

20   Piya Kitthavorn and others, *Findings for Understanding Basic Problems in Pattani, Yala, Narathiwat*.

21   This is the result of a special cabinet meeting held in Pattani on March 16, 2004. It should be noted that on the very same day, another soldier was shot dead in Yala while leaflets accusing the Prime Minister of persecuting Southern Muslims were found. See *Bangkok Post*, March 17, 2004.

22   Wattana Sugunsil, A Research Report on Wage-earners' Consumer Culture in Rural Society, Tak Bai District, Narathiwat. (Bangkok: Thailand's Research Funds, 2000) cited in Srisomphob Jitpiromsri, "The State of Knowledge of Social Science and Humanities Research in the Three Southern Provinces: From the Perspective of Research Conducted at the Prince of Songkhla University, Pattani Campus in the Past Twelve Years, 1987–1999," in Suleeman Narumol Wongsuphab and Yutthanan Kwanthongyim (eds.) *Academic Seminar Proceeding on Status and Direction of Research Concerning the Dynamics of Adaptability of Southern Thai Society.* (Haadyai, Songkhla: Faculty of Liberal Arts, Prince of Songkhla University and Department of Sociology, Social Science Research Council, May 2000), p. 99. (In Thai)

23   Andrew Cornish, *Whose Place is This? Malay Rubber Producers and Thai Government Officials in Yala.* (Bangkok: White Lotus Press, 1997), pp. 111–116.

24   See Omar Farouk Bajunid, "The Muslims in Thailand: A Review," pp. 210–234. The quote is on p. 231.

25   *Bangkok Post* , March 18, 2004.

26   See for example, Prae Sirisakdumkeong, Interrelationship Between Malay Muslims and the Chinese in the Market Place, "Sai Klang", Yala Municipality.(MA thesis, Faculty of Anthropology, Silpakorn University, 2004) (In Thai); Ryoko Nishii, "Emergence and Transformation of Peripheral Ethnicity: Sam Sam on the Thai-Malaysian Border," in Andrew Turton (ed.) *Civility and Savagery: Social Identity in Tai States.* (Richmond, Surrey: Curzon Press, 2000), pp. 180–200.

27   Alexander Horstmann, *Class, Culture and Space: The Construction and Shaping of Communal Space in South Thailand.* (Tokyo: Research Institute for the Languages and Cultures of Asia and Africa, Tokyo University of Foreign Studies, 2002).

28   *Bangkok Post* , March 19, 2004.

29   See my analysis of the cultural meanings of monk killings in Chaiwat Satha-Anand, "Facing the Demon Within," *Bangkok Post*. January 30, 2004. (op-ed.)

30   Raymond Scupin, "Cham Muslims in Thailand: A Model of a Moral Community," in Isma-ae Ali et al., (eds.) *Islamic Studies in ASEAN: Presentations of an International Seminar.* (Pattani: College of Islamic Studies, Prince of Songkhla University, Pattani Campus, Thailand, 2000), pp. 453–464.

31   *Straits Times.* (Singapore) 5 February , 2002.

32   *Straits Times.* (Singapore) 9 February, 2002.

33   Ibid.

34   The journal *Asian Survey* devoted the whole issue to this particular incident. See *Asian Survey*, vol. XXXIII, no. 7 (July 1993). The issue is called "South Asia: Responses to the Ayodhya Crisis".

35   "India's politics of compromise," *Ottawa Citizen* (Canada). 14 March, 2002.

36   "Uproar over minister's call to marry British," *Straits Times* (Singapore). 9 February, 2002.

37   "Many in USA after 9/11 want their Arabic names changed," *USA Today*. 21 March, 2002.

38   See for example, a review of "Pattani in the Eighties " in Omar Farouk Bajunid, "The Muslims in Thailand: A Review," *Tonan Ajia Kenkyu (Southeast Asian Studies)* vol. 37, no. 2 (September 1999), p. 212; and discussions of "Hijab and Moments of Legitimation" in Jamie Hubbard's review in *Journal of Asian Studies*, vol. 53, no. 4 (November 1994), p. 1216; and Frank E. Reynolds' review in *Crossroads*, vol. 9, no.1 (1995), p. 87.

39   See *Sarakhadee (Feature Magazine)*, vol.9, no. 108 (February 1994). (In Thai)

40   The letter from Prawes Khananurak and my response appear in the magazine's letter page. See *Sarakhadee (Feature Magazine)*, vol. 11, no. 126 (August 1995), pp. 73–76. The quote was on p. 73. (In Thai)

41   Wimon Kijwanichkachorn, "When Capitalism Fights Religions," *Matichon* (Daily) 20 May, 1999, p. 12. (In Thai)

42   See Ghazzali Ben Mat's letter in the letter page, *Islamic Guidance Post* (Thang Nam), vol. 17, no. 206 (June–July 1999): 3. (In Thai) It is also interesting to note that the author of the letter chose not to criticize me but "my logic" which led to that *Matichon* column. Perhaps, as a result of this controversy, another Muslim newsmagazine decided to translate my "Spiritualizing Real Estate," into Thai without my prior authorization. Right before they publish their translation, the editor asked for my permission to print it. I insisted on including a note saying that the article was intended to be an academic writing, not a newspaper article. It appears in *Muslim Times*, vol. 1, no. 6 (June 15– July 14, 1999): 18–19 without any footnotes. Later I translated this article into Thai and published it as "Religious Spirituality in Real Estate and the Pilgrimage Business: Globalization and Islamic Responses in Asia-Pacific," in Kanchanee Laongsri and Thanet Apornsuwan (eds,) *Krajok Lai Dan Chai Prawatsastra (Viewing History with Multi-Sided Mirror: Collected Essays in Honor of Charnvit Kasetsiri's Sixtieth Birthday.)* (Bangkok: Matichon Publishers, 2001), pp. 60–74.

43   See this line of argument in Bassam Tibi, *Islam and the Cultural Accommodation of Social Change*. Clare Krojzl (trans.) (Boulder , San Francisco and Oxford: Westview Press, 1991), p.14. Tibi's argument is heavily influenced by Clifford Geertz's understanding of religion as a "cultural system" in his *The Interpretation of Cultures* (New York: Basic Books, 1973).

44   M.B. Hooker, "Introduction: The Translation of Islam into South-East Asia," in M.B. Hooker (ed.) *Islam in South-East Asia*. (Leiden: E.J. Brill, 1983), p. 21. This book has been reprinted by Brill Academic Publishers in 1997.

45   Roy F. Allen, "Social Theory, Ethnography and the Understanding of Practical Islam in South-East Asia," in *Ibid.*, pp.72–73. See also fn.93 on p. 73.

46   This line of reasoning is inspired by Amin Maalouf, *On Identity*. Translated from French by Barbara Bray. (London: The Harvill Press, 2000), pp.14–19.

47   Gilles Deleuze, *Negotiations: 1972–1990*. Martin Joughin (trans.) (New York: Columbia University Press, 1995), p. vii.

48   Oakeshott, *Rationalism in Politics and Other Essays*, p. 491.

49   *Ibid.*, pp. 488–497. The quotations appear on p. 497.

50   Fred Dallmayr, "Conversation Across Boundaries: Political Theory and Global Diversity," *Millennium: Journal of International Studies*, vol. 30, no.2 (2001): 332. It should also be noted that Richard Rorty's celebrated notion of "philosophy in the conversation of mankind" was also inspired by Oakeshott's idea. See Richard Rorty, *Philosophy and the Mirror of Nature*. (Princeton, New Jersey: Princeton University Press, 1979), p. 389.

51   Hans-Dieter Evers and Sharon Siddique, "Religious Revivalism in Southeast Asia: An Introduction," *Sojourn*, vol. 8, no. 1 (February 1993): 1.

52   Charles F. Keyes, Helen Hardacre, and Laurel Kendall (eds.), "Introduction: Contested Visions of Community in East and Southeast Asia," in Charles F. Keyes, Helen Hardacre and Laurel Kendall (eds.) *Asian Visions of Authority: Religion and the Modern States of East and Southeast Asia.* (Honolulu: University of Hawaii Press, 1994), p. 1.

53   Mohamed Ariff, "Islam and the Private Sector: Southeast Asian Perspective," in Mohamed Ariff (ed.) *The Muslim Private Sector in Southeast Asia.* (Singapore: ISEAS, 1991), p. 252.

54   See my "Muslim Social Scientists and the Paradox of Identities," in Chaiwat Satha-Anand (ed.) *Islam and the Quest of Social Science.* (Bangkok: Institute of Asian Studies, Chulalongkorn University, 1989), pp. 48–64. The latter remark is based on an understanding of the *Sunnah* (Traditions of the Prophet) that a Muslim should sit down properly to eat and drink.

Chapter 1

1   "The Clash of Civilizations?" was originally published as an article in *Foreign Affairs*, vol. 72, no. 3 (Summer 1993), pp. 22–49. It was later substantially enlarged into a 350-pp. volume. See Samuel P.Huntington, *The Clash of Civilizations and the Remaking of World Order*. (New York: Simon & Schuster, 1996).

2   Critics of Huntington's article include Fouad Ajami, Kishore Mahbubani, Robert L. Barley, Liu Binyan, Jean J. Kirkpatrick. See their critiques in *Foreign Affairs*, vol. 72, no. 4, (September–October 1993), pp. 2–26. See also Huntington's response in his "If Not Civilizations, What?: Paradigms of the Post-Cold War World," *Foreign Affairs*, vol. 72, no. 5, (November–December, 1993), pp. 186–194. It should be noted that the editors of *Foreign Affairs* informed Huntington that this article stirred up more discussion in three years than any other article published in that journal since the 1940s. See Huntington. *The Clash of Civilization and the Remaking of World Order*, p. 13. See also short reviews of this book by Liu Jinghua, the Chinese Academy of Social Science, Wang Gung Wu of the National University

of Singapore and Abdurrahman Wahid, leader of Nahdatul Ulama and the present President of Indonesia in *Far Eastern Economic Review*, (May 1, 1997).

3   See Francis Fukuyama, "The Primacy of Culture," *Journal of Democracy*, vol. 6, no. 1, (January 1995), pp. 7-14; Harry Eckstein, "Culture as a Foundation Concept for the Social Science," *Journal of Theoretical Politics*, vol. 8, no. 4, (October 1996), pp. 471–497.

4   Fazlur Rahman, *Islam and Modernity: Transformation of an Intellectual Tradition*. (Chicago & London: The University of Chicago Press, 1982).

5   Aziz Al-Azmeh, *Islams and Modernities*. 2nd ed. (London & New York: Verso, 1996).

6   Fazlur Rahman, *Islam and Modernity*, pp. 1–2.

7   *Al-Qur'an*, XCVI: 1–4. The translation of the holy *Qur'an* used here is *The Glorious Qur'an*. Translation and Commentary by A. Yusuf Ali (United States: The Muslim Students' Association of the United States and Canada, 1977).

8   *Al-Qur'an*, X: 37.

9   Al-Azmeh, *Islams and Modernities*, p. 1.

10 Ibid., p. 2.

11 Those who sustain suspicion of some studies are not without historical reasons since demonizing Islam has been recurring, sometimes through writings of those missionaries working in the Muslim world. See for example, the writings of Dr. C. G. Pfander, a missionary working among Indian Muslims at the end of the nineteenth century, quoted in my work which was written as a critique of such demonology: Chaiwat Satha-Anan, "The Islamic Tunes of Gandhi's *Ahimsa*," *Gandhi Marg*, vol. 14, no. 1, (April–June 1992), pp. 107–115. For a discussion of the evil image construction against Islam in the present world using some of the globalize media, see "The Crusades Revisited: The Global Campaign Against Islam," in Farish A.Noor (prepared), *Terrorizing the Truth:The Shaping of Contemporary Images of Islam and Muslims in Media, Politics and Cultures: A report.* (Penang: Just World Trust, 1997), p. 1–35. This book in particular is a learned critique of the demonology of Islamic image by world-renowned scholars, both Muslims and non-Muslims.

12 However, according to some past travelogues, there were reports of non-Muslims who traveled to participate in the Hajj such as the sixteenth century fiction-like *Itenarario* by Ludevico de Varthema, John Lewis Burckhardt's *Travels in Arabia*, (1892); or *A Personal Narrative of a Pilgrimage to al- Madina & Meccah*, (1855) by Richard Burton.

13 See details of the protest and the reasoning from Muslims all over the world in Munawar A. Anees, *The Kiss of Judas: Affairs of a Brown Sahib*. (Kuala Lumpur: Quill Publishers, 1989).

14 See for example, Ali E. Hillial Dessouki, "The Limits of Instrumentalism: Islam in Egypt's Foreign Policy," in Adeed Dawisha, ed., *Islam in Foreign Policy*. (Cambridge: Cambridge University Press, 1985), p. 94.

15 See Chaiwat Satha-Anand, "*Hijab* and Moments of Legitimation: Islamic Resurgence in Thailand," in Charles F. Keyes, Laurel Kenkall and Helen

Hardecre, eds., *Asian Visions of Authority: Religion and the Modern States of East and Southeast Asia*. (Honolulu: University of Hawaii Press, 1994), pp. 279–300.

16 H. A. R. Gibb and J. H. Kramers, eds., *Shorter Encyclopedia of Islam*. (Ithaca: Cornell University Press, 1974), p. 167. See the differences between a Muslim and a "Mu-e-min" in Mohammed Arkoun, *Rethinking Islam: Common Question, Uncommon Answers*. Robert D. Lee, trans. and ed. (Boulder: Westview Press, 1994), pp. 15–17. Here Arkoun also explains the status of prophet Abraham as a Muslim prior to the advent of Islam by the Prophet Muhammad.

17 *Al-Qur'an*, XXIII: 1–6.

18 Chaiwat Satha-Anand, "Radical Political Science," in my *Human Politics:Radical Political Science*. (Bangkok: Dogyar, 1985), pp. 65–66. This article was originally published in *The Journal of Political Science* (Thammasat University), vol. 9, no. 1 (January–April 1983), pp. 1–50. See also a learned critique in Mark Tamthai, "Radical Political Science: Countering What? And How?" and my response: "Radical Political Science: A Rejoinder," in *Thammasat University Journal*, vol. 13, no. 3, (September 1984), pp. 68–72; and 72–76 respectively. (All these are in Thai.).

19 See the differences between "behavior" and "action" in Michael J. Shapiro, *Language and Political Understanding: The Political of Discursive Practices*. (New Haven and London: Yale University Press, 1981), pp. 95–126.

20 Chaiwat Satha-Anand, "The Problems of Political Leadership study: Concepts and Some Observations on Biographical Approach," in my *Human Politics*, pp. 97–138. (In Thai).

21 This type of analysis with three levels of variable is inspired by civilizational theory used in conceptualizing cultural violence advanced by Johan Galtung. See his *Peace by Peaceful Means: Peace and Conflict, Development and Civilization*. (Oslo: PRIO; London: SAGE, 1996), pp. 196–210.

22 *Al-Qur'an*, CIX. See especially A. Yusuf Ali's commentary in footnotes from 6289 to 6291, p. 1800. See also Bernard Lewis, *The Political Language of Islam*. (Chicago and London: The University of Chicago Press, 1991), pp. 4–5.

23 The notion of "alterity," though commonly used interchangeably with "otherness," is different in terms of its focus of analysis. "Otherness" concerns the "epistemic other" or the other which could be known philosophically. "Alterity," on the other hand, concerns more with the "moral other" who exists in a political, cultural, linguistic and religious context. In other words, "alterity" could be understood in terms of "otherness" as a feature in a material and discursive location and therefore, the term is more appropriate with Muslim studies discussed here. See Bili Ashcroft, Gareth Griffiths and Helen Tiffin, *Key Concepts in Post-Colonial Studies*. (London and New York: Routledge, 1999), pp. 11–12.

24 Adriaan Peperzak, "The Other, society and people of God," *Man and World*, vol. 29, no. 2, (April 1996), pp. 109–118.

25 H.D. Rarootunion, "Foucault, Genealogy, History: The Pursuit of Otherness," in Jonathan Arac, ed. *After Foucault: Humanistic Knowledge,*

Postmodern Challenges. (New Brunswick, New Jersey: Rutgers University Press, 1991), pp. 111–112.

26   Paul Rabinow, *Reflections on Fieldwork in Morocco*. (Berkeley: University of California Press, 1984), p. 5. Here Rabinow quotes Paul Ricouer from latter's *"Existence et Hermeneutique."*

Chapter 2

1   Two spellings, "Pattani" and "Patani", are used in this study. This difference will be analyzed as a discourse indicator in constructing different stories with specific political messages later.

2   W. K. Che Man, *Muslim Separatism: The Moros of Southern Philippines and the Malays of Southern Thailand*. (Singapore: Oxford University Press, 1990), pp. 32–33.

3   Werner Kraus, "Islam in Thailand: Notes on the History of Muslim Provinces, Thai Islamic Modernism and the Separatist Movement in the South," *Journal–Institute of Muslim Minority Affairs*, vol. 5, no. 2 (1984), p. 423.

4   A. Teeuw and D. K. Wyatt, *Hikayat Patani: The Story of Patani*. (The Hague: Martinus Nijhoff, 1970), p. 289.

5   David Brown, "From Peripheral Communities to Ethnic Nations: Separatism in Southeast Asia," *Pacific Affairs*, vol. 61, no. 1 (1988), p. 51.

6   Teeuw and Wyatt, *Hikayat Patani*, p. 292.

7   The word "approximately" is needed here because there are cases when journals which were selected could not, however, be thoroughly surveyed due to mailing problems. A thesis completed in 1988 but published in 1990 is also included in this study.

8   Obaid ul Haq, "Islamic Resurgence: The Challenge of Change," in Sharon Siddique and Taufik Abdullah, ed. *Islam and Society in Southeast Asia*. (Singapore: Institute of Southeast Asian Studies, 1986).

9   Omar Farouk, "Malaysia's Islamic Awakening: Impact on Singapore and Thai Muslims," *Conflict*, vol. 8 (1988), p. 157–68.

10   Teeuw and Wyatt, *Hikayat Patani*.

11   Arong Suthasasna, *Problems of Conflict in the Four Southern Provinces*. (Bangkok: Phitakpracha, 1976) (in Thai).

12   Nantawan Haemindra, "The Problem of the Thai Muslims in the Four Southern Provinces of Thailand (Part I and II)," *Journal of Southeast Asian Studies*, vol. 7, no. 2 (1976), pp. 197–225 and vol. 8, no. 1 (1977), pp. 85–105.

13   Surin Pitsuwan, *Islam and Malay Nationalism: A Case Study of the Malay Muslims of Southern Thailand*. (Bangkok: Thai Khadi Research Institute, Thammasat University, 1985), p. 269.

14   Ibid., pp. 271–72.

15   Ibid., p. 282.

16   Chaivivun Prachuamoh, "The Role of Women in Maintaining Ethnic Identity and Boundaries: A Case of Thai Muslims (The Malay-speaking

Group) in Southern Thailand." (Ph.D. dissertation, department of Anthropology, University of Hawaii, 1980), p. 202.

17   Donald L. Horovitz, *Ethnic Groups in Conflict.* (Berkeley: University of California Press, 1985), p. 33. It should also be noted that in addition to Horowitz's explanation, the term *khaek* is used not only for the Malays but includes others such as Pakistanis and Indians as well. Moreover, the official counterpart term "Thai Islam" does not recognize their legitimate status from their point of view because the phrase is linguistically and theologically incorrect. Islam is the name of a religion and its believers are called Muslims. Most Muslims would not qualify their religion with such a parochial adjective. In addition, it is the struggle against the forced Thai-ification, implicitly and explicitly, by the state that the Malay Muslims are engaging in. But for an argument that the word *khaek* is neutral in the minds of the Malay Muslims, see A. V. N. Diller, "Islam and Southern Thai Ethnic Reference," *South East Asian Review*, vol. 13, nos.1–2 (1988), pp. 155–67.

18   Chaivivun, "The Role of Women in Maintaining Ethnic Identity," p. 200.

19   Ibid., p. 223.

20   Ibid., p. 267.

21   Seni Mudmarn, "Language Use and Loyalty among the Muslim Malay of Southern Thailand." (Ph.D. dissertation, State University of New York at Buffalo, 1988).

22   Ibid., p. 23.

23   Ibid., p. 24.

24   Krich Suebsonthi, "The Influence of Buddhism and Islam of Family Planning in Thailand: Communication and Implication." (Ph.D. dissertation, University of Minnesota, 1980). The account of this dissertation is based on its abstract only.

25   Kanniga Sachakul, "Education as a Means for National Integration: Historical and Comparative Study of Chinese and Muslim Assimilation in Thailand." (Ph.D. dissertation, University of Michigan, 1984). The account of this dissertation is based on its abstract only.

26   Panomporn Anurugsa, "Political Integration Policy in Thailand: The Case of the Malay Muslim Minority." (Ph.D. dissertation, Australian National University, 1984), p. 34–35.

27   Ibid., p. 39.

28   Ibid., pp. 50–51.

29   Ibid., pp. 393, 410.

30   Ibid., p. 403.

31   Ibid., p. 476.

32   Uthai Dulyakasem, "Education and Ethnic Nationalism: A Study of the Muslim Malays in Southern Siam.". (Ph.D. dissertation, Stanford University, 1981).

33   Ibid., p. 18.

34   Ibid., p. 188.

35   W. K. Che Man, "Muslim Elites and Politics in Southern Thailand." (Master's thesis, Universiti Sains Malaysia, 1983), p. viii.

36   Che Man, *Muslim Separatism*, p. 172.

37   Ibid., p.109.

38   Ibid., p. 175.

39   Uthai, "Education and Ethnic Nationalism", pp. 17–19.

40   Che Man, *Muslim Separatism*, p. 174.

41   Ibid., p. 175.

42   Ibid., p. 176.

43   It is only fair to note that there are other theses on the subject completed during the last decade but they were inaccessible at the time of writing. Some of these works include Omar Farouk, "The Political Integration of the Thai Islam," (Ph.D. dissertation, University of Kent, 1980), M. Lye, "The Origin of Malay Muslim Discontent in Southern Thailand," (Master's thesis, Australian National University, 1980), J. Rachapaetayakom, "The Demography of the Thai Muslim, with special Reference to Fertility and Nuptiality," (Ph.D. dissertation, Australian National University, 1984), and Anan Tipayarat, "The Perception of Pattani Elementary School: Principals towards the Professional Competencies in Community Education for Pattani Elementary School Teachers from Community Development through Elementary Schools." (Ph.D. dissertation, University of Missouri, Columbia, 1985). From the titles of these works, if they accurately convey the contents, it seems that not all are relevant to story of Pattani discussed here.

44   Chaveewan Vannaprasert, Perayot Rahimmula, and Manop Jittpoosa, *The Traditions Influencing the Social Integration between the Thai Buddhists and the Thai Muslim*, trans. Prachitr Mahahing and Khate Ratanajarana (Pattani: Department of Social Sciences, Faculty of Humanities and Social Sciences and Center for Southern Thailand Studies, Prince of Songkhla University, 1986), p. 2.

45   Ibid., p. 197.

46   Ibid., p. 199.

47   The dating on this work is based on Ibrahim's works about Thai democracy where he writes, "But it has been 17 years since democracy in Siam has been in effect," see Ibrahim Syukri, *History of the Malay Kingdom of Patani*, trans. Conner Bailey and John N. Miksic (Athens, Ohio: Center for International Studies, Ohio University, 1985), p. 76. The change from absolute monarchy to constitutional monarchy in Thailand took place in 1932.

48   Ibrahim, *History of the Malay Kingdom of Patani*, p. xi.

49   Ibid., p. 63.

50   Ibid., p. 74.

51   Ibid., pp. 75–76.

52   Ibid., p. 77.

53   Chaiwat Satha-Anand, *Islam and Violence: A Case Study of Violent Events in the Four Southern Provinces, Thailand, 1976-1981*. (Tampa, Florida: USF Monographs in Religion and Public Policy, 1987).

54   Ibid., p. 41.

55   Chaiwat Satha-Anand, "The Nonviolent Crescent: Eight Thesis on Islam Nonviolent Actions," in Ralph Crow, Philip Grant, and Saad E. Ibrahim, ed. *Arab Nonviolent Political Struggle in the Middle East*. (Boulder and London Lynne Rienner Publishers, 1990).

56   Wayne A. Bougas, *Islamic Cemeteries in Patani*. (Kuala Lumpur: Malayan Historical Society, 1988).

57   Ibid., p. 72.

58   The word "prominent" used here is based upon a recent study which asked 215 political scientists in the United States to evaluate professional journals. Of 78 journals, only two on Asia were highly ranked. They were the *Journal of Asian Studies* and *Asian Survey*, see Michael W. Giles, Francie Mizell, and David Patterson, "Political Scientists' Journal Evaluations Revisited," *PS*, vol. 22, no. 3 (1989), pp. 613–17.

59   Imitiyaz Yusuf, "Review of Surin Pitsuwan's *Islam and Malay Nationalism*," *Journal Institute of Muslim Minority Affairs*, vol. 8, no. 1 (1987), pp. 196–98.

60   Raymond Scupin, "Muslims in South Thailand: A Review Essay," *Journal Institute of Muslim Minority Affairs*, vol. 9, no. 2 (1988), pp. 404–19; Raymond Scupin, "Review of Surin Ritsuwan's *Islam and Malay Nationalism*," *Journal of Asian Studies*, vol. 47, no. 3 (1988), pp. 713–13.

61   Kobkua Suwannathat-Pian, *Thai Malay Relations: Traditional Intra-Regional Relations from the Seventeenth to the Early Twentieth Centuries*. (Singapore: Oxford University Press, 1988).

62   Chaiwat, *Islam and Violence*.

63   Andrew Comish, "Review of Chaiwat Satha-Anand's *Islam and Violence* and Surin Pitsuwan's *Islam and Malay Nationalism*," *SOJOURN: Social Issues in Southeast Asia*, vol. 3, no. 1 (1988), pp. 90–93.

64   Grant Olson, "Review of Chaiwat Satha-Anand's *Islam and Violence*," *Crossroads*, vol. 4, no. 2 (1989), pp. 113–114.

65   Dianne Lewis, "Review of Ibrahim Syukri's *History of the Malay Kingdom of Patani*," *Journal of Southeast Asian Studies*, vol. 18, no. 1 (1987), pp. 154–55.

66   Virginia Matheson, "Review of Ibrahim Syukri's *History of the Malay Kingdom of Patani*," *Review* (Asian Studies Association of Australia), vol. 9, no. 3 (1986), pp. 160–61.

67   Shaharil Talib, "Review of Ibrahim Syukri's *History of the Malay Kingdom of Patani*," *Journal of Asian Studies*, vol. 45, no. 4 (1986), pp. 901–02.

68   Raymond Scupin, "Thailand as a Plural Society: Ethnic Interaction in a Buddhist Kingdom," *Crossroads*, vol. 2, no. 3 (1986), pp. 115–40.

69   M. Ladd Thomas, "Political Violence in Thailand," *Crossroads*, vol. 1, no. 3 (1983), pp. 13–33.

70   Arong Suthasasna, "Occupational Distribution of Muslims in Thailand: Problems and Prospects," *Journal Institute of Muslim Minority Affairs*, vol. 5, no. 1 (1983/84), pp. 234–42.

71   W. K. Che Man, "The Malay Muslims of Southern Thailand," *Journal Institute of Muslim Minority Affairs*, vol. 6, no. 1 (1985), p. 111.

72   David J. Welch and Judith R. McNeill, "Archaeological Investigations of Pattani History," *Journal of Southeast Asian Studies*, vol. 20, no. 1 (1989), pp. 27–41.

73   Che Man, "The Malay Muslims of Southern Thailand," pp. 98–99.

74   Kraus, "Islam in Thailand," pp. 410–25.

75   Raymond Scupin, "Interpreting Islamic Movements in Thailand [1]," *Crossroads*, vol. 3, nos. 2–3 (1987), pp. 78–93.

76   Kraus, "Islam in Thailand," p. 420.

77   Scupin, "Interpreting Islamic Movements in Thailand [1]."

78   Kraus, "Islam in Thailand," p. 423.

79   Howard M. Federspiel, "Islam and Development in the Nations of ASEAN," *Asian Survey*, vol. 25, no. 8 (1985), p. 806.

80   Geoffrey B. Gunn, "Radical Islam in Southeast Asia: Rhetoric and Reality in the Middle Eastern Connection," *Journal of Contemporary Asia*, vol. 16, no. 1 (1986), p. 50.

81   Federspiel, "Islam and Development."

82   David Brown, "From Peripheral Communities to Ethnic Nations: Separatism in Southeast Asia," *Pacific Affairs*, vol. 61, no. 1 (1988), pp. 51–77.

83   Ibrahim, *History of the Malay kingdom of Patani*, p. 88.

84   Uthai, "Education and Ethnic Nationalism," p. 104; Che Man, *Muslim Separatism*, p. 66.

85   Ibrahim, *History of the Malay kingdom of Patani*, p. xvi.

86   M. Ali Kettani, *Muslim Minority in the World Today*. (London and New York: Mansell Publishing, 1986), p. 138.

87   Arong, "Occupational Distribution of Muslims in Thailand," p. 234.

88   Chaivivun, "The Role of Women in Maintaining Ethnic Identity," p. 63.

89   Che Man, *Muslim Separatism*, p. 45.

90   Seni Mudmarn, "Social Science Research in Thailand: A Case of Muslim Minorities." Paper presented at the 2nd ASEAN Forum for Muslim Social Scientists, 1–5 September 1988, in Bangkok. (Mimeographed).

91   Che Man, *Muslim Separatism*, p. 44.

92   M. Ladd Thomas, "Cultural Factors Affecting the Rural Development Interface of Thai Bureaucrats and Thai Muslim Villagers," *Contemporary Southeast Asia*, vol. 7, no. 1 (1985), pp. 1–12.

93   Chaivivun, "The Role of Women in Maintaining Ethnic Identity."

94   Seni, "Language Use and Loyalty among the Muslim Malay."

95   Krich, "The Influence of Buddhism and Islam of Family Planning."

96   Quoted in Diller, "Islam and Southern Thai Ethnic Reference," p. 159.

97   Seni, "Social Science Research in Thailand," p. 29.

98   Surin, *Islam and Malay Nationalism*; Che Man, "The Malay Muslims of Southern Thailand."

99   Che Man, *Muslim Separatism*.

100 Federspiel, "Islam and Development."

101 Gunn, "Radical Islam in Southeast Asia."

102 Chaiwat, *Islam and Violence*.

103 Surin Pitsuwan, "The Lotus and the Crescent: Clashes of Religious Symbolisms in Southern Thailand," in K.M. de Silva, Pensri Duke, Ellen S. Goldberg, and Nathan Katz, eds. *Ethnic Conflict in Buddhist Societies: Sri Lanka, Thailand and Burma*. (London: Pinter Publishers, and Colorado: Westview Press, 1988).

104 Uthai, "Education and Ethnic Nationalism," p. 6.

105 Imitiyaz, "Review of Surin Pitsuwan's *Islam and Malay Nationalism*."

106 Chaveewan et al., *The Traditions Influencing the Social Integration*.

107 Panomporn, "Political Integration Policy in Thailand."

Chapter 3

1   Tej Bunnag, *The Provincial Administration of Siam 1892–1915* (Kuala Lumpur: Oxford University Press, 1977).

2   W. K. Che Man, *Muslim Separatism: The Moros of Southern Philippines and the Malays of Southern Thailand* (Singapore: Oxford University Press, 1990).

3   Omar Farouk, "The Historical and Transnational Dimensions of Malay-Muslim Separatism in Southern Thailand," and Uthai Dulyakasem, "Muslim-Malay Separatism in Southern Thailand: Factors Underlying the Political Revolt," in Lim Joo-Jock and S. Vani, eds., *Armed Separatism in Southeast Asia* (Singapore: Institute of Southeast Asian Studies, 1984); Chaiwat Satha-Anand, *Islam and Violence: A Case Study of Violent Events in the Four Southern Provinces, Thailand, 1976–1981* (Tampa, FL: University of South Florida Monographs in Religions and Public Policy, 1987) (2nd printing, 1990); Che Man, Muslim Separatism.

4   *Pujadkarn Weekly* (Manager Weekly), 11–17 June 1990, (in Thai).

5   Anant Wattananikorn, *Prawat Muang Lankasuka-Muang Pattani* [History of Lankasuka-Pattani]. (Bangkok: Mitr Siam Printing House, 1988), p. 229, (in Thai).

6   Office of the Educational District, District 2, *Kormoon Tang Karn Suksa Karn Sassana lae Wattana tham* [Educational, religious, and cultural data]. Academic year 1990, Document no. 55/1991, 1991, p. 38, (in Thai).

7   Sermsuk Kasitipradit, "Politics and Mosque in Kru-ze," *Bangkok Post*, 23 November 1989.

8   Anant, *Prawat Muang Lankasuka-Muang Pattani*, p. 229.

9   Office of the Educational District, District 2, *Kormoon Tang Karn Suksa*, p. 38.

10   *Sanyaluck*, June 1992, p. 14.

11   Office of the Educational District, District 2, *Kormoon Tang Karn Suksa*, p. 38.

12   Ibid., p. 39.

13   Anant, *Prawat Muang Lankasuka-Muang Pattani*, p. 229.

14   Abdullah Laorman, "Kru-ze Masjid Prawattisastra," [Kru-ze: A Historical Mosque] Insan, vol. 1, no. 3, (July 1990), p. 31, (in Thai).

15   Ibid., p. 32.

16   Sanit Chomcharn, "Kabuan Karn Patiwat Islam nai Prathet Thai" [Islamic revolutionary movement in Thailand]. (A theses, Army Defence College, 1991), pp. 32–33, (in Thai).

17   Ibid., p.38.

18   *Islamic Guidance Post*, August 1990, p. 8.

19   Sanit, "Kabuan Karn Patiwat Islam," p. 34.

20   *Bangkok Post*, 14 July 1991.

21   Sanit, "Kabuan Karn Patiwat Islam," p. 50.

22   *Islamic Guidance Post*, August 1990, p. 8.

23   Sanit, "Kabuan Karn Patiwat Islam," p. 50.

24   Ibid., p. 21.

25   Bangkok Post, 19 June 1990.

26   Sermsuk, "Politics and Mosque in Kru-ze."

27   Sanit, "Kabuan Karn Patiwat Islam," p. 4.

28   Quoted in Chaiwat Satha-Anand, "Bangkok Muslims and the Tourist Trade," in Mohamed Ariff, ed. *The Muslim Private Sector in Southeast Asia* (Singapore: Institute of Southeast Asian Studies, 1991), p 96.

29   *Nation*, 8 June 1990.

30   *Matichon*, 4 June 1990.

31   *Islamic Guidance Post*, July 1990, p. 20.

32   *Islamic Guidance Post*, August 1990, p. 8.

33   Paisal Kaewprasom and Apirath Sama-ae, "Sunni-Shi'ite," *Journal of Development Administration*, vol. 28, no. 1, (January 1988), p. 138.

34   Sanit, "Kabuan Karn Patiwat Islam," p. 36.

35   Office of the Educational District, District 2, Kormoon Tang Karn Suksa, p. 40; Prapon Ruangnarong, *Sombat Thai Muslim Pak Thai* [Southern Thai Muslims' Treasures]. (Bangkok: Charoenwit Printing House, 1984), pp. 57–59 (in Thai); Anant, *Prawat Muang Lankasuka-Muang Pattani*, p. 230; *Institute of Taksin Khadi Suksa* [Institute of Southern Affairs Studies], *Saranukrom Wattanatham Pak Tai* [Encyclopedia of Southern Cultures]. vol. 1. (Bangkok: Sri Nakarinwirote University, 1986), pp. 55–56, (in Thai).

36   Prapon, *Sombat Thai Muslim Pak Thai*, p. 59.

37   Anant, *Prawat Muang Lankasuka-Muang Pattani*, p. 230.

38   Abdullah, "Kru-ze Masjid Prawattisastra," p. 32.

39   Ibrahim Syukri, *History of the Malay Kingdom of Patani* [Sejarah Kerajaan Melayu Patani], trans. Conner Bailey and John N. Miksic. (Athens, OH: Center for International Studies, 1985), p. 31.

40   A. Teeuw and D. K. Wyatt, *Hikayat Patani* [The Story of Patani] (The Hague: Martinus Nijhoff, 1970), p. 154.

41   Ibid., p. 225.

42   Ibid., p. 225; Ibrahim, *History of the Malay Kingdom of Patani*, p. 31.

43   Teeuw and Wyatt, *Hikayat Patani*, p. 224.

44   Ibid., p. 182.

45   Lao Shuan Hua, "The Legend of Lim Kun Yew," *Poo Jad Karn Weekly* [Manager Weekly], 2 September 1991, (in Thai).

46   Ibid.

47   Ibrahim, *History of the Malay Kingdom of Patani*, p. 31.

48   David J. Welch and Judith R. McNeill, "Archaeological Investigations of Pattani History," *Journal of Southeast Asian Studies*, vol. 20, no. 1, (1989), pp. 27–41.

49   G. William Skinner, *Chinese Society in Thailand: An Analytical History* (Ithaca, NY: Cornell University Press, 1962), p. 5.

50   Ibid., pp. 7–8.

51   Ibid., p. 5.

52   While it would be interesting to reread this myth of Lim Kun Yew from a feminist perspective using gender analysis, this is beyond the scope of this paper.

53   Ibrahim, *History of the Malay Kingdom of Patani*, p. 31.

54   Che Man, *Muslim Separatism*, pp. 32–36.

55   Sanit, "Kabuan Karn Patiwat Islam," pp. 7, 32. According to Pirongrong Ramasoota, the Kru-ze movement began in 1988 when an annual Maulid ceremony was organized in Pattani. She, in turn, obtained this information from an interview with the sub-director of Thung Yan Daeng district, see Pirongrong Ramasoota, *Media, State and Ideology: The Case of the Muslim Minority in Thailand* (Master's thesis: University of Hawaii, 1992), p. 114.

57   Ibid.

58   *Bangkok Post*, 2 July 1990. Pornchai Trakulwaranond advanced this idea in a roundtable discussion held at Thammasat University in early July 1990 where both of us served as panel discussants, The *Bangkok Post*, however, mistakenly identified Pornchai as "Witaya." Pirongrong also uses this same line of argument in her thesis, see Pirongrong, "Media, State and Ideology," pp. 110–15.

59   *Bangkok Post*, 29 December 1988.

60   *Bangkok Post*, 30 April 1990.

61   *Bangkok Post*, 2 July 1990.

62   *Royal Thai Government Gazette*, vol. 52. (Bangkok: Office of the Secretariat of the Cabinet, 8 March 1935), p. 3690.

63   *The Royal Act of Historical Sites, Historical Objects, Art objects and National Museum 1961* (Bangkok: Department of Fine Arts, 1970), p. 3, article 4.

64   Ibid., p. 6, article 10.

65   Ibid., p. 29.

66 In an interview in February 1992, Arun Witthayanond, news editor of the *Islamic Guidance Post*, said that the Muslims' discontent stems largely from the commercialization of the mosque which accompanied the promotion of tourism in Pattani, see Pirongrong, "Media, State and Ideology," p. 130. In view of the above discussion, however, one would have to say it was the myth and not the mosque that has been commoditized.

67 Chaiwat, "Bangkok Muslims and the Tourist Trade," p. 90.

68 Karl von Vorys, *Democracy Without Consensus: Communalism and Political Stability in Malaysia* (Princeton, NJ: Princeton University Press, 1975).

69 Susan E. Ackerman and Raymond L. M. Lee, *Heaven in Transition: Non-Muslim Religious Innovation and Ethnic Identity in Malaysia* (Kuala Lumpur: Forum, 1990), p. 57. Ackerman and Lee, however, point out that dakwah in Malaysia has lost its missionary connotations because "many people have associated the movement with religious fanaticism and extremism," see Ackerman and Lee, *Heaven in Transition*, p. 176. But Zainah Answar cautions that it is inaccurate to describe it as a monolithic movement, see Zainah Anwar, *Islamic Revivalism in Malaysia: Dakwah among the Students* (Petaling Jaya: Pelanduk Publication, 1987), pp. 34–35.

70 Ibid., p. 58.

71 Ibid., p. 59.

72 Ibid., p. 60.

73 Pirongrong, "Media, State and Ideology," pp. 43, 61.

74 Ibid., pp. 48–49.

75 Ackerman and Lee, *Heaven in Transition*, p. 57.

76 Hussin Mutalib, "Islamic Revivalism in Asean States," *Asian Survey*, vol. 30, no. 9, (September 1990), pp. 877–91.

77 Omar Farouk, "Malaysia's Islamic Awakening: Impact on Singapore and Thai Muslims," Conflict, vol. 8 (1988), pp. 157–68. Is Conflict a title of book ?

78 Chandra Muzaffar, *Islamic Resurgence in Malaysia* (Petaling Jaya: Penerbit Fajar Bakti, 1987), p. 5.

79 Sanit, "Kabuan Karn Patiwat Islam."

80 The different ways in which the word "Pattani"/"Patani" is spelt is discussed elsewhere, see Chaiwat Satha-Anand, "Pattani in the 1980s: Academic Literature and Political Stories," *SOJOURN: Social Issues in Southeast Asia*, vol. 7, no. 1, (February 1992), pp. 28–29. Suffice it to say here that "Patani" is used with a historical connotation while "Pattani" refers to the present administrative entity in the Thai nation-state.

81 Muhammad Asad, trans. and explained., *The Message of the Qur'an* (Gibraltar: Dar al-Andalus, 1980), pp. 258–59.

82 *Islamic Guidance Post*, November 1989, p. 18.

83 *Islamic Guidance Post*, July 1990, p. 12.

84 *Islamic Guidance Post*, November 1989, p. 9.

85 *Bangkok Post*, 30 April 1990.

86 Pirongrong, "Media, State and Ideology," pp.118–25.

87   *Islamic Guidance Post*, July 1990, p. 11.

88   *Islamic Guidance Post*, November 1990, p. 9.

89   *Sanyaluck*, June 1992.

Chapter 4

1   Chaiwat Satha-Anand, A Letter. *Bangkok Post*, 26 May 1988.

2   Leighton B. Slattery, A Letter. *Bangkok Post*, 4 June 1988.

3   Pantup Danasin, A Letter. *Bangkok Post*, 4 March 1988.

4   Chandra Muzaffar, *Islamic Resurgence in Malaysia* (Petaling Jaya: Penerbit Fajar Bakti Sdn. Bhd., 1987), p. 3. See also Chandra Muzaffar, "Islamic Resurgence: A Global View," in Taufik Abdullah and Sharon Siddique, ed., *Islam and Society in Southeast Asia* (Singapore: Institute of Southeast Asian Studies, 1986), p. 6.

5   Chandra Muzaffar, *Islamic Resurgence in Malaysia*, pp. 2–3; Chandra Muzaffar, "Islamic Resurgence: A Global View," pp. 5–6.

6   Amin Saikal, "Islam Resistance and Reassertion," *The World Today*, November, p. 194; M. Ayoob, ed., *The Politics of Islamic Reassertion* (London: Croom Helm, 1981).

7   Khurshid Ahmad, "The Nature of Islamic Resurgence," in John L.Esposito, ed., *Voices of Resurgent Islam* (New York and Oxford: Oxford University Press, 1983), pp. 218–229; Zainah Anwar, *Islamic Revivalism in Malaysia: Dakwah among the Students* (Petaling Jaya: Pelandok, 1987), p. 9.

8   Muzaffar, *Islamic Resurgence in Malaysia*, p. 2; Chandra Muzaffar, "Islamic Resurgence: A Global View," p. 5.

9   Chandra Muzaffar, "Islamic Resurgence: A Global View," p. 6.

10   James P. Piscatori, *Islam in a World of Nation States* (Cambridge: Cambridge University Press, 1986), p. 24.

11   Chandra Muzaffar, "Islamic Resurgence: A Global View," pp. 12–22; James P. Piscatori, *Islam in a World of Nation States*, pp. 26–34; Obaid ul Haq, "Islamic Resurgence: The Challenge of Change," in Taufik Abdullah and Sharon Siddique, ed., *Islam and Society in Southeast Asia*, p. 343.

12   Khurshid Ahmad, "The Nature of Islamic Resurgence," pp. 219–220.

13   Amin Saikal, "Islam Resistance and Reassertion," p. 191.

14   Ibid., p. 191.

15   *Islamic Guidance Post [IGP]*, October 1987, pp. 5–7.

16   *Siam Rath*, 2 February 1987.

17   *IGP*, April 1987.

18   Ibid.

19   See, for example, the cover of *Asiaweek* for 27 November 1987 with a lead article entitled "The Islam Question: Malaysia's Changing Society." The second sentence of Zainah Anwar's *Islam Revivalism in Malaysia* reads: "In the streets in Kuala Lumpur, the capital city, young women covered from

head to toe in the loose flowing *hijab*" see Zainah Anwar, *Islamic Revivalism in Malaysia: Dakwah among the Students*, p. 1.

20   Chandra Muzaffar, *Islamic Resurgence in Malaysia*, p. 3.

21   Zainah Anwar, *Islamic Revivalism in Malaysia: Dakwah among the Students*. Anwar, p. 59.

22   John McBech, "Thailand: A Long, Though March Towards Total Security," *Far Eastern Economic Review*, 17 April 1986, pp. 30–31.

23   Omar Farouk, "Malaysia's Islamic Awakening: Impact on Singapore and Thai Muslims," *Conflict*, vol. 8, (1988), pp. 157–168.

24   Chaiwat Satha-Anand, *Islam and Violence: A Case Study of Violent Events in the Four Southern Provinces, Thailand 1976-1981* (Tampa, FL: USF Monographs in Religions and Public Policy, 1987)

25   *Sanyaluck*, 10 June 1986.

26   *IGP*, June 1986.

27   The *hijab* crisis described here is based upon reports drawn mainly from the Muslim press, especially the special issue on *hijab* in the *IGP*, (April 1988:16–26 [in Thai]).

28   The Chularajmontri (Shaikh-ul-Islam) is the officially recognized spiritual leader of Muslims in Thailand.

29   *Chao Thai*, 26 December 1987.

30   *Daily News*, 4 February 1988.

31   *Thai Rath*, 19 February 1988.

32   Although the article, "Revealing the Battle at Yala Teachers' Training College," *Siam Rath Weekly*, 20–26 March 1988, pp. 10–11 [in Thai], does not identify that Muslim country, I believe that Iran is implicated.

33   *Daily News*, 11 February 1988.

34   *Daily News*, 18 February 1988. The Room Klao incident, a territorial dispute that took place in early 1988 between Thailand and Laos, resulted in hundreds of casualties on both sides.

35   *Matichon*, 23 February 1988.

36   See Preecha Suwannathat's article in *Naewna*, 3 February 1988 and Narongrit Sakdanarong's article in *Matichon*, 29 January 1988. (Both are in Thai).

37   Chalardchai Ramitanon, "Religion and Conflict," *Siam Rath*, 7–8 March 1988 (in Thai).

38   Nidhi Eiosriwong, "Disunity and Dress," *Matichon*, 2 February 1988 (in Thai).

39   Marvan Sama-oon, "*Hijab*," *Matichon*, 10 February 1988 (in Thai).

40   *Dao Siam*, 16 March 1988.

41   Pagadhamma, "The Yala Case: *Patipatha* for Friends with Different Religious Persuasions," *Matichon*, 15 February 1988 (in Thai).

42   Ibid.

43   The author of an award-winning thesis written for the National Defense College (academic year 1984–1985) points out that according to a survey

done in 1983, 25.7 per cent of civil servants in the four southernmost provinces were not happy to work there, while 24.2 per cent were indifferent. Some of the reasons given for their dissatisfaction include problems arising out of linguistic and religious differences, as well as concern for their own safety, see Viroj Racharak, *Security Promotion in the Four Southernmost Provinces of Thailand*. Individual research projects in the field of Social Psychology, National Defense College, 1984–1985, pp. 143–144.

44   *Siam Rath*, 28, 29 January 1988.

45   These two remarks come from interviews conducted on 12 February 1988, see *IGP*, 1 April 1988, pp. 30–32.

46   All three quotes *IGP*, 1 April 1988, p. 50.

47   P. D. Premasiri, "Minorities in Buddhist Doctrine," in K. M. de Silva, Pensri Duke, Ellen S.Goldberg, and Nathan Katz, eds., *Ethnic Conflict in Buddhist Societies: Sri Lanka, Thailand, and Burma* (London: Pinter; Boulder, CO: Westview, 1988), p. 56.

48   Surin Pitsuwan, "The Lotus and the Crescent: Clashes of Religious Symbolism in Southern Thailand," in K. M. de Silva, Pensri Duke, Ellen S.Goldberg, and Nathan Katz, eds., *Ethnic Conflict in Buddhist Societies: Sri Lanka, Thailand, and Burma*, p. 188.

49   P. D. Premasiri, "Minorities in Buddhist Doctrine," p. 55.

50   Somboon Suksamran, *Buddhism and Politics in Thailand: A Study of Socio-Political Change and Political Activism of the Thai Sangha*. (Singapore: Institute of Southeast Asian Studies, 1982), p. 6.

51   In *Legitimation Crisis*, Habermas's major concern was with crisis in advanced capitalism. Nonetheless, his discussion of the problems of legitimation is applicable here, in part because for Habermas the legitimation crisis is "directly an identity crisis," see Jürgen Habermas, *Legitimation Crisis*, trans. Thomas McCarthy (Boston, MA: Beacon Press, 1975), p. 46. As mentioned previously, Islamic resurgence means, among other things, a reassertion of Muslim identity.

52   Jürgen Habermas, *Legitimation Crisis*, p. 47.

53   Ibid.

54   Chavivun Prachuabmoh and Chaiwat Satha-Anand, "Thailand: A Mosaic of Ethnic Tensions under Control," *Ethnic Studies Report*, vol. 3, no. 1, (1985), pp. 22–31.

55   Benedict Anderson, "Studies of the Thai State: The State of Thai Studies," in Eliezer B.Ayal, ed., *The Study of Thailand* (Athens, OH: Center for International Studies, 1978), pp. 211–213.

56   Chaiwat Satha-Anand, *Islam and Violence: A Case Study of Violent Events in the Four Southern Provinces, Thailand 1976–1981*; Surin Pitsuwan, "The Lotus and the Crescent: Clashes of Religious Symbolism in Southern Thailand," p.198.

57   *Matichon*, 23 February 1988.

58   Michael J. Shapiro, *The Politics of Representation: Writing Practices, Photography, and Policy Analysis* (Madison, WI: University of Wisconsin Press, 1988), pp. 26–27.

59   Ibid., 27.

60   On 16 July 1983 the Office of the Chularajmontri issued a series of religious rulings on various issues pertaining to Muslims' participation in Buddhist rituals and state ceremonies. Questions included whether it was permissible for Muslims to stand up during the lighting of incense and candles by the presiding person at official function; to present wreaths and pay homage to the equestrian statue of King Rama V on the day commemorating his death; and to kneel before the statue of Rama VI during the Boy Scout ceremony. In all these cases the religious rulings are decisively "no." I cannot help but wonder whether such a definitive answer will be possible outside the necessary historical moment, see Surin Pitsuwan, "The Lotus and the Crescent: Clashes of Religious Symbolism in Southern Thailand," pp. 194–198.

61   "Dogmakhua", "*Choom Tang Khru*" [Teachers' Junction]. *Matichon*, 24 February 1988 (in Thai).

62   I wish to thank Professor Helen Hardacre for bringing the possibility of gender analysis of the *hijab* incident to my attention both in a workshop and in her written comments on this essay.

63   Robert John Ackerman, *Religion as Critique*. (Amherst, MA: University of Massachusetts Press, 1985).

Chapter 5

1   *1998 Mid-Year Economic, Review, Bangkok Post Supplement* (June 1988), p. 7.

2   Ibid., p. 36.

3   Chavivun Prachuabmoh and Chaiwat Satha-Anand, "Thailand: A Mosaic of Ethnic Tensions Under Control," *Ethnic Studies Report* (Sri Lanka), vol. 3, no.1, (January 1985), pp. 22–31.

4   Wuthithep Intapanya and Chamlong Atikul, *Economic Significance of Tourism in Thailand*. (Bangkok: NIDA, 1985), pp. 13–14 (in Thai).

5   *Annual Statistical Report on Tourism in Thailand 1985 and Annual Statistical Report on Tourism in Thailand 1986*. (Bangkok: Tourism Authority of Thailand, 1986; 1987), pp. 26; 8; and *1988 Mid-Year Economic Review*, op. cit., p.36.

6   *Siam Rath*, 4 April 1989 (in Thai).

7   *Annual Statistical Report on Tourism in Thailand* 1986, p. 11.

8   Wuthithep Intapanya and Chamlong Atikul, *Economic Significance of Tourism in Thailand*, pp. 23–28.

9   Ubol Topinich, "The Forecasting of the Number of Tourists visiting Thailand, 1975–1979" (Master of Commerce Thesis, Chulalongkorn University, 1975) (in Thai).

10   Chaleeporn Sangboonnum, "A Comparison of the Revenue from Tourism and that from Selected Main Exports" (Master of Commerce Thesis, Chulalongkorn University, 1975) (in Thai).

11   Bang-Omrat Rojwannasin, "Determinants of International Tourist Flows to Thailand" (M.A. Thesis, Thammasat University, 1985).

12   Thai University Research Associates, *Tourism and Economic Development in Thailand*. (Bangkok: NIDA, 1977) (in Thai); See also Prachom Suwatthee, *Job Creation in Tourism Industry*. (Bangkok: Tourism Authority of Thailand, 1980) (in Thai).

13   Wuthithep Intapanya and Chamlong Atikul, *Economic Significance of Tourism in Thailand*.

14   Krikkiat Pipatseridham, "Economic Consequence of Tourism," in *Pu-Tai* (The Messiah), no. 2, (1987), pp. 23–30 (in Thai).

15   Wiriyabha Changrien, "Effects of Tourism on Forms of Arts, Customs and Classical Dancing," *Tourism Journal*, vol. 1, no. 3, (1982), p. 56 (in Thai). It is only fair to note that the author acknowledges the fact that such arts and culture have to be compromised in accordance with the tourists' demand.

16   Preecha Oopyokin and Suriya Weerawong, *Effects of International Tourism on Thai Society and Culture*. (Bangkok: Social Research Institute, Chulalongkorn University, 1978) (in Thai); See also Nattaporn Sangpradab, "Socio-Cultural and Economic Changes Resulted from Tourism Development" (M.A. Thesis, Mahidol University, 1984) (in Thai).

17   Santad Sermsin, "Effects of Tourism on Society and Culture" (M.A. Thesis, Mahidol University, 1986) (in Thai).

18   Thai Khadi Research Institute, *Patterns of Preservation and Revivification of Tourism-Related Festivals and Traditions*. A Research Report submitted to the Tourism Authority of Thailand, Bangkok, September 1986 (in Thai).

19   Vinai Phunampol, "Negative Impacts of the Thai Tourism Industry," *Barn Mai Ru Roey*, vol. 3, no. 6, (July 1987), pp. 90–103 (in Thai).

20   Nidhi Eiosriwong, "Tourism Industry and its Cultural Impacts," *Arts and Culture*, vol. 8, no. 6 (April 1987). This article is reprinted in *Pu-Tai* (The Messiah), no. 2, (1987), pp. 15–21 (in Thai).

21   Thai Khadi Research Institute, *Patterns of Preservation and Revivification of Tourism-Related Festivals and Traditions*, pp. 137–41.

22   Cardinal Meechai Kijboonchu, "Theology of Tourism," in *Pu-Tai* (The Messiah), no. 2, (1987), pp. 4–7 (in Thai).

23   Dr Preeda Prapertchob has called my attention to various verses (e.g., 3:137; 40:21; 12:100; 27:69; 47:10; and 22:46) in the Holy Qur'an that encourage people to travel for reflection and knowledge but not for pleasure or entertainment. I have written a piece on tourism in Thailand with appeared in a monthly magazine. But it was not written from an Islamic perspective. See Chaiwat Satha-Anand, "Visit Thailand Year," *Hi-Class* (December 1987), pp. 68–69 (in Thai).

24   *Annual Statistical Report on Tourism in Thailand 1986*, p. 11.

25   *Thailand and the Muslim World*. (Bangkok: Islamic Center of Thailand, Institute of Middle Eastern and Muslim World Studies, Faculty of Political Science, Chulalongkorn University Under the Sponsorship of the Ministry of Foreign Affairs and the information Division, Supreme Command) (n.d.), pp. 24, 26.

26   Surin Pitsuwan, "The Islamic Banking Option in Thailand," In Mohamed Ariff, ed., *Islamic Banking in Southeast Asia*. (Singapore: Institute of Southeast Asian Studies, 1988).

27   Preeda Prapertchob, "Mobilization of Resources Through Waqf in Thailand." A paper presented at the Workshop on Islam and Economic Development in Southeast Asia Phase, Institute of Southeast Asian Studies, Singapore, 24–25 August 1987.

28   Prayoonsak Chalayondecha, *Muslims in Thailand*. (Bangkok: Tonson Mosque, 1988), p. 163 (in Thai).

29   Puangpetch Suratkavikul, "The Economic Role of Thai Muslims in the Past," *Journal of Social Science and Humanities*, vol. 10, no. 7, (May–June 1980), p. 28 (in Thai).

30   Ibid., p. 30.

31   See for example, Surin Pitsuwan, *Islam and Malay Nationalism*. (Bangkok: Thai Khadi Research Institute, 1985); and Chaiwat Satha-Anand, *Islam and Violence: A Case Study of Violent Events in the Four Southern Provinces, Thailand, 1976–1981*. (Tampa, Florida: USF Monographs on Religion and Public Policy, 1987).

32   Howard M. Federspiel, "Islam and Development in the Nations of ASEAN," *Asian Survey* XXV, no. 8, (August 1985), pp. 805–21.

33   Surin, "The Islamic Banking Option in Thailand."

34   Preeda, "Mobilization of Resources Through Waqf in Thailand."

35   Calculated from ibid. According to Preeda Prapertchob, there are 155 mosques in Bangkok and the average number of Muslim households per mosque in the Central plain is 223 while the average number of household members is eight.

36   International Union of Official Travel Organization (IUOTO), *The United Nations' Conference on International Travel and Tourism*. (Geneva: IUOTO, 1963), p. 14. This definition is most widely accepted and approved by the World Tourist Organization in 1968.

37   *Bangkok Post*, 6 July 1988.

38   See Erik Cohen, "Who is a Tourist?: A Conceptual Clarification," *Sociological Review*, vol. 22, no. 4, (1974), pp. 527–55.

39   I have tried desperately to interview him. All efforts were in vain due to his tight schedule abroad.

40   Pasuk Phongpaichit, "Bangkok Masseuses: Holding Up for Family Sky," *Southeast Asia Chronicle*, no. 78, (1981), pp. 14–15.

41   Charoen Kampeerapab, "Assisting the Thai Parliament in Human Rights Affairs." A Research Report Submitted to the House Affairs Committee, Bangkok, March 1988, p. 17.

42   Pasuk, "Bangkok Masseuses," p. 18.

43   Teppanom Muangmaen and Somsak Santa, "Knowledge, Attitude and Practices of Masseuses in Bangkok". A Research Report, Faculty of Public Health, Mahidol University, Bangkok, 1979, p. 25 (in Thai).

44   When asked whether she knew the meaning of her action, she replied in the negative. I had to relate to them a traditional tale about the incident during the Hijrah when the prophet was leaving Mecca, a lizard signaled the Meccans who pursued him while the spider tried to mislead them. Hence, many Muslims are taught to hate the lizard and appreciate the

spider. However, it was the first time I have heard that killing a lizard is a way of making merit.

45   John Embree, "Thailand: A Loosely Structured Social System," *American Anthropologist*, vol. 52, no. 2, (1950), p. 186.

46   Erik Cohen, "Thai Girls and *Farang* Men," *Annals of Tourism Research*, vol. 9, no. 2, (1982), p. 415.

47   Erik Cohen, "Rethinking the Sociology of Tourism," *Annals of Tourism Research*, vol. 6, no. 1, (January/March 1979), p. 30. [Emphasis in original].

48   Abdur Rehman Doi, "Duties and Responsibilities of Muslims in Non-Muslim States: A Point of View," *Journal Institute of Muslim Minority Affairs*, vol. 8, no. 1, (January 1987), p. 43.

49   Cited in detail in Barbara Freyer Stowasser, "Religious Ideology, Women and the Family: The Islamic Paradigm," in Barbara Freyer Stowasser, ed., *The Islamic Impulses*. (London and Sydney: Croom Helm, 1987), pp. 268–69.

50   Ibid., pp. 286–89.

51   Doi, "Duties and Responsibilities of Muslims," p. 54.

52   Al-Qur'an 31:20. For translation of Qur'anic verses used here, see N. J. Dawood, *The Koran Translation*. (New York: Penguin Books, 1985).

53   Quoted in Doi, "Duties and Responsibilities of Muslims," p. 54.

54   Quoted in Stowasser, "Religious Ideology, Women and the Family," p. 270.

55   Al-Qur'an 2:173. See also Al-Qur'an 6:145.

56   See Doi, "Duties and Responsibilities of Muslims," pp. 43–44.

57   Data obtained from the Bangkok Tourist Police Division.

58   Isma'il Raja al'Faruqi, "Is the Muslim Definable in Terms of His Economic Pursuits?" in Khurshid Ahmad and Zafar Ishaq Ansari, eds., *Islamic Perspectives: Studies in Honor of Mawlana Sayyid Abu A'la Mawdudi* (London and Jeddah: The Islamic Foundation and Saudi Publishing House, 1979), p. 192.

59   The meaning of *darurah* is "necessity". See Doi, "Duties and Responsibilities of Muslims," pp. 50–51. He is cited in the *fatwah* given by Mufti Kifayatullah in 1938.

60   Maxime Rodinson, *Islam and Capitalism*, trans. Brian Pearce (New York: Pantheon Books, 1973).

61   Faruqi, "Is the Muslim Definable in Terms of His Economic Pursuits?" p. 192.

62   Erik Cohen, "The Sociology of Tourism: Approaches, Issue and Findings," *Annual Review of Sociology*, vol. 10 (1984), p. 374.

63   Quoted in Rodinson, *Islam and Capitalism*, p. 239.

Chapter 6

1   Kwame, Anthony Appiah and Henry Louis Gates, Jr., eds., *The Dictionary of Global Culture*. (New York: Alfred A. Knopf, 1997), p. xi.

2   Anthony Giddens, *The Consequences of Modernity*. (Cambridge: Polity Press, 1991), p. 64.

3   Akbar S. Ahmad and Hastings Donnan, "Islam in the Age of Postmodernity," in Akbar S. Ahmad and Hastings Donnan, eds., *Islam, Globalization and Postmodernity*. (London and New York: Routledge, 1994), p. 2.

4   Thomas D. Hall, "The World-System, Perspective: A Small Sample from a Large Universe," *Sociological Inquiry*, vol. 66, no. 4 (November 1996), p. 442.

5   John Naisbitt, *Megatrends Asia: Eight Asia Megatrends That are Reshaping Our World*. (New York: Simon & Schuster, 1996).

6   Jean Chesneaux, "Ten Questions on Globalization," trans. Carolyn O'Brien, *Pacifica Review*, vol. 6, no. 1, (May/June 1996), p. 87.

7   Ibid, p. 88.

8   Giddens, *The Consequences of Modernity*, p. 77.

9   Dennis Altman, "Globalization, The State and Identity Politics," *Pacifica Review*, vol. 7, no. 1, (May/June 1995), p. 69.

10 See also other arguments against the homogenization of culture in Ahmed and Donnan, "Islam in the Age of Postmodernity," p. 3.

11 Mark C. Taylor and Esa Saarinen, *Imagologies: Media Philosophy*. (London: Routledge, 1994), as quoted in Kasian Tejapira, "Consuming Thainess: Global Commodities and National Identity." A research report produced by the Asia Leadership Fellow Program, International House of Japan, and Japan Foundation Asia Center, March 1997, p. 30.

12 *Islamic Guidance Post*, June 1997, front page.

13 See Chaiwat Satha-Anand, "The Internationalization of Conflict: The World According to the Thai Muslims," in K. M. de Silva and R. J. May, eds., *Internationalization of Ethnic Conflict*. (London: Pinter Publishers, 1991), pp. 148–57.

14 *Bangkok Post*, June 1997, Business Section, p. 12.

15 *Islamic Guidance Post*, April–May 1997, p. 3.

16 Muhammad Nejatullah Siddiqi, "Islamic Banking: Theory and Practice," in Mohamed Ariff, ed., *Islamic Banking in Southeast Asia* (Singapore: Institute of Southeast Asian Studies, 1988), p. 34.

17 Muhammad Nejatullah Siddiqi, *Muslim Economic Thinking: A Survey of Contemporary Literature*. (Jeddah: International Center for Research in Economics, King Abdul Aziz University, Leicester: The Islamic Foundation, 1981), p. 63. See pp. 47–51 for a brief review of Muslim writers' critique of modern theories of interest. For an alternative view on the same subject see Abdur Rehman Doi, "Duties and Responsibilities of Muslims in Non-Muslim States: A Point of View," *Journal of the Institute of Muslim Minority Affairs*, vol. 8, no. 1, (January 1987), pp. 50–51.

18 Sayyed Hossein Nasr, *Ideals and Realities of Islam* (London: Unwin Hyman, 1988), p. 116.

19 *Islamic Guidance Post*, April–May 1997, p. 10.

20 See, for example, Ali Shariati, *Hajj*, trans. Ali A. Behzadnia and Najia Denny (n.p.: n.d).

21   Imam Ghazali, *Ibya Ulum-Id-Din (Book 1)*. (Lahore: Sind Sagar Academy, n.d), p. 48.

22   Stuart Ewen, *Captains of Consciousness: Advertising and the Social Roots of the Consumer Culture* (New York: McGraw-Hill Book Company, 1976), p. 48.

23   Charan Maluleem, Kittima Amoratat and Pornpimol Trichote, *Thailand and the Muslim World: A Case Study of Thai Muslims*. (Bangkok: Institute of Asian Studies, Chulalongkorn University, 1996), p. 204. (in Thai)

24   Kasian Tejapira, "Consuming Thainess: Global Commodities and National Identity," p. 6.

Chapter 7

1   Jean L. Cohen and Andrew Arato, *Civil Society and Political Theory* (Cambridge, Massachusetts and London: The MIT Press, 1994).

2   John L. Esposito and John O. Voll, *Islam and Democracy* (New York and Oxford: Oxford University Press, 1996). It should be noted that this study concentrates on issues involving the role of new-style Islamic organizations and their relationship to democratization process. In this sense, it directly deals with "civil society" although the term is nowhere to be seen in the index pages.

3   Dale F. Eickelman and James Piscatori, *Muslim Politics* (Princeton, New Jersey: Princeton University Press, 1996). The authors' notion of "Muslim politics" includes the roles played by intellectuals, mothers, or government leaders, and meanings of concepts such as traditions, protest, or symbolic space are examined. In this sense, it could be argued that "civil society" is dealt with although the term does not appear in the volume's index pages.

4   Samuel P. Huntington, *The Clash of Civilizations and the Remaking of World Order* (New York: Simon & Schuster, 1996).

5   Ibid., pp. 111–12.

6   Ernest Gellner, *Conditions of Liberty: Civil Society and Its Rivals* (London: Allen Lane Penguin Press, 1994).

7   Ibid.

8   John Keane, *Reflections on Violence* (London and New York: Verso, 1996), p. 11.

9   Ibid.

10   See a critical account of Orientalism and the problem of civil society in Islam in Bryan S. Turner, *Orientalism, Post-modernism and Globalism* (London and New York: Routledge, 1994), pp. 20–35.

11   Bernard Lewis, *The Political Language of Islam* (Chicago and London: The University of Chicago Press, 1998), p. 63.

12   According to Lewis, the Greek polis, which he uses the word "city" in English, was rendered madina in Arabic. It should be noted that the Greek term polis means much more than "city" since it is the site or space where a human becomes human because he gains meanings through participation in affairs of polis. See for example, Aristotle's *The Politics*,

trans. T. A. Sinclair (Baltimore, Maryland: Penguin Books, 1975, Book III, Ch.1–2, pp. 101–104). I would think that in terms of the production of meanings and connection between the individual as a part and a political community which is the whole, a polis has more in common with ummah than a city.

13   Edward Said, *Orientalism* (London: Routledge & Kegan Paul, 1978).

14   Keane, *Reflections on Violence*, pp. 98–99.

15   Abdur Rehman Doi, "Duties and Responsibilities of Muslims in Non-Muslim States: A Point of View," *Journal Institute of Muslim Minority Affairs*, vol. 8, no.1, (January 1987), p. 48. Elsewhere I have maintained that these guidelines are not without problems. See Chaiwat Satha-Anand, "Bangkok Muslims and the Tourist Trade," in Mohamed Ariff, ed., *The Muslim Private Sector in Southeast Asia* (Singapore: Institute of Southeast Asian Studies, 1991).

16   This section is based on a case used in a part of my paper: "Muslim Communal Nonviolent Actions: Exemplar of Minorities' Coexistence in a Non-Muslim Society." Presented at the international conference on "Cultural Diversity and Islam" at the American University, Washington, D.C., 20–21 November 1998.

17   *Thai Development Support Committee*, February 1998, p. 60.

18   See a critical view of mainstream development in Saneh Chamarik, *Development and Democracy: A Cultural Perspective* (Bangkok: Local Development Institute, 1993).

19   *Thai Development support Committee*, February 1998, p. 27.

20   *Bangkok Post*, 24 April 2000, p. 1.

21   *Managers' Daily* (in Thai), 25 April 1994.

22   Muslims in Thai society are not monolithic. There are, in fact, at least six lineages of Muslims in the country: Chinese, Persian, Indian/Pakistani, Arab, Cambodian, and Malay Muslims, see Chaiwat, "Bangkok Muslims and the Tourist Trade," pp. 96–97. Using another criterion of classification, Omar Farouk, for example, points out that excluding the Malay Muslims who constitute the majority of Muslims in Thailand, there are at least nine other non-Malay Muslims: Haw, Javanese, Sam Sams, Baweanese, Pathans, Punjabis, Tamils, Bengalis, and Muslim-Siamese. See Omar Farouk, "The Muslims of Southeast Asia: An Overview," in Mohamed Ariff, ed., Islamic Banking in Southeast Asia. (Singapore: Institute of Southeast Asian Studies, 1988).

23   Chalida Tajaroensuk, "Krabuan Karn Kadkarn Krong Karn Tarng Duan Khan Tee 2 (Urupong-Rajdamri) Khong Choom Chon Ban Krua" [Protesting Process of Ban Krua Community on Second Stage Expressway System Project]. M.A. Thesis, National Institute of Development Administration, 1996 (in Thai).

24   *Managers' Daily* (in Thai), 22 April 1994.

25   Ibid., 3 May 1994.

26   Ibid., 22 April 1994, 3 May 1994, and 25 April 1994.

27   Johan Galtung, *Peace by Peaceful Means: Peace and Conflict, Development and Civilization* (Oslo: PRIO; London: SAGE, 1996), Pt II.

28   Charles Taylor, "Invoking Civil Society," in his Philosophical Arguments. (Cambridge, Massachusetts: Harvard University Press, 1997). But there are others who long for the strong role of the state and do not believe that networks of associations could fulfill the tasks that have been the monopoly of the state's. See for example David Rieff's strong criticism of civil society in his "The False Dawn of Civil Society," *The Nation*, 22 February 1999.

Bibliography

English

Ackerman, Robert John. *Religion as Critique*. (Amherst, MA: University of Massachusetts Press, 1985).

Ackerman, Susan E. and Raymond L. M. Lee. *Heaven in Transition: Non-Muslim Religious Innovation and Ethnic Identity in Malaysia*. (Kuala Lumpur: Forum, 1990).

Ahmad, Khurshid. "The Nature of Islamic Resurgence," in John L. Esposito, ed., *Voices of Resurgent Islam*. (New York and Oxford: Oxford University Press, 1983), pp. 18–29.

Ahmed, Akbar S. and Hastings Donnan. "Islam in the Age of Postmodernity," in Akbar S. Ahmad and Hastings Donnan, eds., *Islam, Globalization and Postmodernity*. (London and New York: Routledge, 1994).

Al-Azmeh, Aziz. *Islams and Modernities*. 2nd ed. (London & New York: Verso, 1996).

Al-Faruqi, Isma'il Raja. "Is the Muslim Definable in Terms of His Economic Pursuits?" in Khurshid Ahmad and Zafar Ishaq Ansari, eds., *Islamic Perspectives: Studies in Honor of Mawlana Sayyid Abu A'la Mawdudi*. (London and Jeddah: The Islamic Foundation and Saudi Publishing House, 1979).

Ali, A. Yusuf (Commentary and Trans.). *The Glorious Qur'an*. (U.S.: The Muslim Students' Association of the United States and Canada, 1977).

Altman, Dennis. "Globalization, The State and Identity Politics," *Pacifica Review*, vol. 7, no. 1 (May/June 1995), p. 69.

Tipayarat, Anan. "The Perception of Pattani Elementary School: Principals towards the Professional Competencies in Community Education for Pattani Elementary School Teachers from Community Development through Elementary Schools." (Ph.D. dissertation, University of Missouri, Columbia, 1985).

Anderson, Benedict. "Studies of the Thai State: The State of Thai Studies," in Eliezer B. Ayal, ed., *The Study of Thailand*. (Athens, OH: Center for International Studies, 1978), pp. 193–247.

Anees, Munawar A. *The Kiss of Judas: Affairs of a Brown Sahib*. (Kuala Lumpur: Quill Publishers, 1989).

Annual Statistical Report on Tourism in Thailand 1985 and Annual Statistical Report on Tourism in Thailand 1986. (Bangkok: Tourism Authority of Thailand, 1986; 1987).

Appiah, Kwame Anthony and Henry Louis Gates, Jr., eds., *The Dictionary of Global Culture*. (New York: Alfred A. Knopf, 1997).

Aristotle. *The Politics*, trans. T. A. Sinclair (Baltimore, Maryland: Penguin Books, 1975).

Arkoun, Mohammed. *Rethinking Islam: Common Question, Uncommon Answers*. Robert D. Lee, trans. and ed. (Boulder: Westview Press, 1994).

Suthasasna, Arong. "Occupational Distribution of Muslims in Thailand: Problems and Prospects," *Journal Institute of Muslim Minority Affairs*, vol. 5, no. 1, (1983/84), pp. 234–42.

Asad, Muhammad, trans. and explained, *The Message of the Qur'an*. (Gibraltar: Dar al-Andalus, 1980).

Ashcroft, Bili, Gareth Griffiths, and Helen Tiffin. *Key Concepts in Post-Colonial Studies*. (London and New York: Routledge, 1999).

Asiaweek, 27 November 1987.

Ayoob, M., ed., *The Politics of Islamic Reassertion*. (London: Croom Helm, 1981).

Bangkok Post, 6 July 1988, 29 December 1988, 30 April 1990, 19 June 1990, 2 July 1990, 14 July 1991, June 1997, 24 April 2000.

Bang-Omrat, Rojwannasin. "Determinants of International Tourist Flows to Thailand (M.A. Thesis, Thammasat University, 1985).

Berger, John. *Ways of Seeing*. (London: BBC and Penguin, 1979).

Bougas, Wayne A. *Islamic Cemeteries in Patani*. (Kuala Lumpur: Malayan Historical Society, 1988).

Brown, David. "From Peripheral Communities to Ethnic Nations: Separatism in Southeast Asia," *Pacific Affairs*, vol. 61, no. 1, (1988), pp. 51–77.

Chaiwat Satha-Anand, *Islam and Violence: A Case Study of Violent Events in the Four Southern Provinces, Thailand, 1976–1981* (Tampa, FL: University of South Florida. Monographs in Religions and Public Policy, 1987) (2nd printing, 1990).

———. A Letter. *Bangkok Post*, 26 May 1988.

———. "The Nonviolent Crescent: Eight Thesis on Islam Nonviolent Actions," in Ralph Crow, Philip Grant, and Saad E. Ibrahim, eds., *Arab Nonviolent Political Struggle in the Middle East*. (Boulder and London Lynne Rienner Publishers, 1990).

———. "Bangkok Muslims and the Tourist Trade," in Mohamed Ariff, ed., *The Muslim Private Sector in Southeast Asia*. (Singapore: Institute of Southeast Asian Studies, 1991).

———. "The Internationalization of Conflict: The World According to the Thai Muslims," in K. M. de Silva and R. J. May, eds., *Internationalization of Ethnic Conflict*. (London: Pinter Publishers, 1991), pp. 148–57.

———. "Pattani in the 1980s: Academic Literature and Political Stories," *SOJOURN: Social Issues in Southeast Asia*, vol. 7, no. 1, (February 1992), pp. 1–38.

———. "The Islamic Tunes of Gandhi's *Ahimsa*," *Gandhi Marg*, vol. 14, no. 1, (April–June 1992), pp. 107–115.

———. "*Hijab* and Moments of Legitimation: Islamic Resurgence in Thailand," in Charles F. Keyes, Laurel Kenkall and Helen Hardecre, eds., *Asian Visions of Authority: Religion and the Modern States of East and Southeast Asia*. (Honolulu: University of Hawaii Press, 1994), pp. 279–300.

———. "Muslim Communal Nonviolent Actions: Exemplar of Minorities' Coexistence in a Non-Muslim Society." A paper presented at the international conference on "Cultural Diversity and Islam" at the American University, Washington, D.C., 20–21 November 1998.

Kampeerapab, Charoen. "Assisting the Thai Parliament in Human Rights Affairs." A Research Report Submitted to the House Affairs Committee, Bangkok, March 1988.

Vannaprasert, Chaveewan, Peerayot Rahimmula, and Manop Jittpoosa. *The Traditions Influencing the Social Integration between the Thai Buddhists and the Thai Muslim*, trans. Prachitr Mahahing and Khate Ratanajarana. (Pattani: Department of Social Sciences, Faculty of Humanities and Social Sciences and Center for Southern Thailand Studies, Prince of Songkhla University, 1986).

Chavivun Prachuabmoh and Chaiwat Satha-Anand. "Thailand: A Mosaic of Ethnic Tensions Under Control," *Ethnic Studies Report* (Sri Lanka), vol. 3, no. 1, (January 1985), pp. 22–31.

Chavivun Prachuabmoh. "The Role of Women in Maintaining Ethnic Identity and Boundaries: A Case of Thai Muslims (The Malay-Speaking Group) in Southern Thailand." (Ph.D. dissertation, department of Anthropology, University of Hawaii, 1980).

Che Man, W. K. "Muslim Elites and Politics in Southern Thailand." (Master's thesis, Universiti Sains Malaysia, 1983).

———. "The Malay Muslims of Southern Thailand," *Journal-Institute of Muslim Minority Affairs*, vol. 6, no. 1, (1985), pp. 98–112.

———. *Muslim Separatism: The Moros of Southern Philippines and the Malays of Southern Thailand*. (Singapore: Oxford University Press, 1990).

Chesneaux, Jean. "Ten Questions on Globalization," trans. Carolyn O'Brien, *Pacifica Review*, vol. 6, no. 1, (May/June 1996), p. 87.

Cohen, Erik. "Who is a Tourist?: A Conceptual Clarification," *Sociological Review*, vol. 22, no. 4 (1974), pp. 527–55.

———. "Rethinking the Sociology of Tourism," *Annals of Tourism Research*, vol. 6, no. 1 (January/March 1979), p. 30.

———. "Thai Girls and *Farang* Men," *Annals of Tourism Research*, vol. 9, no. 2 (1982), p. 415.

———. "The Sociology of Tourism: Approaches, Issues and Findings," *Annual Review of Sociology*, vol. 10 (1984), p. 374.

Cohen, Jean L. and Andrew Arato. *Civil Society and Political Theory*. (Cambridge, Massachusetts and London: The MIT Press, 1994).

Cornish, Andrew. "Review of Chaiwat Satha-Anand's *Islam and Violence* and Surin Pitsuwan's *Islam and Malay Nationalism*," *SOJOURN: Social Issues in Southeast Asia*, vol. 3, no. 1 (1988), pp. 90–93.

Dawood, N. J. *The Koran Translation*. (New York: Penguin Books, 1985).

Dessouki, Ali E. Hillial. "The Limits of Instrumentalism: Islam in Egypt's Foreign Policy," in Adeed Dawisha, ed., *Islam in Foreign Policy*. (Cambridge: Cambridge University Press, 1985).

Diller, A. V. N. "Islam and Southern Thai Ethnic Reference," *South East Asian Review*, vol. 13, nos.1–2, (1988), pp. 155–67.

Doi, Abdur Rehman. "Duties and Responsibilities of Muslims in Non-Muslim States: A Point of View," *Journal of the Institute of Muslim Minority Affairs*, vol. 8, no. 1, (January 1987), pp. 50–51.

Eckstein, Harry. "Culture as a Foundation Concept for the Social Science," *Journal of Theoretical Politics*, vol. 8, no. 4, (October 1996), pp. 471–497.

187

Eickelman, Dale F. and James Piscatori. *Muslim Politics*. (Princeton, New Jersey: Princeton University Press, 1996).

Embree, John. "Thailand: A Loosely Structured Social System," *American Anthropologist*, vol. 52, no. 2, (1950), p. 186.

Esposito, John L. and John O. Voll. *Islam and Democracy*. (New York and Oxford: Oxford University Press, 1996).

Ewen, Stuart. *Captains of Consciousness: Advertising and the Social Roots of the Consumer Culture*. (New York: McGraw-Hill Book Company, 1976).

Far Eastern Economic Review, 1 May 1997.

Federspiel, Howard M. "Islam and Development in the Nations of ASEAN," *Asian Survey*, vol. 25, no. 8, (1985), pp. 805–21.

Fenn, Richard K. "Religion, Identity and Authority in the Secular Society," in RolandRobertson and Burkart Holzner, eds., *Identity and Authority*. (Oxford: Basil Blackwell, 1980).

Forbes, A. "Thailand's Muslim Minorities," *Asian Survey*, vol. 22, no. 11, (1982), pp. 1056–69.

Foreign Affairs, vol. 72, no. 4, (September-October 1993), pp. 2–26.

Fukuyama, Francis. "The Primacy of Culture," *Journal of Democracy*, vol. 6, no. 1, (January 1995), pp. 7–14.

Galtung, Johan. *Peace by Peaceful Means: Peace and Conflict, Development and Civilization*. (Oslo: PRIO; London: SAGE, 1996).

Gellner, Ernest. *Conditions of Liberty: Civil Society and Its Rivals*. (London: Allen Lane   Penguin Press, 1994).

Gibb, H. A. R. and Kramers, J. H. eds., *Shorter Encyclopedia of Islam*. (Ithaca: Cornell University Press, 1974).

Giddens, Anthony. *The Consequences of Modernity*. (Cambridge: Polity Press, 1991).

Giles, Michael W., Francie Mizell, and David Patterson. "Political Scientists' Journal Evaluations Revisited," *PS*, vol. 22, no. 3, (1989), pp. 613–17.

Gunn, Geoffrey B. "Radical Islam in Southeast Asia: Rhetoric and Reality in the Middle Eastern Connection," *Journal of Contemporary Asia*, vol. 16, no. 1, (1986), pp. 30–54.

Habermas, Jürgen. *Legitimation Crisis*, trans. Thomas McCarthy (Boston, MA: Beacon Press, 1975), p. 46.

Hall, Thomas D. "The World-System, Perspective: A Small Sample from a Large Universe," *Sociological Inquiry*, vol. 66, no. 4, (November 1996), p. 442.

Hashimoto, T. "The Problems in the Southern Border Provinces of Thailand and the Integration Policy toward the Malay Muslims," *South-East Asian Studies*, vol. 25, no. 2, (1987), pp. 233–53.

Horowitz, Donald L. *Ethnic Groups in Conflict*. (Berkeley: University of California Press, 1985).

Huntington, Samuel P. "If Not Civilizations, What?: Paradigms of the Post-Cold War World," *Foreign Affairs*, vol. 72, no. 5, (November-December, 1993), pp. 186–194.

———. "The Clash of Civilizations?" *Foreign Affairs*, vol. 72, no. 3, (Summer 1993), pp. 22–49.

————. *The Clash of Civilizations and the Remaking of World Order*. (New York: Simon & Schuster, 1996).

Ibrahim Syukri. *History of the Malay Kingdom of Patani* (Sejarah Kerajaan Melayu Patani), trans. Conner Bailey and John N. Miksic. (Athens, OH: Center for International Studies, Ohio University, 1985).

Imam Ghazali. *Ihya Ulum-Id-Din (Book 1)*. (Lahore: Sind Sagar Academy, n.d).

Imitiyaz Yusuf. "Review of Surin Pitsuwan's *Islam and Malay Nationalism*," *Journal Institute of Muslim Minority Affairs*, vol. 8, no. 1, (1987), pp. 196–98.

International Union of Official Travel Organization (IUOTO). *The United Nations' Conference on International Travel and Tourism*. (Geneva: IUOTO, 1963).

James, William. *The Principle of Psychology*. (Vol. I) (1890) (New York: Dover Publication, 1950).

Jay, Martin. *The Dialectical Imagination: A History of the Frankfurt School and the Institute of Social Research, 1923–50*. (London: Heinemann, 1973).

Kanniga Sachakul. "Education as a Means for National Integration: Historical and Comparative Study of Chinese and Muslim Assimilation in Thailand." (Ph.D. dissertation, University of Michigan, 1984).

Kasian Tejapira. "Consuming Thainess: Global Commodities and National Identity," A research report produced by the Asia Leadership Fellow Program, International House of Japan, and Japan Foundation Asia Center, March 1997.

Keane, John. *Reflections on Violence*. (London and New York: Verso, 1996).

Kettani, M. Ali. "The Muslim Minorities," in Khurshid Ahmad and Zafar Ansari, eds., *Islamic Perspectives*. (London: The Islamic Foundation, 1979), pp. 242–45.

————. *Muslim Minority in the World Today*. (London and New York: Mansell Publishing, 1986).

Kobkua Suwannathat-Pian. *Thai Malay Relations: Traditional Intra-Regional Relations from the Seventeenth to the Early Twentieth Centuries*. (Singapore: Oxford University Press, 1988).

Kraus, Werner. "Islam in Thailand: Notes on the History of Muslim Provinces, Thai Islamic Modernism and the Separatist Movement in the South," *Journal Institute of Muslim Minority Affairs*, vol. 5, no. 2, (1984), pp. 410–25.

Krich, Suebsonthi. "The Influence of Buddhism and Islam of Family Planning in Thailand: Communication and Implication." (Ph.D. dissertation, University of Minnesota, 1980).

Lewis, Bernard. *The Political Language of Islam*. (Chicago and London: The University of Chicago Press, 1988).

Lewis, Dianne. "Review of Ibrahim Syukri's *History of the Malay Kingdom of Patani*," *Journal of Southeast Asian Studies*, vol. 18, no. 1, (1987), pp. 154–55.

Lye, M. "The Origin of Malay Muslim Discontent in Southern Thailand." (Master's thesis, Australian National University, 1980).

Mackenzie, W. J. M. *Political Identity*. (Middlesex: Penguin Books, 1987).

Mahathir Bin Mohamad. *The Malay Dilemma*. (Selangor: Federal Publication, 1983).

Matheson, Virginia. "Review of Ibrahim Syukri's *History of the Malay Kingdom of Patani*," *Review* (Asian Studies Association of Australia), vol. 9, no. 3, (1986), pp. 160–61.

McBech, John. "Thailand: A Long, Though March Towards Total Security," *Far Eastern Economic Review*, 17 April 1986, pp. 30–31.

Mutalib, Hussin. "Islamic Revivalism in Asean States," *Asian Survey*, vol. 30, no. 9, (September 1990), pp. 877–91.

Muzaffar, Chandra. "Islamic Resurgence: A Global View," in Taufik Abdullah and Sharon Siddique, ed., *Islam and Society in Southeast Asia*. (Singapore: Institute of Southeast Asian Studies, 1986).

———. *Islamic Resurgence in Malaysia*. (Petaling Jaya: Penerbit Fajar Bakti Sdn. Bhd., 1987).

Naisbitt, John. *Megatrends Asia: Eight Asia Megatrends That are Reshaping Our World*. (New York: Simon & Schuster, 1996).

Nantawan Haemindra. "The Problem of the Thai Muslims in the Four Southern Provinces of Thailand (Part I and II)," *Journal of Southeast Asian Studies*, vol. 7, no. 2 (1976), pp. 197–225 and vol. 8, no. 1, (1977), pp. 85–105.

Nasr, Seyyed Hossein. " Decadence, Deviation and Renaissance in the Context of Contemporary Islam," in Khurshid Ahmad and Zafar Ansari, eds.,*Islamic Perspectives*. (London: The Islamic Foundation, 1979).

———. *Ideals and Realities of Islam*. (London: Unwin Hyman, 1988).

The Nation, 8 June 1990.

Noor, Farish A. (prepared). *Terrorizing the Truth: The Shaping of Contemporary Images of Islam and Muslims in Media, Politics and Cultures: A Report*. (Penang: Just World Trust, 1997).

Olson, Grant. "Review of Chaiwat Satha-Anand's *Islam and Violence*," *Crossroads*, vol. 4, no. 2 (1989), pp. 113–14.

Omar Farouk. "The Political Integration of the Thai Islam." (Ph.D. dissertation, University of Kent, 1980).

———. "The Historical and Transnational Dimensions of Malay-Muslim Separatism in Southern Thailand," in Lim Joo-Jock and S. Vani, ed., *Armed Separatism in Southeast Asia*. (Singapore: Institute of Southeast Asian Studies, 1984).

———. "Malaysia's Islamic Awakening: Impact on Singapore and Thai Muslims," *Conflict*, vol. 8 (1988), pp. 157–68.

———. "The Muslims of Southeast Asia: An Overview," in Mohamed Ariff, ed., *Islamic Banking in Southeast Asia*. (Singapore: Institute of Southeast Asian Studies, 1988).

Paisal Kaewprasom and Apirath Sama-ae. "Sunni-Shi'ite," *Journal of Development Administration*, vol. 28, no. 1, (January 1988), pp. 129–39.

Panomporn Anurugsa. "Political Integration Policy in Thailand: The Case of the Malay Muslim Minority." (Ph.D. dissertation, Australian National University, 1984).

Pantup Danasin. A Letter. *Bangkok Post*, 4 March 1988.

Pasuk Phongpaichit. "Bangkok Masseuses: Holding Up for Family Sky," *Southeast Asia Chronicle*, no. 78, (1981), pp. 14–15.

Peperzak, Adriaan. "The other, society and people of God," *Man and World*, vol. 29, no. 2, (April 1996), pp. 109–18.

Pirongrong Ramasoota. "Media, State and Ideology: The Case of the Muslim Minority in Thailand." (Master's thesis: University of Hawaii, 1992).

Piscatori, Jame P. *Islam in a World of Nation-States*. (Cambridge: The Royal Institute of International Affairs and Cambridge University Press, 1986).

Preeda Prapertchob. "Mobilization of Resources Through Waqf in Thailand." A paper presented at the Workshop on Islam and Economic Development in Southeast Asia, Institute of Southeast Asian Studies, Singapore, 24–25 August 1987.

Premasiri, P. D. "Minorities in Buddhist Doctrine," in K. M. de Silva, Pensri Duke, Ellen S. Goldberg, and Nathan Katz, eds., *Ethnic Conflict in Buddhist Societies: Sri Lanka, Thailand, and Burma*. (London: Pinter; Boulder, CO: Westview, 1988).

Rabinow, Paul. *Reflections on Fieldwork in Morocco*. (Berkeley: University of California Press, 1984).

Rachapaetayakom, J. "The Demography of the Thai Muslim, with Special Reference to Fertility and Nuptiality." (Ph.D. dissertation, Australian National University, 1984).

Rahman, Fazlur. *Islam and Modernity: Transformation of an Intellectual Tradition*. (Chicago & London: The University of Chicago Press, 1982).

Rarootunion, H. D. "Foucault, Genealogy, History: The Pursuit of Otherness," in Jonathan Arac, ed., *After Foucault: Humanistic Knowledge, Postmodern Challenges*. (New Brunswick, New Jersey: Rutgers University Press, 1991), pp. 111–12.

Rieff, David. "The False Dawn of Civil Society," *The Nation*, 22 February 1999.

Robertson, Roland and Burkart Holzner eds. *Identity and Authority*. (Oxford: Basil Blackwell, 1980).

Rodinson, Maxime. *Islam and Capitalism*, trans. Brian Pearce. (New York: Pantheon Books, 1973).

Royal Thai Government Gazette. vol. 52. (Bangkok: Office of the Secretariat of the Cabinet, 8 March 1935).

Sadat, Anwar. *In Search of Identity: An Autobiography*. (New York: Harper & Row, 1987).

Said, Edward. *Orientalism*. (London: Routledge & Kegan Paul, 1978).

Saikal, Amin. "Islam Resistance and Reassertion," *The World Today*, vol. 43, no. 11, (1987), pp. 191–94.

Saneh Chamarik. *Development and Democracy: A Cultural Perspective*. (Bangkok: Local Development Institute, 1993).

Scupin, Raymond. "Thailand as a Plural Society: Ethnic Interaction in a Buddhist Kingdom," *Crossroads*, vol. 2, no. 3, (1986), pp. 115–40.

———. "Interpreting Islamic Movements in Thailand [1]," *Crossroads*, vol. 3, nos. 2–3 (1987), pp. 78–93.

———. "Muslims in South Thailand: A Review Essay," *Journal-Institute of Muslim Minority Affairs*, vol. 9, no. 2, (1988), pp. 404–19.

———. "Review of Surin Ritsuwan's *Islam and Malay Nationalism*," *Journal of Asian studies*, vol. 47, no. 3, (1988), pp. 713–14.

Seni Mudmarn. "Language Use and Loyalty among the Muslim Malay of Southern Thailand." (Ph.D. dissertation, State University of New York at Buffalo, 1988).

————. "Social Science Research in Thailand: A Case of Muslim Minorities". Paper presented at the 2nd ASEAN Forum for Muslim Social Scientists, 1–5 September 1988, in Bangkok. (Mimeographed).

Sermsuk Kasitipradit. "Politics and Mosque in Kru-ze," *Bangkok Post*, 23 November 1989.

Shaharil Talib. "Review of Ibrahim Syukri's *History of the Malay Kingdom of Patani*," *Journal of Asian Studies*, vol. 45, no. 4, (1986), pp. 901–02.

Shapiro, Michael J. *Language and Political Understanding: The Political of Discursive Practices*. (New Haven and London: Yale University Press, 1981).

————. *The Politics of Representation: Writing Practices, Photography, and Policy Analysis*. (Madison, WI: University of Wisconsin Press, 1988).

Shariati, Ali. *Hajj*. trans. Ali A. Behzadnia and Najia Denny. (n.p.: n.d.).

————. *Muslim Economic Thinking: A Survey of Contemporary Literature*. (Jeddah: International Center for Research in Economics, King Abdul Aziz University, Leicester: The Islamic Foundation, 1981).

Siddiqi, Muhammad Nejatullah. "Islamic Banking: Theory and Practice," in Mohamed Ariff, ed., *Islamic Banking in Southeast Asia*. (Singapore: Institute of Southeast Asian Studies, 1988).

Sivan, Emmanuel. *Radical Islam: Medieval Theology and Modern Politics*. (New Haven and London: Yale University Press, 1985).

Skinner, G. William. *Chinese Society in Thailand: An Analytical History*. (Ithaca, NY: Cornell University Press, 1962).

Slattery, Leighton B. A Letter. *Bangkok Post*, 4 June 1988.

Somboon Suksamran, *Buddhism and Politics in Thailand: A Study of Socio-Political Change and Political Activism of the Thai Sangha*. (Singapore: Institute of Southeast Asian Studies, 1982).

Stowasser, Barbara Freyer. "Religious Ideology, Women and the Family: The Islamic Paradigm," in Barbara Freyer Stowasser, ed. *The Islamic Impulses*. (London and Sydney: Croom Helm, 1987), pp. 268–69.

Surin Pitsuwan. *Islam and Malay Nationalism: A Case Study of the Malay Muslims of Southern Thailand*. (Bangkok: Thai Khadi Research Institute, Thammasat University, 1985).

————. "The Islamic Banking Option in Thailand," In Mohamed Ariff, ed. *Islamic Banking in Southeast Asia*. (Singapore: Institute of Southeast Asian Studies, 1988).

————. "The Lotus and the Crescent: Clashes of Religious Symbolisms in Southern Thailand," in K. M. de Silva, Pensri Duke, Ellen S. Goldberg, and Nathan Katz, eds., *Ethnic Conflict in Buddhist Societies: Sri Lanka, Thailand and Burma*. (London: Pinter Publishers, and Colorado: Westview Press, 1988).

Taylor, Charles. "Invoking Civil Society," in Charles Taylor, *Philosophical Arguments*. (Cambridge, Massachusetts: Harvard University Press, 1997).

Taylor, Mark C. and Esa Saarinen. *Imagologies: Media Philosophy*. (London: Routledge, 1994).

Teeuw, A. and Wyatt, D. K. *Hikayat Patani* [The Story of Patani]. (The Hague: Martinus Nijhoff, 1970).

Tej Bunnag. *The Provincial Administration of Siam 1892–1915*. (Kuala Lumpur: Oxford University Press, 1977).

Thai Development Support Committee, February 1998.

Thailand and the Muslim World. (Bangkok: Islamic Center of Thailand, Institute of Middle Eastern and Muslim World Studies, Faculty of Political Science, Chulalongkorn University, n.d.).

The Royal Act of Historical Sites, Historical Objects, Art objects and National Museum 1961. (Bangkok: Department of Fine Arts, 1970).

Thomas, M. Ladd. "Political Violence in Thailand," *Crossroads*, vol. 1, no. 3, (1983), pp. 13–33.

———. "Cultural Factors Affecting the Rural Development Interface of Thai Bureaucrats and Thai Muslim Villagers," *Contemporary Southeast Asia*, vol. 7, no. 1, (1985), pp. 1–12.

Turner, Bryan S. *Orientalism, Post-modernism and Globalism*. (London and New York: Routledge, 1994).

ul Haq, Obaid. "Islamic Resurgence: The Challenge of Change," in Taufik Abdullah and Sharon Siddique, eds., *Islam and Society in Southeast Asia*. (Singapore: Institute of Southeast Asian Studies, 1986).

Uthai Dulyakasem, "Education and Ethnic Nationalism: A Study of the Muslim Malays in Southern Siam." (Ph.D. dissertation, Stanford University, 1981).

———. "Muslim-Malay Separatism in Southern Thailand: Factors Underlying the Political Revolt," in Lim Joo-Jock and S. Vani, eds., *Armed Separatism in Southeast Asia*. (Singapore: Institute of Southeast Asian Studies, 1984).

Viroj Racharak. *Security Promotion in the Four Southernmost Provinces of Thailand*. Individual research projects in the field of Social Psychology, National Defense College, 1984–1985.

von Vorys, Karl. *Democracy Without Consensus: Communalism and Political Stability in Malaysia*. (Princeton, NJ: Princeton University Press, 1975).

Welch, David J. and McNeill, Judith R. "Archaeological Investigations of Pattani History," *Journal of Southeast Asian Studies*, vol. 20, no. 1, (1989), pp. 27–41.

Zainah Anwar. *Islamic Revivalism in Malaysia: Dakwah among the Students*. (Petaling Jaya: Pelanduk Publication, 1987).

"1988 Mid-Year Economic, Review," *Bangkok Post*, Supplement (June 1988).

Thai

Abdullah Laorman. "Kru-ze: Masjid Prawattisastra," [Kru-ze: A Historical Mosque] *Insan*, vol. 1, no. 3, (July 1990), p. 30–32.

Anant Wattananikorn. *Prawat Muang Lankasuka-Muang Pattani* [History of Lankasuka-Pattani]. (Bangkok: Mitr Siam Printing House, 1988).

Arong Suthasasna, *Problems of Conflict in the Four Southern Provinces*. (Bangkok: Phitakpracha, 1976).

Chaiwat Satha-Anand. "Radical Political Science: A Rejoinder," *Thammasat University Journal*. vol. 13, no. 3, (September 1984), pp. 72–76.

———. "Radical Political Science," in Chaiwat Satha-Anand, *Human Politics: Radical Political Science*. (Bangkok: Dogyar, 1985), pp. 65–66.

———. "The Problems of Political Leadership study: Concepts and Some Observations on Biographical Approach," in Chaiwat Satha-Anand, *Human Politics: RadicalPolitical Science*. (Bangkok: Dogyar, 1985), pp. 97–138.

———. "Visit Thailand Year," *Hi-Class* (December 1987), pp. 68–69.

———. "Social Integration and Problems of State Security: Some Observations on the Four Southern Provinces, Thailand," in Kusuma Snidvongse, ed. *Cracks in Thai Society?: Integration and Problems of National Security*. (Bangkok: Institute of Security and International Studies, Chulalongkorn University, 1988), pp. 250–279.

Chalardchai Ramitanon. "Religion and Conflict," *Siam Rath*, 7–8 March 1988.

Chaleeporn Sangboonnum. "A Comparison of the Revenue from Tourism and that from Selected Main Exports." (Master of Commerce Thesis, Chulalongkorn University, 1975).

Chalida Tajaroensuk. "Krabuan Karn Kadkarn Krong Karn Tarng Duan Khan Tee 2 (Urupong-Rajdamri) Khong Choom Chon Ban Krua" [Protesting Process of Ban Krua Community on Second Stage Expressway System Project]. (M.A. Thesis,National Institute of Development Administration, 1996).

Chao Thai, 26 December 1987.

Charan Maluleem, Kittima Amoratat, and Pornpimol Trichote. *Thailand and the Muslim World: A Case Study of Thai Muslims*. (Bangkok: Institute of Asian Studies, Chulalongkorn University, 1996).

Daily News, 4 February 1988, 11 February 1988, 18 February 1988.

Dao Siam, 16 March 1988.

"Dogmakhua," "*Choom Tang Khru*" [Teachers' junction]. *Matichon*, 24 February 1988.

Institute of Taksin Khadi Suksa (Institute of Southern Affairs Studies), *Saranukrom Wattanatham Pak Tai* [Encyclopedia of Southern Cultures]. vol. 1, (Bangkok: Sri Nakarinwirote University, 1986).

Islamic Guidance Post, June 1986, April 1987, October 1987, April 1988, November 1989, July 1990, August 1990, November 1990, April–May 1997, June 1997.

Krikkiat Pipatseridham, "Economic Consequence of Tourism," in *Pu-Tai* (The Messiah), no. 2 (1987), pp. 23–30.

Lao Shuan Hua, "The Legend of Lim Kun Yew," *Poo Jad Karn Weekly* [Manager weekly], 2 September 1991.

Mark Tamthai. "Radical Political Science: Countering What? And How?" *Thammasat University Journal*, vol. 13, no. 3 (September 1984), pp. 68–72.

Marvan Sama-oon, "*Hijab*," *Matichon*, 10 February 1988.

Matichon, 4 June 1990, 23 February 1988.

Meechai Kijboonchu, Cardinal. "Theology of Tourism," in *Pu-Tai* [The Messiah], no. 2 (1987), pp. 4–7.

Narongrit Sakdanarong's article in *Matichon*, 29 January 1988.

Nattaporn Sangpradab. "Socio-Cultural and Economic Changes Resulted from Tourism Development" (M.A. Thesis, Mahidol University, 1984).

Nidhi Eiosriwong. "Tourism Industry and its Cultural Impacts," *Arts and Culture*, vol. 8, no. 6 (April 1987).

——. "Disunity and Dress," *Matichon*, 2 February 1988.

Office of the Educational District, District 2, *Kormoon Tang Karn Suksa Karn Sassana lae Wattana tham* [Educational, religious, and cultural data]. Academic year 1990, Document no. 55/1991, 1991.

Pagadhamma. "The Yala Case: *Patipatha* for Friends with Different Religious Persuasions," *Matichon*, 15 February 1988.

Prachom Suwatthee. *Job Creation in Tourism Industry*. (Bangkok: Tourism Authority of Thailand, 1980).

Prapon Ruangnarong. *Sombat Thai Muslim Pak Thai* [Southern Thai Muslims' treasures]. (Bangkok: Charoenwit Printing House, 1984).

Prayoonsak Chalayondecha. *Muslims in Thailand*. (Bangkok: Tonson Mosque, 1988).

Preecha Oopyokin and Suriya Weerawong. *Effects of International Tourism on Thai Society and Culture*. (Bangkok: Social Research Institute, Chulalongkorn University, 1978).

Preecha Suwannathat's article in *Naewna*, 3 February 1988.

Puangpetch Suratkavikul. "The Economic Role of Thai Muslims in the Past," *Journal of Social science and Humanities*, vol. 10, no. 7, (May–June 1980), p. 28.

Pujadkarn Raiwan [Managers' Daily], 22 April 1994, 25 April 1994, 3 May 1994.

Pujadkarn Weekly [Managers' Weekly], 11–17 June 1990.

Sanit Chomcharn. "Kabuan Karn Patiwat Islam nai Prathet Thai" [Islamic revolutionary movement in Thailand]. (A thesis, Army Defence College, 1991).

Santad Sermsin. "Effects of Tourism on Society and Culture." (M.A. Thesis, Mahidol University, 1986).

Sanyaluck, June 1986, June 1992.

Siam Rath, 2 February 1987, 28, 29 January 1988, 4 April 1989.

Siam Rath Weekly, 20–26 March 1988.

Teppanom Muangmaen and Somsak Santa. "Knowledge, Attitude and Practices of Masseuses in Bangkok." A Research Report, Faculty of Public Health, Mahidol University, Bangkok, 1979.

Thai Khadi Research Institute. *Patterns of Preservation and Revivification of Tourism-Related Festivals and Traditions*. A Research Report submitted to the Tourism Authority of Thailand, Bangkok, September 1986.

Thai Rath, 19 February 1988.

Thai University Research Associates. *Tourism and Economic Development in Thailand*. (Bangkok: NIDA, 1977).

Ubol Topinich. "The Forecasting of the Number of Tourists visiting Thailand, 1975–1979." (Master of Commerce Thesis, Chulalongkorn University, 1975).

Vinai Phunampol. "Negative Impacts of the Thai Tourism Industry," *Barn Mai Ru Roey*, vol. 3, no. 6, (July 1987), pp. 90–103.

Wiriyabha Changrien. "Effects of Tourism on Forms of Arts, Customs and Classical Dancing," *Tourism Journal*, vol. 1, no. 3 (1982), p. 56.

Wuthithep Intapanya and Chamlong Atikul. *Economic Significance of Tourism in Thailand*. (Bangkok: NIDA, 1985).

Index